HAWAI'I

Moana Tregaskis

photography by Wayne Levin and Paul Chesley

Hong Kong

First published in Great Britain in 1993
Copyright © 1993 Compass American Guides Inc
Maps copyright © 1992 Compass American Guides Inc

Distribution in the United Kingdom, Ireland, Europe and certain Commonwealth countries by Hodder & Stoughton, Mill Road, Dunton Green, Sevenoaks, Kent TW13 2YA

British Library Cataloguing-in-Publication Data
A catalogue record for this book is available from the British Library

Series Editor: Kit Duane
Editors: Kit Duane, Jamie Jensen, Jamie Robles
Photography Editor: Christopher Burt
Designers: David Hurst, Christopher Burt
Map Design: Eureka Cartography, Berkeley, CA

Photography by: Wayne Levin, cover, 10, 43, 45, 49, 57, 68, 69, 76, 77, 83, 90, 98, 101, 113, 148, 166, 173, 197, 213, 214, 221, 227, 246, 253, 268, 276, 287, 349; Paul Chesley 3, 42, 65, 72, 73, 80, 85, 88–89, 99, 103, 106–107, 117, 129, 144, 149, 153, 156, 157, 164–165, 168, 169, 172, 179, 183, 190, 208, 209, 221 (bottom), 238, 239, 244, 248 (both), 269, 282, 283, 286; Don King, Pacific Stock 22–23; Greg Vaughn 116, 241, 256, 257, 260, 261; Reg Morrison 56, 81, 193, 231; Bancroft Library, University of California, Berkeley 12, 25, 26, 29, 34, 35, 219, 225, 271; Bishop Museum, Honolulu 191; Cornelia M Foley 132; Hawaiian Historical Society 205; Hawaii State Archives, Honolulu 27, 139, 167, 177; Honolulu Academy of Arts 7, 53; Library of Congress 170, 171, 185, 188, 196; Mission Houses Museum, Honolulu 182; The Oakland Museum History Department, Oakland, CA 38, 123, 267; Scientific Research Museum of the Academy of Arts, St Petersburg, Russia for the Mikhail Tikhanov painting 31; Taito Co, Tokyo 125; and Joe Bisignani for permission to use the illustrations of reef fish by Louise Foote 262–265.

Production House: Twin Age Limited, Hong Kong
Printed in China

To the mana of another, brave warrior and man of courage,
that granted me the power to write this book.
Ho'o mana'o.

C O N T E N T S

Maps

Topical Essays

Literary Extracts

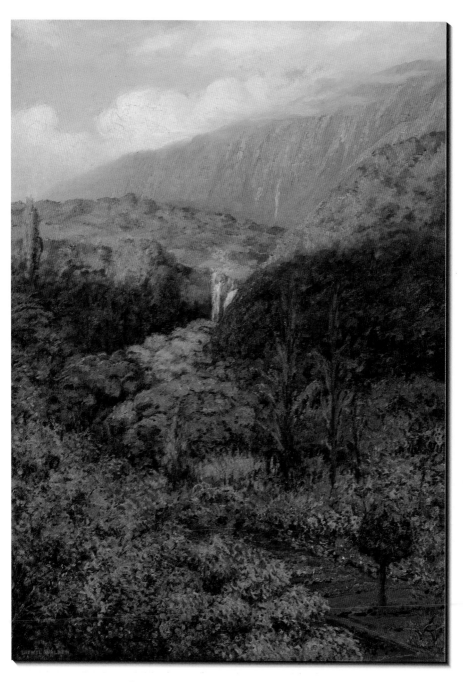

*Evening in the Nuʻuanu Valley above Honolulu; by Lionel Walden, 1916.
(Honolulu Academy of Arts)*

FACTS ABOUT HAWAI'I

Aloha State

Capital: Honolulu

Entered Union: Aug. 21, 1959

First Settled: A.D. 300-600

State Flower: Hibiscus

State Bird: *Nene* (goose)

State Tree: *Kukui* (candlenut)

Population: 1,108,000 (1990)

		Five Largest Cities: (1990)	
Hawaiian/part Hawaiian	31%	Honolulu, O'ahu	365,300
White	25%	Hilo, Big Island	37,800
Japanese	24%	Kailua, O'ahu	36,800
Filipino	12%	Kaneohe, O'ahu	35,450
Other	8%	Waipahu, O'ahu	31,450

GEOGRAPHY:

Size:	6,425 sq. miles (16,641 sq. km)
Highest point:	Mauna Kea, Hawai'i 13,796 ft. (4,205 m)
Lowest point:	Sea level
Highest temp.:	100° F (38° C), Pahala, Hawai'i, April 27, 1931 (recorded)
Lowest temp. :	12° F (-11° C), Mauna Kea, Hawai'i, May 17, 1979 (recorded)
Wettest place:	460 in. (1,168 cm) per annum, Mt. Wai'ale'ale, Kaua'i
Driest place:	14.01 in (35.58 cm) Mahukona, Big Island

ECONOMY:

Major industries:	Tourism, defense, sugar refining, fishing
Chief crops:	Sugar, pineapple, macadamia nuts, fruits, coffee
Per capita income:	$18,306
Tourism:	$9.2 billion spent by more than 7 million out-of-state visitors, or $8,400 (highest ratio in nation) for each resident

EDUCATION: Student teacher ratio is 21.1 to 1

FAMOUS HAWAIIANS:

King Kamehameha the Great, Bernice Pauahi Bishop, Duke Kahanamoku, Queen Lili'uokalani, Gabby Pahinui, Ellison Onizuka, Sen. Daniel K. Inouye

FACTS ABOUT THE HAWAIIAN ISLANDS

ISLAND	AREA	POPULATION	PRINCIPAL CITY	HIGHEST MOUNTAIN
Hawai'i	4,037 sq. miles 15,582 sq. km	121,000	Hilo 37,800	Mauna Kea 13,796 ft 4,205 m
Kaua'i	549 sq. miles 2,119 sq. km	54,000	Lihu'e 4,700	Mt. Kawaikini 5,243 ft 1,598 m
Lana'i	140 sq. miles 540 sq. km	2,200	Lana'i City 2,100	Lana'ihale 3,370 ft 1,027 m
Maui	728 sq. miles 2,810 sq. km	85,000	Kahului 15,600	Haleakala 10,023 ft 3,055 m
Moloka'i	260 sq. miles 1,004 sq. km	7,000	Kaunakakai 2,200	Kamakou 4,961 ft 1,512 m
O'ahu	594 sq. miles 2,293 sq. km	839,000	Honolulu 365,300	Mount Ka'ala 4,020ft 1,598 m

THE HAWAIIAN ISLAND CHAIN

ACKNOWLEDGMENTS

MAHALO NUI TO SERIES EDITOR KIT DUANE whose friendly advice and piercing questions kept me on a straight course and eager to have her comments. She knows the gift of *aloha*.

I am grateful for the invaluable assistance of David Forbes, curator of "Encounters with Paradise" at the Honolulu Academy of Arts and good friend, and for the *kokua* of the Academy's Carol Khewhok. Grateful recognition for technical advice goes to my husband Capt. Tom McGlaughlin for his knowledge of the sea, to my friend Dr. Yvonne Bickerton for reference to her study on *awa,* and to Dr. Scott Medbury, botanist at Foster Botanic Gardens. I am indebted to many National Park Service rangers at Volcanoes National Park and to geologists at the U.S. Geologic Survey on the Big Island for their invaluable discussions.

Institutions providing help through publications are the Bishop Museum Press, Friends of 'Iolani Palace, Kauai Historical Society, Lahaina Restoration Foundation, Mission Houses Museum, and the University of Hawaii Press. I appreciate the treasure-houses of information at the Archives of the State of Hawaii and the Hawaiian Historical Society.

With much *aloha* I acknowledge the steadfast support and literary experience of Lt. General Victor H. Krulak, U.S.M.C. (ret), and James L. Greenfield at the editorial board of the *New York Times.*

■ PUBLISHERS ACKNOWLEDGMENTS

The publisher wishes to thank the following people for their generous contributions to this book: Rena Kalehua Nelson, producer and host of "Na Mele 'O Ka Oina," KPFA radio, Berkeley, for her invaluable assistance in understanding Hawaiian music; Thomas Farber for excerpts from *On Water,* Okeanos Press, Berkeley, 1991 © Thomas Farber; Manuel Abascal for his essay, "Cane Cutter's Journey"; Bamboo Ridge Press of Honolulu for assistance in finding modern Hawaiian writers of merit and for these selections from *The Best of Bamboo Ridge* published in 1986: *The Mango Tree,* © Eric Chock; *Teapot Tales,* excerpts from the biography of a Japanese homesteader, © Clara Mitsuko Jelsma; and "Water Born," © Norman Hindley. *After Iniki,* by Rick DelVecchio, reprinted by permission © *San Francisco Chronicle.* We also wish to express our gratitude to Gil Reavill, author of Compass American Guides' *Los Angeles* for his lively essay on movies made in Hawai'i, and to Joan Komura for reading over the manuscript. Thanks also to Jan Hughes and Julia Dillon for help with the final editing process.

The king and queen of Aloha Day in traditional royal robes at Pu'uhonua O Honaunau on the Big Island.

J.Webber del.   *J.K.Sherwin sc.*

A YOUNG WOMAN of the SANDWICH ISLANDS.

Young Hawaiian woman; by John Webber, artist with Captain Cook's expedition, 1778-1779. (Bancroft Library)

INTRODUCTION

HAWAI'I OVERFLOWS WITH NATURAL BEAUTY. Piercing up through the surface of the Pacific from the ocean floor, the Hawaiian Islands are ringed by turquoise and purple waters. Each isle is garlanded in strands of soft sand beaches that may run from pure white to ebony. On the land lie jagged volcanic cliffs slashed by lush green valleys and deep gorges, snowfields and deserts, green palms and red *lehua* blossoms, black lava and the heavy scent of tropical flowers.

There is also another kind of natural beauty in Hawai'i. It is her people—everyone is a part of a minority, and we live in extraordinary rapprochement. The islands have absorbed wave after wave of immigrants, each bringing bits and pieces from homelands to create a mixture of taste, sound, and blended ancestry that is unique to these islands. It is her people who have learned from Hawai'i, assimilated the gentle spirit and Hawaiian heritage, and made these islands the Land of *Aloha*. "*Aloha*" has many definitions and no single one. The Reverend Abraham K. Akaka said it best in his speech on the day Congress granted statehood in 1959:

> *Aloha ke Akua,* God is *aloha* . . . . We do not do good only to those who do good to us. One of the sweetest things about the love of God, about aloha, is that it welcomes the stranger and seeks his good. A person who has the spirit of *aloha* loves even when the love is not returned . . . the real Golden Rule is *aloha*.

In the coastal cities and rural towns, Hawai'i's people are ingrained from generation to generation with this certain beauty, this spirit named *aloha*. Visitors can experience it today at ancient sites, and through hula, music, arts and crafts, and especially in *aloha*.

It is this real and living culture, coupled with ethnic diversity, that places the Hawaiian Islands apart. It explains the rise of tourism and the large numbers of visitors (52 percent) who return again and again. Honolulu today is the eleventh largest city in the nation and the prime visitor destination in the U.S.A.

Yet the natural beauty remains. With the number of annual visitors passing the seven million mark, few realize that tourist destination areas are a fraction of the Hawaiian landscape and that the major portion of the islands is wilderness or rural. On Maui, for example, 75 percent of the land is protected in one type or another of wilderness preserve. Mountainous interiors on each island are largely pristine. Hikers may choose from an abundance of trails in unblemished backcountry.

Hawai'i is crowded with polarities and bizarre extremes—the world's highest mountain measured from the seabed, Mauna Kea; the wettest spot on earth, atop Wai'ale'ale; the most active volcano on earth, Kilauea; the largest dormant volcano, Haleakala; the highest sea cliffs, on Moloka'i; and rainfall that may vary by hundreds of inches within a radius of just a few miles. Many thousands of flora and fauna species emerged in these isolated islands and some 90 percent are found no other place on earth. The *po'ouli* is a bird so rare it was not seen until 1975, living in the cloud-shrouded forests of Maui. Some of nature's weirdest mutant changes and diversification of a species from a single ancestor live only here.

Hawai'i's tropical climate is benign due to cooling northeast trade winds throughout the year. The year-round average ocean temperature is nearly constant, fluctuating between 75 and 82 degrees F (24°–28° C). The caressing air of coastal areas is nearly the same; between 66 and 88 degrees F (19°–31° C) year-round. Rainbows glistening in sunshine follow brief daylight showers. Hawai'i gave birth to surfboarding, sport of Pacific kings, and the warm ocean draws windsurfers and bodysurfers, snorkelers, divers, and game-fishing fans.

On the six major islands of Hawai'i, leeward (western and southern) shores are sunny and dry, with soft sand beaches and limpid aquamarine seas. The windward [eastern and northern] coasts are lined with sharp cliffs, waterfalls, lush rainforests, and heavy crashing surf. In the cool and misty highlands are green undulating meadowlands, ranches, and farms.

The Big Island of Hawai'i is the home of Pele, the volcano goddess, and here volcanoes erupt and snow whitens the mountain peaks. On this island that encapsulates every type of climate on earth are orchards growing macadamia nuts and coffee, and farms that cultivate velvety orchids. Astronomers study the heavens, *paniolo* (cowboys) ride herd on cattle, and sport fishing fans tag leaping marlin. Kaua'i is the island of the most spectacular lush scenery, with a verdant collar, jagged cliffs of the Na Pali Coast, and a Grand Canyon-like gorge (Waimea Canyon). Lana'i, once the Pineapple Island, is newly engaged in tourism, with two luxury hotel-resorts. Maui takes second place in visitor destination development. This island with the vast crater of Haleakala, its twisting drive to Hana, and glitzy mega-resorts, is top rated for whale-watching and upland farming. Rural Moloka'i, with the largest percentage of Hawaiians living on a major island, has just one luxury hotel.

The most populous island is Oʻahu, the capital island, site of government and Waikiki Beach, where one-half of the visitor accommodations in the state are located and nightlife is lively and hip. On this island you can eat many of the world's cuisines at family restaurants or indulge in gourmet continental wining and dining. Oʻahu is the surfing island of famed international competitions. Traffic in Honolulu and windward suburbs is staggering, yet a mile away lies a quiet rural countryside.

Writers have always been captivated by Hawaiʻi's unique cultural and ethnic mix. Nineteenth-century literary figures captured the Hawaiian magic, creating tales as absorbing today as they were long ago. The vivid descriptions and sensitive, sometimes bumptious tales spun by Jack London and Robert Louis Stevenson, as well as Mark Twain's accounts of his rovings, testify to the seductive witcheries of this chain of Pacific islands.

Newer testaments to Hawaiʻi's magic have come from James Michener and James Jones, and from that storyteller of men in war, Richard Tregaskis, all attesting to the continuing allure of modern Hawaiʻi.

Each island has a separate chapter in this book, beginning with its history and geography. The chapters lead readers to what stood or happened at ordinary places, to sites where Hawaiian gods accomplished fearsome deeds, and to sites where famous writers worked and stayed. In referring to their perceptions and observations, I hope the readers' experiences are enhanced. Each island's special qualities, its art and activities are described. "PRACTICAL INFORMATION," including accommodations, restaurants, and much more, can be found at the back of the book.

This guide is intended for modern pathfinders who I hope will sense the voluptuous island magic that courses through Hawaiian culture and myth, its blend of oriental and occidental energy, and fascinating history. It is for those readers and travelers who, like the writers, would go beyond a balmy beach to discover the legend, fabric, and environment that bestow Hawaiʻi's magic.

ABOUT GLOTTAL STOPS

You may notice in this travel guide that the names of certain places and historical figures are marked with a glottal stop or hamsa (ʻ) which indicates a pause in a word's enunciation. However, these punctuation marks are a relatively recent addition to the written Hawaiian language and may not appear consistently on Hawaiian street signs, maps, institutional names, or other literature about Hawaiʻi.

BASIC HAWAIIAN

Although the Hawaiian spoken today is vastly different from the Old Hawaiian, the roots of the language can be traced back to the early Polynesian colonists and the later Tahitian influences.

The language was further modified by the development of a local dialect known as pidgin. Originated by landowners who wanted to communicate with their Chinese, Japanese, and Portuguese migrant workers, pidgin has become a strong current in the island's sub-culture—a language of the people—which is still evolving today.

PRONUNCIATION

Syllables in Hawaiian words do not end in consonants. When referring to the capital city, say Ho-no-lulu, not Hon-o-lulu—an immediate sign of an outsider. On the Big Island, the volcano Ki-lau-e-a commonly is mispronounced Kil-au-e-a.

When Protestant missionaries arrived in 1920, they began the task of transcribing Hawaiian into written form, assembling an alphabet of 12 letters—H, K, L, M, N, P, and W—to represent the consonants. The five vowels were to be pronounced identically to the Latin-based Spanish or Italian.

Over time, enhancements were added. A hamsa {'} marked the glottal stop—often written today with an apostrophe. The macron followed, a line above a vowel indicating a long sound. The stress (or accent) is easy enough. All vowels with macrons are sounded, and in short words, the stress is on the next-to-last syllable: wa-HI-ne (woman), or ka-ma-AI-na (native born or old-timer). Long, multi-voweled words are composed of groups of syllables and each has a stress.

Hawaiian is robust and eloquent, especially in the grouped syllables: mo-A-ni le-HU-a is the breeze (*moani*) that wafts the fragrance of lehua blossoms.

COMMON WORDS AND EXPRESSIONS

Ae	Yes
Aloha	Greeting and farewell, spirit of affection
Haole	Foreigner/ white person or Caucasian
Hocomalimali	Flatter, use soft words
Hula	Native Hawaiian dance
Itai! itai!	Ouch! ouch! (Japanese)
Kama'aina	Native born or old-timer
Kane	Man

Kapu	Forbidden
Keiki	Child
Komo mai	Come in
Lanai	Veranda
Lei	Necklace of flowers
Luau	Traditional Hawaiian feast
Mahalo	Thank you
Makai	Toward the sea
Mauka	Toward the mountains
Mele Kalikimaka	Merry Christmas
Okole maluna	Cheers!
Pali	Cliffs
Poi	Staple food made from taro root
Pilikia	Trouble
Wahine	Woman

HOW TO INTERPRET HAWAIIAN DIRECTIONS

The old Hawaiian way of locating a place is still practiced. *Makai* is toward the ocean and is *mauka* toward the mountains. (Ma means "to"; *ma-kai* to the ocean; *ma-uka* to the uplands.)

Directions are given from the point where one is located when asking the way. For example, if you are in Waikiki and ask for directions to the University, you'll be told to go *mauka* (toward the mountains). Or if you ask how to get downtown from the National Cemetery in Punchbowl, you will be directed to head *makai* (toward the ocean). Because these two words are so wonderfully efficient, new residents quickly adopt the Hawaiian way.

Similarly, there are directions specific to every island, where actual sites are used to guide you to your destination. On Oahʻu, *ewa* is to the west, a direction taking its name from a sugar plantation area on western Oʻahu. Diamond Head, Waikiki, and Koko Head are to the east. If, for instance, you are at the Ala Moana Shopping Center and ask the way to ʻIolani Palace, you will be told to go *ewa* (west). Or if you're at the Prince Hotel and are looking for the Royal Hawaiian, you will be directed to go *Diamond Head,* or *Waikiki* (east). If you are not standing within the boundaries of these sites, the directions are adaptable. If, for example, you are at the Kahala Hilton, a location beyond (or east of) Diamond Head, and are planning to visit Hanauma Bay, you will be directed to head "Koko Head" (farther east).

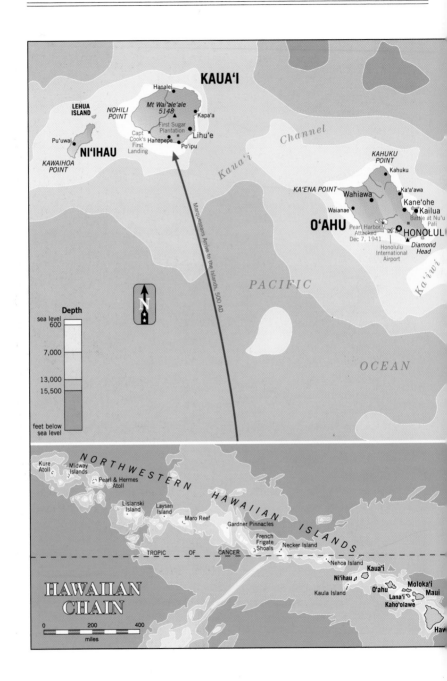

KAUA'I

Hanalei

Mt Wai'ale'ale
5148 ▲

Kapa'a

First Sugar
Plantation

**LEHUA
ISLAND**

*NOHILI
POINT*

Capt
Cook's
First
Landing

Lihu'e

Pu'uwai

Hanapepe

Po'ipu

NI'IHAU

*KAWAIHOA
POINT*

Channel

Marquesans Arrive to the Islands, 500 AD

Kaua'i

*KAHUKU
POINT*

Kahuku

KA'ENA POINT

Wahiawa

Ka'a'awa

Kane'ohe

Kailua

Waianae

Battle at Nu'u
Pali

O'AHU

Pearl Harbor
Attacked
Dec 7, 1941

HONOLUL

PACIFIC

Honolulu
International
Airport

*Diamond
Head*

Ka'iwi

OCEAN

Depth

sea level
600

7,000

13,000
15,500

feet below
sea level

N

NORTHWESTERN

Kure
Atoll

Midway
Islands

Pearl & Hermes
Atoll

Lisianski
Island

Laysan
Island

Maro Reef

HAWAIIAN

Gardner Pinnacles

ISLANDS

French
Frigate
Shoals

Necker Island

TROPIC   OF   CANCER

Nehoa Island

Kaua'i

Ni'ihau

Moloka'i

O'ahu

Lana'i

Kaula Island

Maui

Kaho'olawe

**HAWAIIAN
CHAIN**

Haw

0   200   400

miles

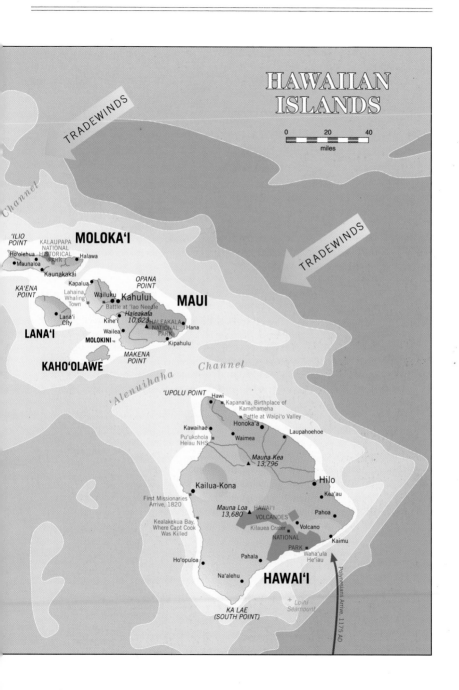

HAWAIIAN ISLANDS

0   20   40
miles

TRADEWINDS

TRADEWINDS

Channel

MOLOKA'I

'ILIO POINT

KALAUPAPA NATIONAL HISTORICAL PARK

Ho'olehua
Maunaloa
Kaunakakai
Kapalua
Halawa

OPANA POINT

KA'ENA POINT

Lahaina, Whaling Town
Wailuku **Kahului**
Battle at 'Iao Needle
Haleakala 10,023
HALEAKALA NATIONAL PARK

MAUI

Lana'i City
Kihe'i
Wailea
Hana

LANA'I

MOLOKINI

Kipahulu

MAKENA POINT

KAHO'OLAWE

Channel

'Alenuihaha

'UPOLU POINT   Hawi
Kapana'ia, Birthplace of Kamehameha
Battle at Waipi'o Valley
Honoka'a
Kawaihae
Pu'ukohola Heiau NHS
Waimea
Laupahoehoe

Mauna Kea 13,796

Kailua-Kona
Hilo

Kea'au

First Missionaries Arrive, 1820

Mauna Loa 13,680 HAWAI'I VOLCANOES
Pahoa
Kealakekua Bay, Where Capt Cook Was Killed
Kilauea Crater Volcano
NATIONAL
Kaimu

Ho'opuloa
Pahala
Waha'ula He'iau

Na'alehu   **HAWAI'I**

KA LAE (SOUTH POINT)

+ *Loihi Seamount*

Polynesians Arrive 1175 AD

HISTORY AND CULTURE

■ GEOLOGY

The Hawaiian Islands are more than the land you see. They are peaks of massive volcanoes, which began coughing up molten rock some 25 to 40 million years ago from a crack in the earth's seabed mantle. The ocean floor at Hawai'i is part of the Pacific Plate, which stretches out from California and moves northwest some three inches (8 cm) a year. The crack, or hot spot, is stationary. Each volcano was created when a weak spot in the earth's crust moved over the crack. Piling liquid magma layer upon layer, the lava pierced the surface of the sea and continued to mold the peaks, creating an archipelago with eight main islands. As the volcanoes crawled beyond the hot spot, their activities decreased, finally cooling to become dormant, and at the final stage, extinct.

Hawai'i's volcanoes are "shield volcanoes" that build up gradually with wide-based gentle slopes, rather than by rapid explosion. There is little gas emitted as the molten rock streams down in flows that may spread over several miles. You can see the tapering slopes dropping down off the summits of Mauna Kea and Mauna Loa on the Big Island of Hawai'i—the youngest of the islands, which is still in the process of being created. Kilauea is its most active volcano, spurting lava directly above the hot spot. Its current eruption series, which has thrown out more than a billion cubic yards of lava since it began in 1983, shows no signs of abating.

Two types of lava pour from volcanoes and their Hawaiian names are used throughout the world: *pahoehoe* and *'a'a*. You can walk on *pahoehoe*. It is smooth, flowing in flat billows that wrinkle when the liquid flow beneath a cooling crust drags it forward. The fiery stream forms tubes under the crust, sometimes large enough to walk through, like the Thurston Lava Tube in Hawai'i Volcanoes National Park on the Big Island. *'A'a* lava is rough and knife-sharp, cast up in jagged boulders with solid interiors. If you try to walk or climb on it, your shoes and hands may well be cut.

When a volcano stops spewing lava, other forces of nature take hold. Rain, wind, and wave action erode the land. In this way the uninhabited northwest islands, oldest in the Hawaiian chain, have been eroded down from mountains to flat-tops that now barely break the surface of the water. This process is clearly evident on Kaua'i, oldest of the main islands, where the Na Pali cliffs are eroded by wind and rain into sharp, serrated ridges, and wave-carved caves meet the sea.

The active volcanoes in the Hawaiian Islands are Kilauea and Mauna Loa on the Big Island. Mauna Kea and Hualalai on the Big Island, and Haleakala on Maui are dormant. All of the volcanoes on the other islands are considered extinct.

■ GEOGRAPHY

The Hawaiian archipelago slices through the Tropic of Cancer, extending in a line from southeast to northwest for 1,523 miles (2,437 km), from the Big Island of Hawai'i at 19 degrees north latitude to Kure Island at 28.5 degrees north latitude. All of the eight main Hawaiian islands are in the tropics. The 28 northwest islands are a National Wildlife Refuge strewn across one thousand miles (1,600 km) of Pacific Ocean. With the exception of the five Midway islands (geographically a part of the archipelago administered by the U.S. Navy), the chain of shoals, reefs, and islands is the State of Hawai'i.

The land area of the main islands and offshore islets is 6,425 square miles. Hawai'i is the biggest and Maui is next, followed by O'ahu, Kaua'i, Moloka'i, Lana'i, Ni'ihau, and uninhabited Kaho'olawe. Mauna Kea on the Big Island rises to 13,796 feet (4205 m), but when measured from the ocean floor to its summit, it is higher than Mount Everest.

■ POLYNESIAN VOYAGERS

Hawai'i is the northern point of the triangle spread across the North and South Pacific which is known as Polynesia, or "many islands." The southern point is New Zealand, home of the Maori, and Easter Island (Isla de Pascua, a possession of Chile) is the eastern apex of the vast triangle. The generally accepted theory of the prehistoric roots of Polynesians is that they followed a migration pattern out of South Asia, down into Southeast Asia, moving into Indonesia and across Melanesia to settle in the islands of Samoa and Tonga in about 1000 B.C. Later settlements were formed over the next 1,500 years in the Marquesas and Tahiti, Rapa Nui (Easter), and other islands of Polynesia.

(following pages) Eruption of lava at Pu'u O'o vent on the Big Island. (Don King, Pacific Stock)

The Polynesians crossed the vast empty waters of the world's largest ocean in double-hulled canoes up to 80 feet (24 m) long and mounted with woven sails. Navigating with extraordinary skill by the stars and sun, clouds, ocean swells, and currents, they sought "Havaiti," the ancestral home in the sun. (The word also meant the underworld.) In the canoes they brought the food staple taro, dogs, pigs, breadfruit, and the uninvited Polynesian rat. The last island group to be settled, Hawai'i marks the end of the great era of Polynesian exploration and colonization.

■ EARLY HAWAIIANS

Between A.D. 500 and 700, the warring, tattooed Marquesans beached their canoes on Hawaiian shores. Around A.D.1000 the first Tahitians arrived and probably conquered the Marquesans. By about 1175, a Tahitian priest or *kahuna* (in Hawaiian) arrived on the Big Island. Named Pa'ao in the ancient oral chants, he founded the *kahuna nui,* or high-priest line, and introduced the institution of a king for each island. From Tahiti he brought Pili, who sired the royal line that led to Kamehameha. These two ruling forces formed a dynasty that continued unbroken for 700 years.

Religion centered on four gods: Ku, Lono, Kane, and Kanaloa. Ku was the ancestor of humanity and took many forms—he could be Ku'ula, god of fishing, or Kuka'ilimoku, the war-god-who-snatched-land worshipped by Kamehameha. Lono, the god of peace and fertility, ruled the elements, bringing rain for food plants. Kane made man from dust and gave him life (*kane* is the Hawaiian word for male). Kane, Lono, and Ku made the earth and ocean, the moon and stars. Their downfall was an addiction to the alcoholic drink *kava,* and for this they were banished to the underworld, where Kanaloa ruled the dead.

The Tahitian priest Pa'ao hoped to improve upon the way the Hawaiians worshipped their gods *(akua)* by instituting a new order of things. At Puna, Pa'ao built Waha'ula He'iau, the first temple of human sacrifice, and introduced gods and demigods, including the war god Kuka'ilimoku and the fire goddess Pele. He initiated a social order which divided the people into royalty *(ali'i)* and high priests *(kahuna),* commoners *(maka'ainana),* and the lowly outcast *(kauwa)* class. The division was enforced by rigid sanctions of the *kapu,* or taboo system that controlled daily life. The ruling chief possessed the greatest degree of *mana,* or supernatural force, and towered over commoners, who were required to fall prostrate when a conch shell hailed his presence.

Commoners could not eat the same food as *ali'i*, walk on the same ground, or cross the king's shadow. Women could not eat with men and were forbidden to take coconut or bananas, pork, or certain fish. Unless the *kapu*-breaker could reach a sanctified place of refuge, or *pu'uhonua*, the penalty always was death. *Pu'uhonua* were used by chiefs and commoners alike, and everyone believed that violating the sanctity of a refuge would bring the wrath of the gods—and retribution in the form of a volcanic eruption or a *tsunami* (tidal wave). If a pursuer dared enter, he was slain at once by the resident *kahuna* for breaking a *kapu*.

The *kahuna* proclaimed religious laws, or *kapu* (both murder and making distracting noises during religious ceremonies were *kapu*). *Ali'i*, or chiefs, proclaimed the non-religious laws, or *kanawai*—such as a proclamation sparing the lives of warriors of a defeated chief.

From the twelfth to fifteenth centuries a long list of essentials was brought to Hawai'i from Tahiti: the large *pahu* or coconut tree temple drum with a head of sharkskin; the *pulo'ulo'u*, a *tapa* ball on a stick used as a symbol of *kapu;* the *'awa,* or *kava* plant for making liquor; the *pa'u* or *kapa* skirt; the nose flute; and probably the sweet potato.

Life was not all grim. Hawaiians lived in a pleasurable harmony with nature, worshiping gods of lesser rank inspired by the world around them. These included Pele's sister Laka, goddess of that paean to nature, the hula. Mitigating the rigid *kapu* system were the pleasures of surfing, kite flying, and most importantly, the concept of *aloha*. Permeating life and meaning "love," *aloha* was a profound sense of compassion, kinship, and friendly spirit. The most important element in Hawaiian life, the spirit of *aloha* imprinted upon Hawaiian culture a communal sense so strong that it has survived into modern times. If

Young man in a helmet, drawn by John Webber of Captain Cook's expedition, 1778-1779. (Bancroft Library)

human sacrifice and *aloha* seem to derive from antithetical impulses, one can only say that this is typical of human nature and especially typical of Hawai'i. The kind nature of early Hawaiians was coupled with ferocious antipathies toward enemies, and terrible, bloody wars, a combination clearly reflected in the way Hawaiians treated Captain James Cook.

■ CAPTAIN JAMES COOK

On his third voyage into the Pacific, in 1778, the English explorer Captain James Cook sailed his ships *Resolution* and *Discovery* into Waimea Bay at Kaua'i. He was welcomed as Lono, the god prophesied to return on a "floating island." Cook recorded in his journal, that "all fell flat on their faces, and remained in that humble posture till . . . [I] made signs to them to rise."

Cook is the first Pacific explorer to leave a record of reaching Hawai'i, although he may have been preceded by Spanish galleons on their voyages between the Philippines and Mexico. He found many similarities between Hawai'i and Tahiti in language and culture, and was welcomed in the same way—with canoe-loads of

Ancient hula combined chanting, dancing, and myth; by Louis Choris, 1812. (Bancroft Library)

fresh food. Cook's reciprocal gifts included iron goods, and from the moment Hawaiians saw metal for the first time, they were uninterested in trading for beads or trinkets.

After spending two weeks re-provisioning at Waimea, Cook set sail for the Arctic, where his mission was to find a northwest passage that might connect the Atlantic and Pacific Oceans. Unable to find it, he returned to Hawai'i one year later, discovered the other main islands and named the group the Sandwich Islands to honor the Earl of Sandwich, First Lord of the Admiralty and patron of the expedition. On this second voyage, Cook dropped anchor in Kealakekua Bay, on the Big Island of Hawai'i.

One thousand canoes circled his ships, and again he was welcomed as Lono. What Cook did not realize was that both times he had arrived during

English explorer Captain James Cook, who, on his third expedition headed north from Tahiti through uncharted waters, and in January of 1778 came unexpectedly upon the Hawaiian Islands. Engraving by Wright. (Hawaii State Archives)

the annual Makahiki—a festival held each January to honor the harvest god Lono. Cook and his crew thought every day in Hawai'i was festive, and after months in the Arctic, it's no wonder Hawai'i was paradise. Crewmen were invited to join in sport competitions, and women took them to their beds. Despite Cook's orders that they abstain from sex, the men indulged, infecting Hawai'i's women with venereal disease. The ship's artist John Webber roamed about at will, and today his precise fine-point drawings offer us an excellent visual record of that period.

With his ships replenished and artifacts and idols taken aboard, Cook set sail some three weeks later. Soon afterwards, in a violent storm, the foremast of the *Resolution* was cracked, and he ordered the ships back to Kealakekua Bay for repairs. It was a fatal decision. The *kahuna* (priests) were upset—Lono should not

JOURNAL OF CAPTAIN COOK

Captain James Cook set sail from England on his third voyage to circumnavigate the globe in July of 1776. His mission was to find a Northwest Passage that might connect the northern Pacific and Atlantic oceans. The ships he chose were two converted coal ships, Resolution *and* Discovery. *Together they traveled south of Australia and past New Zealand and Tahiti, trying out the relatively new Harrison chronometer, which made it possible for sailors to find longitude even if they were away from land for over a month. Cook left Bora Bora in December of 1777 and began to head north through uncharted seas.*

*F*riday 2nd January. We continued to see birds every day of the sorts last mentioned, sometimes in greater numbers than at others: and between the latitude of 10 and a 11 we saw several turtle. All these are looked upon as signs of the vecinity of land; we however saw none till day break in the Morning of the 18th when an island was descovered bearing NEBE and soon after we saw more land bearing North and intirely ditatched from the first; both had the appearence of being high land.

Monday 19th January. . . . At this time we were in some doubt whether or not the land before was inhabited, this doubt was soon cleared up, by seeing some Canoes coming off from the shore towards the Ships, I immediately brought to to give them time to come up, there were three and four men in each and we were agreeably surprised to find them of the same Nation as the people of Otahiete [Tahiti] and the other islands we had lately visited. It required by very little address to get them to come along side, but we could not prevail upon any one to come on board; they exchanged a few fish they had in the Canoes for any thing we offered them, but valued nails, or iron above every other thing; the only weapons they had were a few stones in some of the Canoes and these they threw overboard when they found they were not wanted. Seeing no signs of an anchoring place at this part of the island, I boar up for the lee side, and ranged the SE side at the distance of half a league from the shore. As soon as we made sail the Canoes left us, but others came off from the shore and brought with them roasting pigs and some very fine Potatoes, which they exchanged, as the others had done, for whatever was offered them; several small pigs were got for a sixpeny nail or two apiece, so that we again found our selves in the land of plenty, just as the turtle we had taken on board at the last island was nearly expended. We passed several villages, some seated upon the sea shore and other up in the Country; the inhabitants of all of them crowded to the shore and on the elevated places to view the Ships.

. . . As soon as the Ships was anchored I went a shore with three boats, to look at the water and try the disposition of the inhabitants, several hundreds of whom were assembled on a sandy beach before the Village. The very instant I leaped ashore, they all fell flat on their faces, and remained in that humble posture till I made signs to them to rise. They then brought a great many small pigs and gave us without regarding whether they got any thing in return or no indeed the most of them were present[ed] to me with plantain trees, in a ceremonious way as is usual on such like occasions, and I ratified these marks of friendship by presenting them with such things as I had with me. After things were a little settled I left a guard on the beach and got some of the Indians to shew me the water, which proved to be very good and convenient to come at.

. . . Our guide proclamed our approach and every one whom we met fell on their faces and remained in that position till we had passed. This as I afterwards understood, is done to their great chiefs.

. . . No people could trade with more honisty than these people, never once attempting to cheat us, either ashore or along side the ships. Some indeed at first betrayed a thievish disposition, or rather they thought they had a right to any thing they could lay their hands upon but this conduct they soon laid aside.

—Captain James Cook, *The Journals of Captain Cook*, 1778-1779.

Curious Hawaiians come out to visit Captain Cook's ships in 1778; by John Webber. (Bancroft Library)

have sailed in from an anti-clockwise direction, the timing was not auspicious, and the god's mast was broken.

In their passion for iron, Hawaiians took to absconding with anything metal they could pilfer, which led to a tragic series of misunderstandings, unfortunate diplomatic decisions, and a final confrontation in which Cook was slain on the beach. Enraged, Cook's men rampaged through villages, killing dozens of Hawaiians. As the violence waned, King Kalaniopu'u, aware that a great man had fallen, conveyed belated esteem by returning some of Cook's bones, which had been distributed for their *mana*. The remains were buried at sea while Hawaiians respectfully chanted ashore, and the two ships sailed from Hawai'i in February of 1779 under the command of James Clerke, captain of the *Discovery*. At a high price, Hawai'i had entered the modern world.

James Cook is considered one of history's finest explorers. His journals evoke a wise, merciful, and ingenious seafarer who feared European contact with Pacific peoples would bring them disease and forever alter their cultures. Young officers on the Cook expedition later would return to the Pacific with their own ships—the infamous William Bligh in command of the *Bounty*, and Captain George Vancouver, who brought the first cattle to Hawai'i and became a confidante of Kamehameha the Great.

■ KAMEHAMEHA THE GREAT

Twelve years after Cook's death, the young warrior Kamehameha defeated in battle the heir to the island of Hawai'i and became its ruler. Believing he was the man destined in a prophecy to unite the islands under one king, he waged uncompromising war on the rulers of the other islands. Impressed by Cook's cannon power (which he'd seen as a young man), he shrewdly acquired an armory of western weapons. In 1795, Kamehameha the Great defeated his last enemies in Nu'uanu Valley on O'ahu, and his mission to form a united kingdom was accomplished. Only Kaua'i remained unconquered militarily, and a pact was made with Kaumauali'i, King of Kaua'i, that allowed him to remain governor, while giving up overall power to Kamehameha. After the great king's death in 1819, his son Liholiho, who became Kamehameha II, lured the Kaua'i ruler aboard a ship, kidnapped him, and forced him to marry Kamehameha's widow. With this maneuver, the grand design of unification was completed.

Boki, chief of the Hawaiian Navy, (far right) and Chief Kahekili (center, facing away) with two Hawaiian chieftesses, visit the Russian sloop, Kamchatka in 1818; painting by Mikhail Tikhanov. (Scientific Research Museum, Academy of Arts, St. Petersburg)

Kamehameha I was known for wise decisions and athletic feats. Biographer Richard Tregaskis describes his "strength and grace—surfing in tropical seas, pursuing beautiful women and voluptuousness, living among palms and flowers, mountains, rainbows, volcanoes, tropical lagoons and trade winds." Acting with humanistic and peaceable wisdom, he proclaimed a law still revered:

> *K*now ye and reverence your God. Have an understanding heart that you may regard the small as you would the big man. Love one another, lest your affections wither away and die. Let the old man and the woman and the little child, traveling, sleep unmolested on the King's Highway. Let none disturb them or harm them as they walk or sleep. The penalty is death.

Soon after the death of Kamehameha the Great, his favorite wife Ka'ahumanu, and his sacred wife Keopuolani, engineered the overthrow of the *kapu* system by convincing the new king, Liholiho (Kamehameha II), to eat with them. Hawaiians were shocked to see that the gods didn't retaliate, and in the ensuing upheaval, idols were smashed and the *kapu* system was toppled. With the old beliefs in disarray, the Hawaiians found themselves adrift in a spiritual vacuum.

■ WHALERS AND MISSIONARIES

Within a few months the vacuum rapidly was filled by American Protestant missionaries who arrived from New England in 1820, armed with Christian fervor and a plan to rescue the pagans from sin. About this time abundant whaling grounds were being discovered in waters off Japan, whose ports were closed to foreigners. Soon hundreds of whaling ships out of New England put in for replenishment at Lahaina Roads on Maui, and at Honolulu on O'ahu. The whalers' crews also had more personal forms of replenishment in mind and bolted ashore in search of grog and women.

In the space of less than two years, fate had thrown the Hawaiians a triple punch. It was just a matter of time until whalers, missionaries, and a kingdom undergoing great change would wear away at the old Hawaiian customs. In the inevitable collision of the two New England factions, the whalers' motto, "No God west of the Horn," led to violent confrontations with the missionaries, who were gaining Hawaiian converts. Within an hour of her death in 1823, Queen

Keopuolani was baptized a Christian. By 1825, dancing and horseback riding on the Sabbath had been forbidden. Drinking, gambling, and ship visits by women were outlawed. Under a succession of monarchs during the rest of the nineteenth century, the missionaries banished Hawai'i's hula, through which Hawaiians told the great stories and myths of their race; covered the women in baggy *mu'umu'u* gowns; and sermonized against adultery—a previously unknown concept. They convinced Hawaiians that the *haole* (Westerners) were somehow superior. To their credit, the missionaries created a 12-letter alphabet and put the Hawaiian language on paper, established schools, and began the process of intermarriage which has culminated in Hawai'i's beautiful part-Hawaiian people.

KAMEHAMEHA IN PERSON

In 1816, a Russian brig, the Rurik, *sailed into Kealakekua Bay on the Island of Hawai'i, and its captain, Otto von Kotzebue, visited with Hawai'i's great king, Kamehameha I. It was at Kealakekua Bay that Captain Cook had been killed in 1779, when Kamehameha was a powerful young warrior and nephew to the island's chief. By the time Captain von Kotzebue arrived 37 years later, Kamehameha was not only king of the Big Island, he had conquered all of the islands and unified them under his rule. Once a ferocious warrior, he was now a wise older statesman, who'd returned to his home island to live out the final years of his life. Not only does von Kotzebue give us an intimate portrait of the king and his family, but the ship's artist, Louis Choris, sketched one of the few portraits in existence of Kamehameha and of his favorite queen, Ka'ahumanu.*

The king came to meet us as far as the landing place with some of his most distinguished warriors, and when we got out of the boat he came up to me and cordially shook me by the hand. Curiosity brought the people from all sides, but the greatest order prevailed, and no noise or importunity was permitted. I now stood at the side of the celebrated Kamehameha, who had attracted the attention of all Europe, and who inspired me with the greatest confidence by his unreserved and friendly behavior. He conducted me to his straw palace, which, according to the custom of the country, consisted only of one spacious apartment, and like all the houses here, afforded a free draft both to the land and sea breezes, which alleviates the oppressive heat.

continues

He conversed with a vivacity surprising at his age, asked us various questions respecting Russia, and made observations. Cook [von Kotzebue's translator] was not always able to translate the words that the king used, which were peculiar to the Hawaiian language and so witty that his ministers often laughed aloud.

One of Kamehameha's wives passed by our house, and in a friendly manner wished me a good morning through the door, but she was not allowed to enter, it being the king's eating house. With the king's permission, we took a walk, accompanied by Cook and a guard of honor of five naked soldiers. We visited the favorite queen Ka'ahumanu mentioned by Vancouver; we found her with the two other wives, and were very politely received by all. The house which Ka'ahumanu inhabits is built very neatly, and is very cleanly in the interior; the entrance hall, in which the three wives were seated according to the Asiatic fashion, was covered with fine and elegant mats, and she herself was pretty closely wrapped up in the finest cloth of the country. Ka'ahumanu was seated in the middle, and the two other ladies on either side; and I had the honor to be invited to sit down opposite them, likewise on the ground. They put to me several questions, which I answered to their satisfaction through Cook. Watermelons were brought and Ka'ahumanu was polite enough to cut one and hand me a piece.

The chief employment of the royal ladies consists in smoking tobacco, combing their hair, driving away the flies with a fan, and eating.

Kamehameha the Great later in his life; by Louis Choris, 1812. (Bancroft Library)

After we had left the king's wives, we visited his son. Cook informed me that this prince, as successor to the throne, had already begun to exercise the rights of his father, which consist in the fulfilling of the most important tabus. Kamehameha has ordered this from political motives, that no revolution may arise after his death; for as soon as the son fulfills the most important tabu, he is sacred, is associated with the priests, and nobody dare dispute the throne with him. The prince, as soon as he is admitted into the rights of his father, receives the name of Liholiho, that is, dog of all dogs [a mistake; it means fiery]; and such we really found him.

We entered a neat and small house, in which Liholiho, a tall, corpulent, and naked figure, was stretched out on his stomach, and just indolently raised his head to look at his guests; near him sat several naked soldiers armed with muskets, who guarded the monster; a handsome young native, with a tuft of red feathers, drove away the flies ʿrom him and from his interesting countenance and becoming behavior, I should rather have taken him for the king's son. Kamehameha, who, by his wise government, has acquired permanent glory, and has laid the foundation for the civilization and improvement of his people, ought to have a successor capable of prosecuting with zeal and judgment the work which he has begun.

The dog of all dogs at last rose very lazily, and gaped upon us with a stupid vacant countenance. My embroidered uniform seemed to meet his approbation, for he held a long conversation about it with a couple of naked chamberlains. I could not learn his age, as no account is kept of it. I guess it may be about twenty-two years, and am of the opinion that his enormous corpulency is occasioned by his constant lying on the ground.

continues

Queen Kaʻahumanu, who loved surfing, battles, and men, was Kamehameha the Great's favorite wife; by Louis Choris, 1812. (Bancroft Library)

Kamehameha's first walk was to the morai; he embraced one of the statues, which was hung round more than the others with fruits and pieces of a sacrificed hog, saying, "These are our gods, whom I worship; whether I do right or wrong, I do not know; but I follow my faith, which cannot be wicked, as it commands me never to do wrong." This declaration . . . indicated much sound sense, and inspired me with a certain emotion.

Cook told us that Kamehameha never regarded the rank of his subjects; that he generally chose his confidants from the lower classes, and was seldom deceived in his choice. He behaves to his great men with justice indeed, but with rigor, and as he places little confidence in them, they are obliged to accompany him on his journeys, by which he deprives them of the opportunity to throw off his authority by a conspiracy. They have not forgotten that Kamehameha is the conqueror of their lands, and is now sole monarch, and they would certainly attempt to conquer their property if he did not know so well how to keep them in his power.

—Captain Otto von Kotzebue,
A Voyage of Discovery into the South Sea and Behring's Strait, 1821

■ RISE OF SUGAR

Having done well with Bibles, descendants of the missionaries set about doing well in financial enterprises. They took a sweet route—sugarcane, and it led to the establishment of Hawai'i's five wealthiest *haole* companies. The first of the great sugar plantations was begun on Kaua'i in 1835.

In 1848, Kamehameha III proclaimed the Great *Mahele* (division), and changed the concept of land ownership. The king, until now the owner of all land, gave up much of it. Before the act, commoners had lived off the land, working it for their personal use and paying chiefs, who controlled lands for the king, in labor or crops. Now chiefs were allowed to buy those lands, and smaller crown plots were offered to commoners. To gain title, all were required to pay a tax and register the land. While the *Mahele* was intended to distribute the land, few commoners understood the concept of private land ownership and most failed to complete registration. Two years later foreigners were permitted to purchase land, and in the 1850s Westerners plunged in. Within a couple of generations, 80 percent of all private land lay in large estates, most of them owned by *haole* or the children of *haole* and native Hawaiians. Meanwhile, by the mid-1800s only 50,000 Hawaiians survived, down from the approximately 300,000 reported by Captain Cook in 1778. They had died in droves from imported diseases—venereal disease contracted from Cook's crew, cholera and smallpox from whalers.

When plantation-style agriculture went into full swing in the islands, there weren't enough Hawaiians to work the fields (nor were they enamored of giving up what was left of their traditional life to help those who were destroying it). The sugar companies began bringing in foreign contract laborers. Between 1852 and 1856 Chinese arrived, and in 1885, Hawai'i's king signed a treaty with Japan which allowed large-scale immigration, and 70,000 Japanese arrived. Between 1878 and 1887, Portuguese came from the islands of Madeira and the Azores. As most of the workers stayed on and established families, Hawaiians became a landless minority in their own land.

■ ANNEXATION

Hawai'i's last king, David Kalakaua was elected to the throne in 1874. A world traveler known as the "Merry Monarch," his greatest legacy was the revitalization of Hawaiian culture. After years of missionary suppression of the "heathen dance," Kalakaua brought back the hula and compiled ancient legends. However, the moment Kalakaua died in 1891, American planters plunged into plots against his successor and sister, Queen Lili'uokalani. Hawaiian sugar sales to the U.S. had been severely restricted due to a hefty tariff imposed by Congress, and to protect their profits the planters connived for an end to the monarchy and a takeover by the United States. By now the sugar barons, descendants of the missionaries, had taken the land and held key governmental positions. In 1893, the Queen was deposed and replaced by a Provisional Government, which in turn was replaced by the **Republic of Hawai'i**.

The Republic of Hawai'i was little more than a governorship controlled by Sanford Dole, the most powerful of the American sugarcane planters. The U.S. president at the time of the coup, Grover Cleveland, called it "not merely wrong, but a disgrace." In 1898, at the urging of Teddy Roosevelt and others, Congress annexed the Islands and created the Territory of Hawai'i. That same year, in the aftermath of the Spanish-American War, the U.S. acquired the Philippines and

After a series of questionable political maneuvers by prominent Americans, on July 4, 1894 the Kingdom of Hawai'i and the Provisional Government of Hawai'i were replaced by the Republic of Hawai'i, with Stanford Dole as its first president. (Oakland Museum)

Guam. Since Japan was seen as expansionist, the U.S. Navy set its eye on the finest sheltered harbor in the Pacific, Pearl Harbor, where access had been permitted by Kalakaua. Construction of naval facilities began in 1908.

Meanwhile, the planters increased their profits with the newly arrived pineapple, planted and picked by imported contract laborers. The earlier waves of plantation laborers were augmented by Puerto Ricans who arrived in 1900, Koreans in 1903, and between 1907 and 1931, Filipinos. While working conditions were poor and wages minimal, the planters unwittingly preserved ethnic cultures by setting up plantation camps in native groupings.

■ TOURISM BEGINS

Extraordinary events affected the growth of tourism. The roots of the industry took hold well before the twenties. Just 14 years after the widely publicized annexation of the islands, the Hawaiian swimmer Duke Paoa Kahanamoku (1890-1968) placed Hawai'i again in the international limelight. At the Stockholm Olympic Games in 1912, he shattered the world record in the 100-meter freestyle. In the same year he introduced surfboard riding to Australia where "The Duke" is known as the Father of Surfing. Kahanamoku brought another Olympic gold home in 1920, and more Olympic medals in 1924 and 1928. With his new fast "Hawaiian Crawl" style, the Duke's fame spread Hawai'i's name. A popular song, *On the Beach at Waikiki,* was sung across the mainland at the onset of World War I, implanting the romance and allure of Hawai'i's islands and Waikiki Beach in the public mind.

The development of Waikiki and its tourist industry are tied to Matson shipping in a convoluted web of business and foresight. Matson built the deluxe passenger ship SS *Malolo* (Flying Fish), which entered service on the San Francisco-Honolulu run in conjunction with the opening of Waikiki's new Royal Hawaiian Hotel in 1927.

Despite the stock market crash of 1929, and the pall which descended across the nation, the business barons of Honolulu continued to flourish in well-heeled bliss. They were prepared to invest in the growth of tourism. Matson contracted for two more ships, placed the *Lurline* in service to Hawai'i, and bought out the Los Angeles Steamship Company which had entered the Hawai'i trade in the early twenties. Liner travel flourished until World War II. It did not recover rapidly in following years. Today, Matson no longer carries passengers; it plies the waters of the Pacific with giant ships carrying freight.

■ PAN AM AND TOURISM

The most decisive factor in the growth of Hawaiian tourism came in 1936 when a Martin M-130 flying boat, the *Hawai'i Clipper,* soared out over San Francisco Bay with seven paying passengers ($360 one-way). Flying 2,270 air miles (3,632 km), she settled down on Honolulu waters in the amazing time of 21 hours, 33 minutes, introducing an era of luxurious air travel with private compartments and sleeping berths, dining room tables heaped with gourmet delicacies, and gracious service. The 26-ton giant brought Hawai'i nearer to the mainland by three and a half days. Overnight, modern tourism was born. With the Moana, the Royal Hawaiian, and the new Halekulani hotels, Waikiki in the thirties began to develop into the center of island tourism.

With demand escalating for more and larger aircraft, Pan Am replaced its three Martins with the *California Clipper,* a 74-passenger Boeing B-314. By 1941, with five more Boeings, Pan Am's flying boats were racing the skies on a daily service run from San Francisco to Honolulu.

The great body of lore that fills the logs of aircraft pilots includes an entry for December 7, 1941. While en route from San Francisco and just one hour out from the Pan Am base at Pearl Harbor, the pilot of Pan Am's clipper learned the Japanese had attacked. Diverting to Hilo on the Big Island, instead of laying over, the crew broke every rule for speed, and within two hours had unloaded passengers and mail, refueled the plane by hand, and had taken off as daylight faded. (What the passengers thought of this is unrecorded.) By making a dangerous nighttime takeoff, the pilot avoided Japanese patrols and returned safely to San Francisco (and government wartime service).

Four years later, on November 16, 1945, commercial flights to Honolulu resumed. North, south, and west from Honolulu, Pan Am flying boat clippers trail-blazed the Pacific Ocean area, prying open far-away Pacific destinations. Now time and progress ordained that the era of the flying boat was coming to an end: by early 1946, land-based aircraft (Douglas DC-4s) entered service on the route to Honolulu.

Pan Am's trail-blazing wasn't finished yet. The dawn of the jet age also belongs to Pan Am. In 1958, just one year before Hawai'i achieved statehood, the airline flew a Boeing 707 to Honolulu, revolutionizing international travel. When its inaugural 747 flight touched down at Honolulu in 1970, Pan Am was first again, and some aircraft historians claim that if Pan Am had not had the foresight to order the 747 in 1966, the modern era of flight would have been delayed.

■ MODERN HAWAI'I EVOLVES

While Pan Am was fostering tourism, two upheavals profoundly altered the political power structure in the Territory of Hawai'i. The clique of "Big Five" companies was forced to negotiate wages and working conditions with unions, made legal by the National Labor Relations Act of 1935. The other change came after World War II, when the Veterans Act provided education funds for returned servicemen. Men of Hawai'i's highly decorated 100th Infantry and the all-Japanese 442nd Regimental Combat Team enrolled in mainland universities, returned home, and joined the Democratic Party. Labor-supported Democrats swamped Republicans in the election of 1954 and have dominated Hawaiian politics ever since.

Hawai'i has paid a price for social equality. As wages climbed to acceptable levels, Hawaiian sugar and pineapple could no longer compete with low-cost labor plantations abroad. Both industries began moving out of Hawai'i. Some Hawaiians do not rue their passing. Today there are new ways to earn a living—through large-scale tourism, service industries, and high-tech oceanographic programs.

■ MASS TOURISM

When Congress granted Hawai'i statehood in 1959 and a fiftieth star was added to the nation's flag, the islands entered a building boom which shows few signs of abating. New hotels and condominiums stabbed the skyline of Waikiki on O'ahu. Maui followed, and by the mid 1970s, tourism had overtaken the military as Hawai'i's largest industry. Mass tourism flourished in Waikiki, cramming it with restaurants, nightclubs, snack bars, and endless shops. While the giant hotels were expanding, still more construction squeezed into the area between the beach and the Ala Wai Canal. Within the 618 acres of Waikiki, the room count rose to more than 25,000, and is now close to 33,500.

By the eighties, residents began to wake up, wondering at what they had allowed to happen. Many pointed to the district as an example of what must not be repeated on neighbor islands, and outsiders railed that Waikiki was another Miami Beach. While that comparison is far off the mark, the fact stands that Waikiki *is* over-developed. In the nineties, "controlled development" has become the watchword of legislators and conservationists. Despite its over-development, Waikiki

An inter-island luxury liner pulls up off Lahaina on the Maui coast. Passengers are brought into the historic harbor on small boats.

offers a long list of delights. Amid the ubiquitous concrete, trees and greenery flourish. Though rife with commercialism, Waikiki is clean, the sun is bright, and there are no billboards or neon signs protruding above the street. (They're both banned throughout Hawai'i.) Crowds of visitors stroll the shops clad in beach togs; restaurants abound; and a saunter at night in caressing tradewinds delivers the proof that somehow Hawai'i's magic still reigns.

■ HAWAI'I'S PEOPLE

Tourism made the magic of Hawai'i known the world round, yet advertising hyperbole cannot capture its essence. With diverse cultures in islands of great beauty, Hawai'i is a microcosm of the future, and it is her people who make it so. Nearly one-third of marriages in Hawai'i mix, blend, and produce beautiful offspring. In his novel *Hawaii,* James Michener called Hawai'i's modern people "Golden Man." With a population of 1,108,000, Hawai'i is about 25 percent Caucasian, 24 percent Japanese, 31 percent Hawaiian and part-Hawaiian, 12 percent Filipino, and five percent Chinese; (other Asians and African-Americans make up the remaining three percent). Today the most politically powerful group is Hawai'i-born Japanese and part-Japanese, and the most free-spending tourists are the Japanese as well. Japanese from Japan now own more than half of Hawai'i's hotels and condos, and continue to buy service industries and private homes.

■ HAWAIIAN CULTURE

Hawaiians are the fastest-growing ethnic community in the state. While their culture was vulgarized in the early days of tourism, today few Hawaiians, or visitors, have much interest in imitations. Hawaiians strive to preserve their culture and its traditions, which

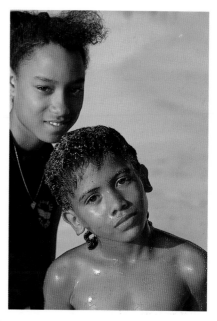

The people of Hawai'i are a beautiful blend of many races.

always have been interwoven with the natural environment. Since 1974, when a *kumu hula* (hula master) led a male troupe through an authentic, vigorous hula, a renaissance of Hawaiian culture has taken root and blossomed. The hula originated, legend says, when the volcano goddess Pele commanded her younger sister Laka to dance. In time, schools sprang up in honor of the goddess of the dance, and temples were dedicated to her. Dancers lived within the confines of the temple grounds, under strenuous training regimes and *kapu* (taboos), for hula was a sacred art; it represented the heart of the people, with its oral tradition carrying history, custom, ceremony, and genealogy. They trained in the classical hula or *kahiko*—the ancient form of chanting and dance—which tells of knowledge seen, known, and felt, that travels through generations in oral and dance form.

Some surviving hula chants allow rare glimpses into the past and give clues to the future. In the *Kaulilua* chant, the unknown composer saw Hawai'i as the homeland of many people fused together in the manner of coral.

To Hawaiians, hula celebrates life. For decades the words of Kalakaua were forgotten; now they are recognized: "Hula is the language of the heart and therefore the heartbeat of the Hawaiian people." Today, *kahiko* is a highly regarded wellspring, and it takes a long stretch of imagination to consider this hula mere popular entertainment. Hula *halau* (house of hula instruction) troupes practice nights and weekends to compete in annual dance contests that are held throughout the islands and followed avidly by the general population. Winners take home a ribbon or a medal, and enormous prestige. Architects, nurses, teachers and attorneys, clerks and artisans—whatever their careers, Hawaiians are eager to study and be a part of this resurgent Hawaiian heritage.

The basic concept of Hawaiian culture is best translated as sharing. It flows from respect and love, which is the hula. And it flows from *ho'opono,* which is communal counseling and problem solving that is non-judgmental, truth-seeking, and solution-oriented. With the renaissance of the hula, and of *ho'opono,* present-day Hawaiians learn from the wisdom of their ancestors.

(opposite) Bodysurfers diving under an outside wave at Mokapu Beach, O'ahu.

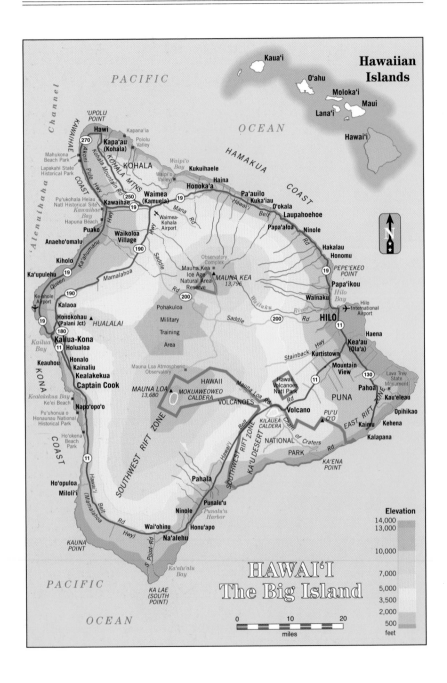

H A W A I ' I
T H E   B I G   I S L A N D

PELE, GODDESS OF FIRE, DOMINATES THE HEARTLAND OF HAWAI'I, dwelling in her firepit home at the summit of the world's most active volcano, Kilauea. Since the latest series of eruptions began nearly a decade ago her outpourings of red burning lava have added new acres of black-sand coastline to Hawai'i—geologically the youngest, and by far the largest, of all the Hawaiian islands.

Since Hawai'i is twice the size of all the other islands put together, you won't be able to see all of its turtle-like shape from your airplane window. Nor is it easy to begin to grasp its great variety. This most diverse island in the Hawaiian chain is something of a miniature planet, enfolding almost all the varieties of topography and climate found on earth. Cool and misty ranch pastures blanket the volcanic slopes of the north at Waimea and North Kohala. In the mountainous center, active volcanoes have shaped arid moonscapes of lava tubes, craters, and volcanic mounds called *pu'u;* smoky plumes rise from rift cracks in the earth. To the south the island swells toward lava flows spilling into the sea. Beaches run in colors from deep black (formed when lava cinders exploded at the water line) to brilliant white to green sands laced with olivine and obsidian tossed up by volcanoes.

As your plane approaches, you will see Hawai'i's mountains, tallest in the island chain. At nearly 14,000 feet (4,200 m) above sea level, they are only the peaks of massive mountains rising 32,000 feet (9,700 m) from the ocean floor. Because they create a barrier to wind and rain, the mountains keep the northeasterly tradewinds on the windward east flank of Hawai'i, watering rain-swept valleys, pastel-green sugarcane fields, forests, and the orchid farms of the Hamakua Coast. To the dry west, volcano lands slope down to coffee farms stretching above the sunny beaches of the leeward Kona and South Kohala coasts. Sometimes called the Gold Coast, the landscape here alternates between fields of barren lava and the gleaming emerald grounds and golf courses of luxury hotels. Palm-backed beaches face warm blue snorkeling waters where rainbow-colored fish dart in coral reefs. Beyond the reefs, the cooler navy-blue sea is the domain of game fish—bill fish (also called swordfish or blue, black, and striped marlin); *mahimahi* (dorado) and *ono* (wahoo); and skipjack, bluefin, and yellowfin tuna.

The Big Island is so big you can drive all day without encountering a mega-resort. Hawai'i Belt Road outlines the island's contour, yet some sections remain untouched. While tourism is well-established, it blends into the landscape most successfully on Hawai'i, and there are miles and miles of pristine wilderness. Whether you arrive at Hilo, the county seat in the wet tropical east, or at Kailua-Kona in the dry volcanic west, it's well to realize these two main towns are far apart. One hundred thirty-one miles (210 km) stretch between them when you drive up into the middle and down around the southern end of the island. By the northern route, the drive is 116 miles (186 km).

Hawai'i is an island that claims time. Within 300 miles (480 km) of coastline lie centuries of history and the climates of a hemisphere. Beach, volcano, a sunset blue-water sail, game fishing, snorkeling, elegant dining, or trekking through rainforest and cowboy country—all are available. Take time on the Big Island. Hawai'i's magic is here.

■ HISTORY

The history of the Big Island of Hawai'i is very nearly the history of all Hawai'i. Here the Polynesians first beached their voyaging canoes some 1,400 years ago. Following tradition, they built a *he'iau*, or temple of sacrifice, and continued the Polynesian system of social laws, or *kapu*.

Here too Kamehameha the Great was born (probably in 1750) and spent his boyhood. He would have been in his early twenties and may well have been present in 1779 when the strange, high-masted ship of Captain James Cook sailed into Kealakekua Bay—where Cook later was killed. A fearsome warrior, Kamehameha was nephew to Kalaniopu'u, chief of the island, and soon became his most successful general. A pleased Kalaniopu'u made the young warrior the keeper of the god of war—a carved statue of Kuka'ilimoku. As Kamehameha carried the gory, red-mouthed god into battle, it supposedly emitted horrible screams.

At the death of his uncle, Kamehameha battled with the old king's son Kiwala'o, who had inherited his father's lands and title. After defeating Kiwala'o, Kamehameha emerged as the ruler of the northern half of Hawai'i. This worried his rivals, Kahekili, king of Maui, and Keoua, a cousin, both of whom ruled over southern parts of the island.

Kamehameha had just begun. In 1790, to help fulfill a prophecy that he would rule all the islands, he began construction of Pu'ukohola He'iau, a temple of sacrifice in northwest Kohala. In the prophecy, war would end (and presumably he would dominate) when the *he'iau* was completed and he had sacrificed a major chief. As building progressed, Kamehameha learned that Keoua was sailing a fleet of war canoes up the east coast, planning to come around the top of Kohala to attack him and stop construction. Kamehameha met and defeated the invading forces off the sacred eastern valley of Waipi'o—where he had received his war god Ku. This time, in the Battle of the Red-Mouthed Gun, the war god had the assistance of a cannon manned by two British sailors on the captured schooner *Fair American*.

Construction of the controversial *he'iau* continued. A contingent of Keoua's warriors, returning to south Hawai'i by way of Kilauea volcano, encountered the goddess Pele near her Halema'uma'u firepit. Here she came to Kamehameha's aid, heaving rock and cinders in clouds of choking gas in the only explosive eruption known. You still can see the footprints in solidified ash where the warriors tried to

Hawaiians dressed in traditional costume at Pu'ukohala He'iau, which Kamehameha built to fulfill a prophecy that he would rule all the islands and where he made his cousin, Keoua, its first sacrifice. North Kohala Coast.

run. When the temple was completed in 1791, Keoua, Kamehameha's cousin, was its inaugural human sacrifice.

By the late eighteenth century the warrior king who would be known as Kamehameha the Great filled the horizons with fleets of immense war canoes; with them he subdued and unified the other islands and named the Kingdom of Hawai'i for his home island. When all was secure, he returned to the Big Island, where he died at Kailua in May of 1819. After his death, the remains of Kamehameha were prepared in the ancient way, by separating flesh from bone. To protect the *mana* of his sacred bones, they were hidden in secret—perhaps in a cave; no one knows where. The site never has been revealed, nor discovered.

Six months after Kamehameha's death his strong-minded, favorite wife Ka'ahumanu engineered the breaking of a *kapu* (the rules of social behavior) which forbade women to eat with men. When the gods didn't retaliate against this intrepid woman, the Hawaiians began to doubt both gods and *kapu*. A wave of destruction and violence swept the island, as the laws which had long supported Hawaiian social structure came crashing down. Idols were smashed and one after another the *kapu* were broken, leaving the people bewildered. Into this vacuum sailed a shipload of missionaries aboard the *Thaddeus,* out of New England. Landing at Kailua in April of 1820, they stepped ashore almost on top of the very spot where the great king had died less than a year earlier. They brought a new god and a new restrictive social system that destroyed much of Hawaiian culture, particularly the hula, heartbeat of the Hawaiian people.

What followed on Hawai'i mirrors the modern history of the Hawaiian Islands: a catastrophic decline in population through disease; domination over Hawaiian culture by the new religion; and the arrival of sugar, ranching, and tourism. Yet the Big Island, steeped in mythology of the fire goddess, preserves the fragments of early Hawai'i, of Kamehameha and the first contacts with foreigners, and is a treasure trove of history and ancient belief.

■ HILO

Visitors landing in Hilo arrive on the lush windward side of the island, where tropical growth is rampant and rain feeds waterfalls, leafy tree ferns, and enough flowers to fill a rainbow. The trick is to snare a sunny day—when it also can be hot and humid.

Perhaps named for the first night of the new moon, or for an ancient Polynesian navigator, Hilo is the second largest city (after Honolulu) in the state, and the Big Island's main seaport. The town curves around the broad rim of Hilo Bay and stretches up *mauka* (inland) into lush hills. Rainfall is well over 100 inches (254 cm) annually, making Hilo the wettest city in the United States. Rain usually falls in the afternoon and is responsible for rich greenery and a slower pace of resort development. Flowers and more flowers are everywhere—orchids, anthurium, and bromeliads bloom in gardens and shops and push up through roadside growth. This part of the island is the heart of the world's orchid business, growing some 30,000 species.

Hilo is a town with spirit. In 1960, a *tsunami* deluged the waterfront, sweeping an organ console out the stage door of the Palace Theater, depositing fishing boats in streets, and killing 61 residents. Businesses rebuilt. By 1985, Hilo's downtown was sliding into disrepair, an affliction suffered by the core of many cities. The city responded by turning the old waterfront into a park. Despite the changes, Hilo has managed to retain the aura of Pacific trading ports between 1920 and 1940— its buildings sporting vintage wood and metal roofs. You still can park your car or tie up your horse at a five-cent meter.

Downtown Hilo is centered at the west end of Hilo Bay. On a patch of grass in front of the Hilo Public Library on Wai'anuenue Street lies the **Naha Stone**. Nearly unknown to visitors, this monstrous rectangular block of lava—heavy as a 40-man war canoe or about three tons (2,700 kg)—marks the beginning of the career of Kamehameha. It was here, at the age of 14, that he sought to fulfill a prophecy that the man who could move the Naha Stone would be the greatest king of Hawai'i.

If he could move it, he would gain fame and status. If he could not, the *kahuna* of the Hilo king might beat him to death for violating a mortal *kapu*. Before high chiefs, a prophetess, and the assembled people, Kamehameha lifted the stone. Appropriately, his star rose.

A round, up-ended stone stands beside the Naha. Called the Pina'o, it is said to have been an entry pillar of a nearby temple named Pina'o, where the Naha originally stood. No plaque marks the stones; ask for a flyer at the front desk inside the library.

To delve into old Hilo, visit the **Lyman House Museum**, one block away on Haili Street. This was the home of the Reverend David and Sarah Lyman who arrived in Hilo from New England in the early 1830s. Half the museum is the

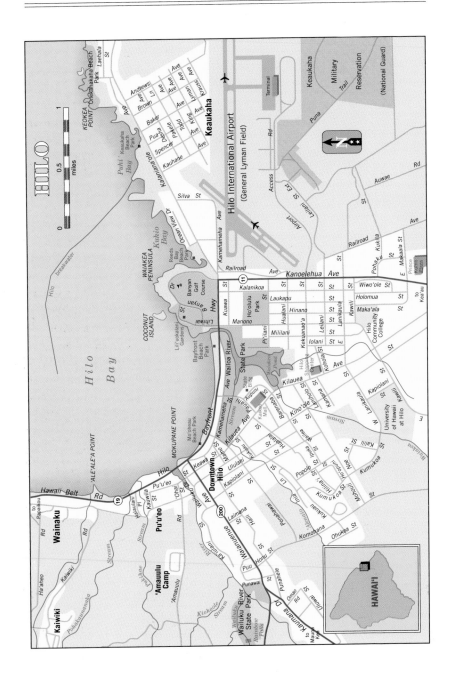

home, furnished as though the Lymans still lived there, with clothing, a cradle, quilts, photos, and curios in a Victorian parlor; there are children's rooms, dining and sitting rooms, kitchens and pantry. The other half is an adjoining modern museum building opened in 1973 to house an extensive collection of volcanic mineral rocks, and period pieces associated with the waves of immigration to Hawai'i—Japanese, Chinese, Portuguese, Korean, and Filipino. Look for the *braginha*, ancestor of the ukelele from Portugal, and a Taoist shrine from China.

Off upper Wai'anuenue Avenue, **Wai'anuenue (Rainbow-Seen-in-Water) Falls** drops 80 feet (25 m) into a large pool. Behind the falls lies a deep cave, a legendary home of Hina, mother of Maui. For the best rainbows, go in the morning. Many tour buses may be there, too.

If you get up early, drive over to the **Suisan Fish Auction** at the mouth of the Wailoa River on Kam Avenue, about a half mile from downtown. The Hilo commercial fishing fleet chugs in at sunrise every morning except Sunday. Here, between 8:00 and 8:30, an auction is conducted in a polyglot of languages at Hawai'i's last open-air fish market. By the time the final bell rings, the Wednesday and Saturday **Farmers' Market** nearby has been underway for hours. Look for breadfruit, Chinese crack seed, papaya, avocados, and stalks of ginger flowers.

Visitors who stay at the hotels on the **Wai'akea Peninsula**, which juts out into the bay, will enjoy taking in harbor life and the clear view of Mauna Kea. On the

View of Hilo in 1852; by James G. Sawkins. (Honolulu Academy of Arts)

peninsula, ringed by Banyan Drive, are great brooding trees planted by movie stars, athletes, and other celebrities who came here by ship in the thirties. Look for those planted by Amelia Earhart and Louis Armstrong; and note the Babe Ruth plaque in front of the Hilo Hawaiian Hotel. At **Lili'uokalani Park** walk in the 30 acres of Japanese gardens, with bridges, lagoons, and stone lanterns. A footbridge leads across to a small islet named Coconut, once a place of healing.

■ PUNA

Hawai'i is one of the few places on earth where spectators rush *to* volcanic eruptions instead of running from them. South of Hilo in the Puna region, you can experience Pele's raw power at close range, as she pours flaming lava from Kilauea Volcano into the sea in loud hissing columns of white steam. Hawaiian volcanoes don't blow their tops in the unpredictable manner of Mount St. Helens in the state of Washington. Rather, due to the composition of the lava, the flows are not termed "explosive," and volcanologists, measuring Pele's mood with their high-tech equipment seem to have the leisure of anticipation. Native Hawaiians have their own ways of knowing when an eruption is about to occur: Pele often appears to them in the cloudy night just before an eruption—perhaps on a deserted moonscape, or on the road. She may be an old crone asking for a lift, or a beautiful woman. Sometimes she will send her white dog in the misted moonlight.

To see flowing lava, take the Volcano Road (HI 11) from Hilo up to Kea'au and turn south on HI 130. The road travels through plantation towns, past orchid farms, and down into Puna, the southeastern district of Hawai'i. After continuing past old, weathered lava flows, at about 25 or 30 miles (45 km) from Hilo, the road (which once curved around the southern end of Puna and now is overrun with lava) stops abruptly at a barricade. The barricade is moved from time to time for safety—as Pele hurls her molten cascades downward and wide rivers of fast-moving lava slither over the pavement. The lava moves relentlessly toward the sea, consuming homes and churches, beach parks, whole villages, and sacred Hawaiian sites. Rangers of the Hawai'i Volcanoes National Park are stationed at the barricade to provide travelers with information, including daily updates on the state of the lava flow, and to direct them toward areas that can be reached on foot for safe viewing. At no other place on earth can you safely come so close; sometimes walking right beside flowing *pahoehoe*—the smooth, unbroken lava. Out on newly cooled lava, park rangers (outfitted, of course, in sturdy boots) walk around to determine its condition. Below the grey, slightly cooled crust the lava still is molten. Often there are places—if you can stand the heat—where you can stir it with a twig and the flow will consume the twig in a sudden brief spurt of flame. Above the sound of the molten river you hear sharp pops and bangs. Bushes and trees are exploding in the heat.

At a safe distance from the unstable area where lava enters the sea, you can view and walk on new black sand beaches. Unlike the narrow strips of earlier eruptions, as the latest series of eruptions goes on—some 650,000 cubic yards of molten material daily—wide, tumbling flows of lava meet the water to explode into tiny bits, and new black sand beaches hundreds of yards wide are made instantly. The Big Island grows bigger.

On January 3, 1983, Pu'u O'o vent opened in the east rift zone on the slopes of Kilauea Volcano some 10 miles (16 km) below the summit. A curtain of red lava shot into the air. Geysering tall one day, spewing steadily the next, the magma came up, and continues to come up, from the earth's core. Vog—volcanic smog—hovers over the vent, and when winds come the vog is carried over the island. Before Pu'u O'o opened its fiery mouth, the Chain of Craters Road looped down from the summit of Kilauea to Puna's shores. Now it is cut off, and when volcanologists determine that the eruption is surely done, road reconstruction will begin. Again. Until then, we must return to Hilo.

If you look up from the road barricade toward the high ridge above, cloud cover often confuses the view, and visitors sometimes wonder whether they are looking at Kilauea Volcano or Mauna Loa Volcano. Nearest to you is Kilauea rising to 4,093 feet (1,227 m). It is Kilauea that is erupting from Pu'u O'o vent on its slope to pour lava down into Puna. The tall peak you see actually is behind Kilauea. Often shrouded in cloud, this is the much taller mountain of Mauna Loa, towering to 13,680 feet (4,104 m). Mauna Loa and Kilauea are the two active volcanoes that make up Hawai'i Volcanoes National Park.

■ HAWAI'I VOLCANOES NATIONAL PARK

In Hawai'i Volcanoes National Park fire fountains roar, heat radiates from molten *pahoehoe* and *'a'a* (sharp, rough broken chunks of lava), and cinders laden with olivine and obsidian fall in fast-rising cones. The air smells of sulphur, and slashes in the earth waft steam. The park was established in 1916 to decipher and give access to the eerie volcanic lands of Mauna Loa and Kilauea; and the place itself is a lesson in geology. Rare plants and birds are carefully protected, and previously unknown species of insects still are being discovered.

Within park boundaries there are two volcanoes, scenic drives, 150 miles (240 km) of hiking trails, campgrounds, an observatory, a visitor center, a museum, and an art gallery. To visit the park take Volcano Road (HI 11) from Hilo. (As mentioned above, the alternate road from Puna has been covered over with lava flow.) On the 30-mile (48-km) drive, you'll see a rainforest nourished by volcanic soil where fragrant ginger threatens to smother the roadside pavement. Near the top, a turnoff leads to the tiny village of **Volcano**. The road continues through the gate of the national park, bordered in rainforest where *hapu'u* tree ferns, thick-boled and covered in soft red hair, sprout curled fiddleheads that unfurl to enormous size. A couple of miles past the gate the landscape unfolds in an arid plain of steaming rift cracks. A pervading spiritual presence seems to emanate here—the sacred home of the goddess Pele.

The best way to orient yourself is to drive straight to the **Visitor Center** at the park headquarters, a mile (1.6 km) from the gate. The free film shown hourly is a

Lava from Pu'u O'o vent engulfing a house along Chain of Craters Road. (Reg Morrison)
(opposite) Slopes of the Kohala Mountains at the north end of the Big Island, looking southwest.

fine introduction to volcanoes and park rangers are available to answer questions. Here you can buy maps and ask for directions, and can choose from a multitude of mini-expeditions. These include driving the Crater Rim Road (11 miles/18 km) circling the summit caldera through desert, rainforest and past old eruption sites; or walking one of three trails, each about one mile (1.6 km) long. They are Thurston Lava Tube, a huge tunnel 400 feet (120 m) long crossing Devastation Trail—a boardwalk through a cindered moonscape; Petroglyph Trail, which takes one to petroglyphs etched in rock; and the Bird Park Trail. (Bring a jacket to wear in the cooler air of these higher elevations.)

Directly across the road from the Visitor Center are viewing sites of the Kilauea caldera. Here the Volcano House Inn sits on the rim. Kilauea holds in its caldera, or large crater, the deep firepit named Halema'uma'u, the "enduring fire-house" home of Pele. From 1823 until 1924, the pit held a bubbling lake of fluid lava, and intrepid travelers once rode horses or mules up from the coast to the burning red-hot hole, among them visiting nineteenth- and twentieth-century writers—including Isabella Bird, Mark Twain, and later, James Michener. The lake vanished in 1924, swallowed whole by a rapid drain-off into a subterranean network of tubes and channels. The pit now lies exposed to a depth of some 500 feet (150 m).

Standing at the caldera rim you can look across it and decide if you'd like to take the trail down to the caldera floor to Halema'uma'u firepit. That trailhead can be reached by driving on Crater Rim Road to the far side of the caldera. If you visit the firepit, offer a handful of 'ohelo berries to the goddess Pele—or a bottle of gin. Some claim it's her favorite drink. In ancient times kahuna (priests) brought food and flowers here, never human sacrifices. Today, offerings still accumulate. The awesome force and beauty of Pele's work inspire respect.

An arid plateau stretches out behind the rim of the caldera. On it, clouds of hot steam snake up from wide cracks onto the cool plateau, and ferns drip with moist heat in the fissures. You can drive out onto the plateau, which is well marked with signs. Recently, the foolhardy have taken to steam bathing at the cracks. Don't try it; you could slip in the mud and fall in. Intense heat prevents rescue, so keep behind the safety rails.

Madame Pele frequently shrouds her home in mist and drifting cloud. Covering, then revealing her ghostly works, moving shadows chased by shafts of sunlight float across the caldera. Gnarled or standing tall, Pele's 'ohi'alehua trees form matte green clusters on the plateau. Sometimes its red pompom flowers fly away, inexplicably transformed into small *i'iwi* birds. When you leave Pele's region, it's unwise to take away pieces of lava rock. Tradition has it that bad luck will hound you. Park rangers say that parcels of rocks arrive in the mail every day. Enclosed are notes telling of dire events that have plagued the lives of visitors since they took rocks away with them, and they implore the rangers to give them back to Pele. (If you find yourself having inadvertently made off with a piece of Pele's rock, and you want to send it back, the address is: Headquarters, Hawai'i Volcanoes National Park, Volcano, HI 96785.)

■ KA'U AND THE ROAD TO KONA

The Hawai'i Belt Road (HI 11) descends southwest from Hawai'i Volcanoes National Park to loop down around the southern tip of the island and turn north along the west coast. In this 101-mile (162-km) journey toward Kailua-Kona, the road travels first through the uninhabited Ka'u Desert on the southwest rift zone, then passes Pahala, a tiny plantation colony leading to **Wood Valley Temple,** a Tibetan Buddhist retreat. (Visitors are permitted.) It continues past Na'alehu, the most southerly town in the U.S. (its 19-degree latitude is the same as Mexico City), to the village of Wai'ohinu, where the canopy-shaped **Mark Twain Monkeypod Tree** stands at the roadside. The original tree, planted by the author in 1866, was felled long ago by strong winds and the present tree rose from the roots. At the **South Point** turnoff, South Point Road leads 11 miles (17 km) through pasturelands to the nation's most southerly jut of land, rocky Ka Lae Point, where fishermen drop ladders off sheer cliffs to reach baited pots, or boats that pull up below.

Bending around the bottom of the island, the road crosses an ancient lava plain at the southwest shores of Ka'u district, where a new kind of resort is in the making. The **Hawaiian Riviera,** near the sandy-bottomed cove of Pohue (Gourd) Bay, is designed for visitors on extended stays. Set on 1,172 acres of land, slated to open in 1996, the resort will have its own airport, three hotels, marina apartments, sidewalk cafes, elegant shops, and restaurants near a 22-acre lagoon.

■ SOUTH KONA COAST

While the west side of the island can't hold a candle to the east when it comes to tropical vegetation, the sun always shines on the golden Kona and South Kohala coasts. From the macadamia nut orchards of South Kona to Kawaihae in South Kohala, more than 80 miles (130 km) of coastline mark the sunsoaked coast. Even afternoon showers in the coffee fields seldom reach the shore a short two miles (3 km) away. Sometimes called Kamehameha's Coast, it is lined with some of the most important sites in Hawaiian history, and boasts the best water-sport activities on the island.

Ho'okena Beach Park is north of Ka'u and about 22 miles (36 km) south of Kailua. A sign marks the Ho'okena paved road, and it is two miles (3 km) to the beach. The soft black sands of Ho'okena are rimmed by sheer lava walls. Its wide strand, lined with coco palms, opens a broad view of the South Kona coastline. Straight out from a wave-battered landing once used to ship cattle to market in Honolulu, there's good swimming and deepwater snorkeling above coral groupings. Look for spectacled angelfish and silvery wrasses that bump sea urchins upside down to eat their meat. Sometimes schools of dolphins swim into the bay.

It was toward this tiny fishing community that Robert Louis Stevenson headed in a whaleboat from Kailua in 1889, arriving in a heavy squall and disembarking near a point of

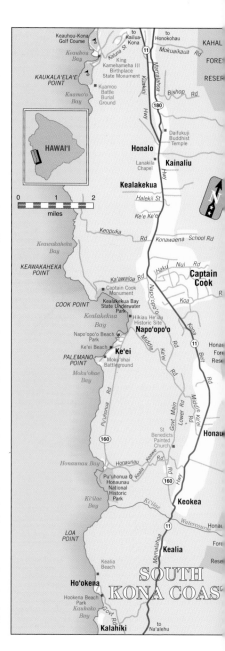

reef in knee-deep water. Drenched by rain and sea, Stevenson waded ashore where he was met by D. H. Nahinu, a former judge who "with a hat band of peacock feathers, a face like an old trusty dog's, no eyes, and no English," was to be his host. He led the writer to an open shed which served as the village store. No one paid the slightest attention to Stevenson, and while Nahinu shopped, the writer waited, talking and "flirting with a little maid of seven." Stevenson stayed alone here for a week, in comfortable quarters, with no interruptions, enjoying the solitude, and writing at the end of the stay that he no longer felt "oppressed with civilization." His journal entries later were integrated into his book, *Travels in Hawaii.*

While he was in the Ho'okena store, Stevenson heard a story of Hawaiians who were buying 60,000 acres in the mountains for $4,000. As Hawaiians seldom bought land, Stevenson wanted to see the site, and the next day the writer, despite his poor health, endured five hours on a mule, riding to the land in "the place of the

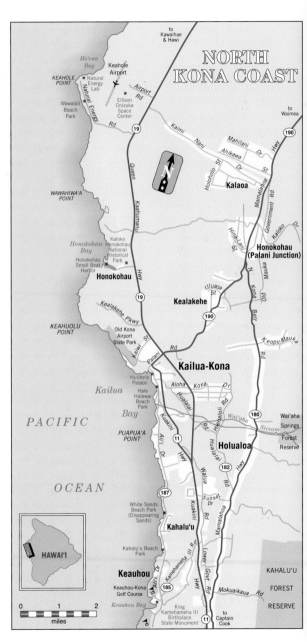

mist," and reaching "the region of the gods and goblins." On the descent, Stevenson rode a tortuous path above the sea through forest dappled with lichens, dripping with vines, and mysterious cave entrances. As this was sacred territory, where bones of chiefs were interred and could not be disturbed, he did not tarry.

North of Hoʻokena is **Puʻuhonua O Honaunau National Historical Park** (Place of Refuge at Honaunau Bay), one of the largest and most important places of refuge in the islands. It can be visited by taking the *makai* (seaward) turnoff at the 104-mile marker on the belt road for 3.5 miles (5 km), or on the secondary Middle Keʻei Road from Kealakekua Bay, four miles (6 km) to the north.

The sanctuary or "place of refuge at Honaunau" was a site of absolution for *kapu* or lawbreakers—if they could reach it. If not, they met with immediate death. A stone wall built in 1550 marks the refuge boundary. Dry-laid and held in place by friction, it is 1,000 feet (300 m) long, 10 feet (3 m) high, and 17 feet (5 m) wide. Tide pools built of *pahoehoe* lava meet the L-shaped wall and form the 12-acre refuge into a triangle.

Adjacent to the north wall lay the palace grounds. If a *kapu*-breaker was on the run from the north, he had to skirt the grounds and swim through stiff currents and shark-haunted waters to reach sanctuary. If making a dash from the south, and if the king's pursuers didn't grab him, he entered by land.

Along the ocean side of the north wall, Hale O Keawe, the *heʻiau*, or temple of Keawe, still stands—built about 1650 in honor of ruling chief Keawe. Because the *mana* of a chief continued to be associated with his remains after death, the wrapped bones of Keawe were carefully stored in the *heʻiau*. Over succeeding generations, the bones of 23 chiefs were interred, adding spiritual force to the puʻuhonua.

Robert Louis Stevenson recounted a tale of these bones in *The Eight Islands:*

> . . . Since his death he [Keawe] has wrought miracles. As late as 1829 Kaʻahumanu sent messengers to bring the relics of the kings from their long repose at Honaunau. First to the keeper's wife and then to the keeper the spirit of Keawe appeared in a dream, bidding them prevent the desecration. They rose trembling . . . exchanged the bones of Keawe with those of some less holy chieftains; and were back in bed . . . before the messengers arrived. So it comes that to this hour the bones of Keawe . . . sleep in some unknown crevice of that caverned isle.

Hale O Keawe, carefully reconstructed in 1985, is flanked by towering carved images called *kiʻi*, incarnate spirits of the ancient gods.

At the Visitor Center near the entrance, pick up a brochure describing a self-guided walk passing Hale O Keawe, the ruins of two older *heʻiau*, a petroglyph, lava tree molds, thatched huts, and a hand-carved koa-wood canoe. Beside the center a "story wall" with audio messages describes the migration of Polynesians to Hawaiʻi. As some of the park rangers are Hawaiian, you may see them garbed in *kapa* cloth while demonstrating thatch, *haku hulu* (featherwork), canoe or *kiʻi* carving; they present 20-minute orientation talks six times a day. On the weekend nearest July 1, a three-day cultural festival features ancient hula, *hukilau* (community net fishing), crafts and games, food, and processions led by a royal court.

Each year on the Labor Day weekend (September), Hawaiʻi's biggest long-distance **outrigger canoe races** take place between Honaunau and Kailua. In six-person single- and double-hull canoes, men and women race 18 miles (29 km). There's a torchlight parade in Kailua on the second night.

KEALAKEKUA BAY

The small town of **Captain Cook** edges the belt road above Kealakekua Bay about 12 miles (20 km) south of Kailua. Take Middle Keʻei Road down to Napoʻopoʻo on the bayshore. On the way, you might stop at the Kona Coast Macadamia Nut & Candy Factory to try your hand at cranking a husking machine and nut cracker, one nut at a time. Samples of the roasted macadamias are offered, and it's a good place to buy slightly over-roasted nuts at a reduced price.

At its mouth, Kealakekua (Pathway of the God) Bay is a mile wide. Napoʻopoʻo and Hikiʻau *heʻiaus* lie at the south end. It was into this bay that the English explorer Captain James Cook sailed in January of 1779, as the Hawaiians were holding feasts in honor of the god Lono. Thinking Cook might be Lono himself, the Hawaiians welcomed him joyously, and honored him with a great feast. After an initial period of welcome, however, the Hawaiians began to suspect that the Englishmen might not be gods after all. (Kamehameha the Great, not yet king but a trusted warrior to his uncle the chief of Hawaiʻi, most likely was at the feasting and saw Cook.) The Englishmen, reprovisioned, set sail, but were soon caught in a storm, found their foremast broken, and were forced to return. Cook's reappearance convinced Hawaiians that the English were mere mortals. Good will degenerated into thievery, tempers rose on both sides, and Cook was killed on Kealakekua Beach.

The actual place where Cook was killed, at the north end of the bay, is enclosed by steep cliffs, and is accessible only by water or trail. (It takes about an hour and a half each way to travel the little-used trail, through tall grass, and it's uphill all the way back. It starts from a dirt track off Napo'opo'o Road.) Here, when the main bay is roiled by storms, the northern cove offers calm waters in one of the best natural boat shelters on the Kona Coast. Deep waters, dark blue and sparkling over coral reefs, glint with tropical fish, drawing snorkelers and divers. Glass-bottom boats cruise the cove, and tour operators bring snorkelers to some of the best viewing waters of Hawai'i.

The entire Kealakekua Bay is a state underwater park and marine life conservation district. Underwater caves, sunken lava flows, and coral reefs shelter parrot and goat fish and night-swimming big-eyed reddish squirrel fish. In clear blue waters 30 feet (10 m) deep, they flash rainbows on the sea bed.

From Napo'opo'o you can see the Captain Cook Monument in the northern cove, a 27-foot (8-m) white obelisk surrounded by single-chain railing. Its plaque reads: "In memory of the great circumnavigator Captain James Cook, RN, who discovered these islands on the 18th day of January AD 1778 and fell near this spot on the 14th day of February AD 1779. This monument was erected in November AD 1874 by some of his fellow countrymen." In later times the Commonwealth of Australia erected a jetty and plaque in front of the monument in memory of Cook, "the discoverer of both Australia and these islands."

At **Napo'opo'o,** the beach of the small, six-acre park is strewn with bits of lava and rock, yet it is a popular spot, with facilities and excellent deep-water swimming. While fishing is restricted, the boat ramp receives heavy use. Tour buses bring visitors to **Hiki'au (Moving Current) He'iau** in the park and the whole area has quite a lot of traffic.

Around Palemano Point at the south end of Kealakekua Bay the white sand of tiny **Ke'ei Beach,** speckled with shreds of lava, draws water-sports fans. At night, torch fishermen congregate. During the day, snorkelers find the medium-sized grey snappers *(uku)* and perhaps a black-tailed snapper (introduced from Tahiti) swimming in clear waters of a broad shallow reef. Surfers are drawn to some of the longest surfing rides on this part of the Kona Coast. Mark Twain once paused here, and wrote with characteristic ebullience: "We came upon a large company of naked natives, of both sexes and all ages, amusing themselves with the national pastime of surf-bathing."

Coconut palms rim a black-sand beach.

Ke'ei is the site of the Battle of Moku'ahai, Kamehameha's first offensive in his bid to dominate the Big Island. By devious measures, Kiwala'o—the weak son who had succeeded Kalaniopu'u as ruling chief—had taken temple lands belonging to his cousin, Kamehameha. Insults mounted, and the two young chiefs soon were riding a collision course. After the land and sea battle at Ke'ei, with Kiwala'o slain and his forces on the run, Kamehameha ruled over the northern half of Hawai'i.

From Ke'ei, the Hawai'i Belt Road cuts north past small upland towns. This is **Kona coffee country,** the only place coffee is grown commercially in the U.S. These coffee trees were brought to Hawai'i via Brazil, and they thrive in the fertile volcanic earth of the Kona Coast. Tropical evergreens do not do well in direct sunlight, and in other coffee-growing parts of the world shade trees are planted to protect them. In Kona, however, afternoon clouds that form on the slopes of Hualalai protect the coffee plants. They are kept pruned to a height of 12 feet (4 m) for ease in hand-picking. An average plant yields about five pounds (2 kg) of coffee cherries a year, or one pound (.45 kg) of roasted coffee from the beans contained in the cherries. The berries turn from green to red from September until mid-December.

At the south end of Captain Cook town the Captain Cook Coffee Company operates a visitor center where you can sample the brew. Samplings also are offered at the Royal Kona Coffee Mill on the two-mile (3-km) road down to Kealakekua Bay. About a mile farther, an HVB (Hawai'i Visitors Bureau) sign marks a turnoff to an area where the coffee plants may be examined up close.

■ NORTH KONA

The hub of activity on the Kona Coast is at mid-point, in **Kailua-Kona town.** Surrounding Kailua Bay at the foot of Hualalai mountain, eight miles (13 km) south of Keahole Airport, Kailua-Kona is a still-quaint old village smothering under the onslaught of souvenir shops and malls in the vicinity of moderate to budget-priced hotels. Stacks of condos and larger hotels follow a five-mile strip of secondary coast road directly south to Keauhou.

The town is famous for its proximity to deep-sea sport fishing, especially the Hawaiian International Billfish (Marlin) Tournament which takes place out of Kailua every summer. You've probably seen photos of catches taken at the hanging scales on Kailua Pier: a Pacific blue marlin may weigh over 1,000 pounds (450 kg).

HAWAIIAN VIEW OF CAPTAIN COOK

More than eighty years after the arrival of Captain Cook, the native Hawaiian writer S. M. Kamakau described events leading to the explorer's death at the island of Hawai'i in 1779. Kamakau, who was educated at a school established to train young Hawaiians as Congregational ministers, reflects both the way native Hawaiians remembered Cook and a nineteenth-century Christian view of why Cook was implicated in his own death.

*W*hen Captain Cook went ashore at Kealakekua the kahuna, believing him to be a god, [Lono], led him to the he'iau, and seated him above the altar where sacrifices were offered . . . Now it is doubtful whether Captain Cook consented to have worship paid to him by the priests. He may have thought they were worshiping as in his own land. But he was a Christian and he did wrong to consent to enter an idolator's place of worship. He did wrong to accept gifts offered before idols and to eat food dedicated to them.

On February 4, Lono [Cook] sailed away in his ship and had got beyond Kawaihae when he discovered that one of the masts was decayed and he had to put back to Kealakekua to repair it. The natives saw him return, and the women took up once more their association with the sailors, but not in such numbers as before. The natives had begun to be suspicious, and some said, "these are not gods; these are men, white men from the land of Kukanaloa." . . . One man said, "The woman who was on the ship says that they groan when they are hurt."

After one of Cook's longboats was stolen, a series of misunderstandings occurred, and an English sailor shot a chief named Kalimu. The Hawaiians were outraged by this and a warrior named Kalanimanookahoowaha tried to block Cook's way with a club.

Captain Cook struck Kalanimanookahoowaha with his sword, slashing one side of his face from temple to cheek. The chief with a powerful blow of his club knocked Captain Cook down against a heap of lava rock. Captain Cook groaned with pain. Then the chief knew that he was a man and not a god, and, that mistake ended, he struck him dead together with four other white men.

When the strangers on the ship knew that their chief was dead, they shot their guns from the ship while the natives tried to ward off the shots with sleeping mats. The bodies of Captain Cook and the four men who died with him were carried to Kalaniopuu at Manualoia, and the chief sorrowed over the death of the captain. He

continues

dedicated the body of Captain Cook, that is, he offered it as a sacrifice to the god with a prayer to grant life to the chief (himself) and to his dominion. Then they stripped the flesh from the bones of Lono.

Captain Cook . . . had been but a short time in Hawaii when God punished him for his sin. It was not the fault of the Hawaiian people that they held him sacred and paid him honor as a god worshiped by the Hawaiian people. But because he killed the people he was killed by them without mercy, and his entrails were used to rope off the arena, and the palms of his hands used for fly swatters at a cock fight. Such is the end of a transgressor. The seeds that he planted here have sprouted, grown, and become the parents of others that have caused the decrease of the native population of these islands. Such are gonorrhea, and other social diseases; prostitution; the illusion of his being a god [which led to] worship of him; fleas and mosquitoes [erroneous]; epidemics. All of these things have led to changes in the air which we breathe; the coming of things which weaken the body; changes in plant life; changes in religion; changes in the art of healing; and changes in the laws by which the land is governed.

—S. M. Kamakau, *The Floating Islands and the Return of Lono,*
[about] 1865

Hale Keawe, Pu'uhonua O Honaunau He'iau, or Place of Refuge at Honaunau Bay, South Kona, a sanctuary for kapu *or law-breakers who could escape the death penalty by swimming through stiff currents to safety.*

(opposite) A Hawaiian kupuna *(elder), at Pu'uhonua O Honaunau He'iau.*

Every May, Kailua-Kona hosts the **Ironman Triathlon World Championship,** which includes a 2.4-mile (4-km) swim, 112-mile (180-km) bike ride, and a 26.2-mile (42-km) run. It's arduous, some say the world's most arduous. Records to beat were set in 1989. Mark Allen of the U.S. set the men's time: 8 hours, 9 minutes, 15 seconds; and Paula Newby-Fraser, a U.S. resident from Zimbabwe, set the women's time: 9 hours 56 seconds.

Kailua overflows with history. When Kamehameha returned from Honolulu to Kailua-Kona in 1812, the kingdom was secure and at peace. In his last years, Kamehameha wanted to come home—to the Kona coast. He lived at Kamakahonu, his home on Kailua Bay, until his death on May 8, 1819.

When the first batch of Congregational missionaries stepped ashore at Kailua Bay in April of 1820, almost a year after Kamehameha's death, they could not know that the ancient religion of the warrior king of Hawai'i, based in part on the *kapu* system, had been battered, denied, and broken at this same place just six months earlier. They lost no time in making converts among a bewildered people who had come to doubt the power of ancient gods. It was not long before a series of thatched churches arose on the site, in what is now the center of town.

In 1836, the Big Island's governor, John Adams Kuakini, decided to tear down the last of these weathered thatch structures and build the first stone church in the islands, **Mokuaikaua Church.** To accomplish this task, he sent every male in the district into the mountains to cut and haul 'ohi'a trees, which were to serve as beams. These spanning beams were cut 50 feet (15 m) long, and the name of the church is probably taken from the forest where they were cut. The walls of the stone church were held in place by mortar made from coral dragged ashore and burned for its lime. Built with intensive labor, primitive tools, and massive effort, the church was dedicated in February of 1837.

Mokuaikaua Church is notable for its simple, well-proportioned mass, and it was soon to be imitated by missionaries on the other islands—Kawaiahao Church in Honolulu takes advantage of this engineering design. Modern architects note with admiration that the roof was designed so as to require no trusses. Still in service, Mokuaikaua Church marks the influence of pioneer missionaries in Hawai'i, and in 1978 it received a National Historic Landmark designation.

Governor Kuakini not only built a fine house of worship, he also issued laws for the so-called betterment of its congregation. Women were to wear bonnets to service; dogs were not permitted inside; and anyone caught sleeping received a rap on the forehead with a long cane.

In 1838, Governor Kuakini built Hulihe'e Palace across from the church. Meant to be his home, it became instead a royal summer residence. Built of the same lava block as the church, this two-story home was plastered smooth by King Kalakaua in 1885. By 1916, it was abandoned, and left to deteriorate until the 1950s, when the state-owned palace was leased to the Daughters of Hawai'i (read daughters of missionaries) who have since guided its restoration. Now a somewhat stuffy museum, it displays furniture and antiques acquired by Hawaiian royalty on visits to Europe. The most interesting pieces are Hawaiian: Kamehameha's own war spears, a table inlaid with 25 varieties of Hawaiian woods, and an armoire of Hawaiian sandalwood carved in China.

Near Hulihe'e Palace, at the northern end of Kailua Bay is **Kamakahonu (Turtle Eye) Beach,** which fronts the King Kamehameha Hotel and is the only swimming strand in town. Calm, shallow, and usually safe for children, it was named for a turtle-shaped *pahoehoe* lava formation, now buried under Kailua Pier, onto which the first missionaries stepped ashore. It is also the same sandy little cove where Kamehameha made his last home and dealt with affairs of state. In his time, a heavy stone wall extending from Ahu'ena He'iau to the present pier enclosed the royal grounds; the beach was his canoe landing.

Five miles (8 km) upslope from Kailua sits the village of **Holualoa.** At 1,400 feet (427 m), it is cooler than the beach and the lifestyle still is rural, with slowed pace and few tourists. Some find their way to a couple of galleries, evidence of a small colony of artists who have gathered in the little town. Holualoa was also home to astronaut Ellison Onizuka, who died in the 1986 *Challenger* space shuttle explosion. His portrait hangs prominently at the Imin senior center. A four-suite inn called the Holualoa, elegant and relaxed with sweeping views above Kailua, nestles in these cooler uplands.

From Kailua town, two highways lead north, one to luxury hotels of the South Kohala coast (HI 19), the other straight inland to the cool upland ranches of Waimea (HI 190).

The coast road cuts across ancient lava flows where mega-resorts lie in the distance like green sequins on a cloth of barren brown. Along its 35 mile (56 km) length north to Kawaihae, the road passes *makai* (seaward) turnoffs down to the luxurious (and expensive) Kona Village Resort north of the airport, then the Waikoloa complex where Hyatt operates a popular theme-park type of hotel. An ancient site, fish ponds, petroglyph trails, and golf courses lie here. In the Hyatt lagoon you can swim with silky-skinned dolphins—if you're lucky and have $50 to spend. Daily drawings are held to select the lucky swimmers who then pay the fee.

Continuing north across ribbons of razor-sharp *'a'a* lava, the drive passes roadside plantings of bougainvillea, flowering a brilliant crimson against the stark and arid landscape. Because the road is smooth and well-engineered, speeding is a temptation. Beware! Unmarked police cars monitor this part of the highway.

Four miles (7 km) south of Kawaihae, upscale tourism on the Big Island arose from the lava flows in the 1960s. Here, Laurance Rockefeller leased lava-covered land and after much bulldozing, building, and watering (the lava turns to soil so rich anything grows), the Mauna Kea Beach Hotel opened in 1965, the first luxury hotel outside O'ahu. Two features of the Mauna Kea—art pieces decorating an atrium-centered hotel design—have become models for many luxury hotels in Hawai'i and around the Pacific. While other world-class hotels have blossomed on the naked lava of South Kohala, the Mauna Kea remains its elegant, understated doyen.

Swimmers begin the first leg of the Ironman Triathalon on the Kona Coast. After a 2.5-mile (4-km) swim, participants face a 112-mile (180-km) bike ride, then a 26.2-mile (42-km) run.

Just north of the Mauna Kea Hotel is the **Hapuna Beach State Recreation Area,** one of the most beautiful beaches in all Hawai'i. The beach is divided in half by a tongue of lava, and the recreation area occupies the southern portion, where a smooth lawn dotted with cocos, hala, and kiawe trees unfolds down to a half-mile (750-m) strand of soft white sand some 200 feet (60 m) wide. This is the island's most popular beach and is often crowded with bodysurfers, snorkelers, and sunbathers. Board surfing is not permitted. Swimmers, partial to the gradual slope of the seabed, rush in and out from the water's edge. At a small cove near the top end, diving instructors work with beginners during the summer, and it is usually a good, safe, water-play area for children.

If **Hapuna Beach** is calm throughout the spring and summer, it is pounded by heavy waves from October to April. There is no lifeguard, and it is not advisable to swim at Hapuna during high surf periods. Hapuna's six A-frame cabins may be reserved from the Division of State Parks in Hilo. (No tent camping.)

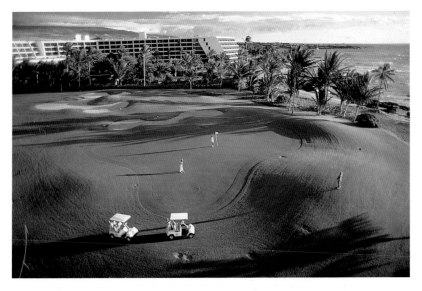

The Mauna Lani, one of the exclusive resorts of the north Kona Coast.

■ NORTH KOHALA

Visitors tend to skirt right past the North Kohala peninsula. A mistake. The cool uplands of Kohala are the one place in the islands where a feeling of ancient Hawai'i is all-pervasive and rural Hawai'i is still natural, not contrived. Continue north on the rising coast road, here called Akoni Pule Highway (HI 270). You can loop back down to Waimea on an inland route.

Pu'ukohola He'iau National Historic Site is a mile above Kawaihae Harbor. The main war temple, Pu'ukohola ("Hill of the Whale"), was the focal point of a dramatic final confrontation between Kamehameha and his rival and first cousin, Keoua Ku'ahu'ula.

After he had battled for years with Keoua, Kamehameha was advised by a prophet that success would come after he built a high temple to Ku at this site and sacrificed an important chief. Temple construction was undertaken by hundreds of Hawaiians who passed heavy, water-smoothed stones from hand to hand for a distance of up to 14 miles (22 km), to be dry laid, without mortar. Down south in Ka'u, Keoua and kings of the other islands heard of the prophecy and believed they must stop the construction to prevent Kamehameha from acquiring unbeatable *mana*.

Once the massive temple platform (224 feet by 100 feet/65 m by 30 m) was complete, it required a human sacrifice. Kamehameha thought Keoua would be a good candidate, and he invited his cousin to attend ceremonies at the *he'iau*. Believing all the signs pointed toward Kamehameha as the leader chosen by the gods, and knowing it would mean his death, Keoua accepted Kamehameha's invitation. As he stepped from the canoe a spear was thrown. Keoua and 11 of his men were killed, their bodies sacrificed at the consecration. With Hawai'i under his control, Kamehameha turned toward his ultimate goal—uniting the islands under his rule.

At the Visitor Center brochures describe the 77-acre park. If you walk the trail, plan to take an hour; or you can drive the beach road to the *he'iau* towering above the trail.

Old Hawai'i is recreated ten miles (16 km) north at **Lapakahi State Historical Park.** Extending four miles (6.5 km) inland and a mile (1.6 km) along the shore, the long chunk of land is called an *ahupua'a*—a land division from the mountains to the sea. From 1968 through 1970, the state conducted archaeological studies here, discovering settlements dating back to the fourteenth century. Despite it being a somewhat bleak place of little rain or vegetation and brackish drinking water, its main village, called Koai'e, carried on successfully until late in the nineteenth century. A highway sign marks the park entrance. There, pick up a self-guided trail brochure for a walk past reconstructed ruins of canoe shelters, animal enclosures, *hale* (houses) and salt pans. The park shoreline was designated a Marine Life Conservation District in 1979.

Mahukona Beach Park a mile (1.5 km) north is an insider's secret. Despite the name, there isn't any beach, yet Mahukona has some of the best swimming and snorkeling on Hawai'i. Long ago it was a harbor where a railroad brought in raw sugar from Kohala plantations to be loaded onto ships and sent to O'ahu. It fell into disuse in 1956 when bulk-sugar trucks began making the 90-mile (144-km) run to Hilo Harbor. Structural relics of the port still are visible in the lucid blue water. These railroad wheels, cables, and slabs of metal have become fish havens and make ideal conditions for snorkelers and scuba divers. There's an anchor chain adorned with sea growth out to a sunken boiler and ship in about 25 feet (8 m) of water and visibility is excellent. At the concrete landing, boats can be launched with the chain hoist and winch. In winter, a heavy surge prevents all water activities. Camping is allowed at a grassy area bordered by small tide pools and swaying cocos.

Beyond Mahukona, the road veers east around the top of the island and away from miles of rugged coastline, a wild area where wind and heavy seas pound the shore year-round and no beaches beckon. Yet Hawaiians lived there long ago, leaving evidence of villages and canoe landings.

Near **'Upolu Point** at the northernmost tip of the island, Kamehameha was born in secret at **Kapana'ia,** probably in 1750. Because there had been a prophecy that this infant would become a killer of kings, Kamehameha's mother Kekui'apo'iwa (of royal Kona lineage), went in the night to the cave of birthing stones. She then gave the baby to a trusted servant, probably named Naeole, with instructions to hide him. Raiding parties sent out by King Alapai of Hawai'i, and Kahekili, a prince of Maui, tried to find and kill the newborn child. As his *kahu,* or tutor, Naeole reared the boy in the remote and mountainous district of Kapa'au.

To reach the birthplace, take the almost-deserted paved road to 'Upolu Airport (used infrequently by commuter aircraft), and turn left onto the jeep trail.

Before looping down to Waimea from the small old plantation town of Hawi (Ha-WI), continue east on Highway 270 for another six miles (10 km) to discover a surprise. Through green and cool rolling countryside where horses graze in front yards, the road dips down and then up again. As you come up over the rise, suddenly, like a curtain lifting, the horizon fills with a sweeping line of verdant, purple-shadowed cliffs and valley, falling away before an expanse of blue ocean: Pololu. At the end of the road the scene from **Pololu Valley Lookout** stretches down into the lush valley and out along the remote valley-slashed scarps of the Hamakua Coast.

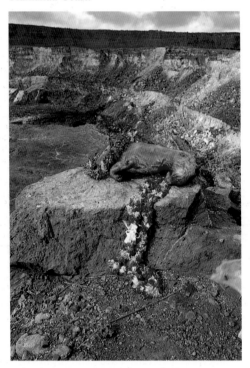

It's common to see offerings left to the Goddess Pele at Halemaumau firepit in Kilauea Crater in Hawai'i Volcanoes National Park. Leaving gifts brings good luck, but removing Pele's volcanic rock is known to bring trouble. Hawaiian traditional beliefs have maintained a rocky co-existence with Christian orthodoxy and churches are ubiquitous throughout the Hawaiian islands. This is Christ's Church Episcopal (opposite), established 1867 at Kealakekua.

When you return on the same road, stop at the **Kohala District Courthouse,** standing along the road in the tiny plantation community of Kapa'au. A single-story frame building with corrugated iron roof, an eight-foot wrap-around lanai, and ornamented eliptical arches, the building is a good example of late nineteenth-century plantation architecture. Built in 1889 under King Kalakaua, it is one of fewer than six surviving monarchy period courthouses. Since 1975, it's been used as a civic center.

In front of the courthouse stands a bronze **statue of Kamehameha the Great,** the warrior king who has been called the Napoleon of the Pacific and the George Washington of Hawai'i for his brilliant strategy in war. The 8½-foot (2.5-m) statue depicts the king in his *a'ahu*

(feather cape), *malo* (loin cloth), and *mahiolo* (feather helmet). One arm is outstretched and the other holds an upright spear. The statue was commissioned by the Hawaiian legislature in 1878, oddly enough to commemorate the centennial of Captain Cook's discovery of the islands. The Boston sculptor Thomas R. Gould was chosen to undertake the work, and for a fee of $10,000 he set about forging it in Italy. In 1880, the statue was shipped for Honolulu from Germany aboard a vessel that was lost at sea off the Falkland Islands. Those who commissioned it must have congratulated themselves for taking out a $12,000 insurance policy to cover the casting of a second statue from the original mold. This statue at the courthouse isn't that second casting. It's the first and was "found" by a sea captain familiar with Hawai'i who came face to face with it while strolling in the streets of Port Stanley, capital of the Falkland Islands. Captain Jervis inquired if he might buy the statue and was able to do so for $500, whereupon he took it off to Hawai'i and sold it at a profit. The Hawaiian government replaced the statue's damaged arm, and the original Kamehameha statue was unveiled here in 1912. The bronze and gold monument to Kamehameha that stands fronting Ali'iolani Hale (the Judiciary Building) in Honolulu is the second casting, installed in 1883.

The route from Hawi to Waimea is one more reason to visit here. Highway 250 passes through the eroded Kohala mountains, where cattle and horses graze on meadows undulating over knolls and *pu'u* (mounds), and where sighing ironwood trees cluster in pastures and tower at roadside. At the highest point, 3,500 feet (1,050 m), stop at a lookout to enjoy the crisp air and a panoramic view stretching from the high green meadows, down across sloping parched mountainsides to the Kona-Kohala coast and out to a sparkling sea.

■ WAIMEA: THE PARKER RANCH

In the cool, sometimes cloudy, mist-laden uplands 15 miles (24 km) above the sunny luxury hotels of South Kohala, is **Waimea** cowboy country and the home of **Parker Ranch**—the largest family-owned ranch in the U.S. From a two-acre site purchased for $10 in 1847, the Parker Ranch has burgeoned into a swath of 225,000 acres, ranging down from 3,000 feet (915 m) to long seacoasts and valleys. Its 700 miles (1,120 km) of fence encloses forests, pastures, 50,000 head of cattle, and 400 working horses. Kekuya grass, a bright almost electric green, forms clumps and unrolls like a gigantic sculpted carpet on the pasturelands.

The original homestead served as a payment to its founder, John Parker, for rounding up feral cattle (which were running around since Captain George Vancouver gave a bull and cow to King Kamehameha in 1793) as well as horses—offspring of a mare and foal given as gifts in 1803. (The mare, frightened, rolled her eyes, and Hawaiians called this startling behavior *lio*, or wild-eyed, and it became the word for horse.) More animals followed, and the king's *kapu* decreed that none might be killed for 10 years. When the *kapu* ended, the animals that had been rounded up formed the nucleus of the first stock to graze at Parker Ranch. That meant cowboys, and the ranch brought men from the Azores to join Mexicans already in Hawai'i. To Hawaiians they all were "espagniolos," or *paniolo*, Hawaiian cowboys. Today the 27 *paniolo* who herd cattle at the Parker Ranch ride horses that are a special breed developed here from imported and local stock. While the horses are the main ranch tool, the *paniolo* also use motorized all-terrain vehicles known as "Japanese quarterhorses."

In 1989, the ranch and home of Richard Smart, the sixth-generation owner, were opened to visitors. Visitors to the **Parker Ranch** must go on guided tours in small groups (reservations required; call 885-7655). While you can't mount a horse and go galloping off on your own, the tour gives you a lot of riding around in the Japanese quarterhorses, on bumpy dirt trails, up mountain slopes, through forests and across pastures, in the vicinity of working *paniolo*. Visits to the **Parker home**, called Pu'uopelu, may be enjoyed at your own pace, and a curator is always available to answer questions. The home is in town, off the belt road less than a mile south of the intersection with HI 190. Touring the main house, one is startled to find a fine collection of art ensconced in the agricultural highlands. The home displays Venetian art, French impressionist works, Chinese jade, and luminous, sunflower-yellow "Peiping glass."

Waimea town usually is known as **Kamuela**, Hawaiian for Samuel (Parker). The ranch town offers a visitor center and somewhat dreary mini-museum, polo, an elegant theater for stage productions, and a couple of wonderful restaurants. Over the past 20 years the area has grown dramatically with a mix of artists, upscale transplants from the mainland and Europe, retirees, and Honolulu part-timers.

East of Kamuela the Hawai'i Belt Road crosses the island and veers south, down the windward Hamakua Coast 54 miles (86 km) to Hilo.

■ HAMAKUA COAST

Where past lava flows have weathered into fertile soil, the waning sugarcane industry still reigns over tens of thousands of rain-fed acres. Called the Hamakua Coast, in the late 1800s and well into the twentieth century it was known as the Scotch Coast, in tribute to the many Scots who came to work as managers, or "lunas" on the sugar plantations.

North of the plantations, the eastern slopes of Mauna Kea tumble down to the sea in emerald valleys ridged by volcanic cliffs. Extravagant tropical growth fills the valleys and no road intrudes. Under leafy canopies rare birds chirp, the beauty of their calls vying with the musical sound of the water coursing through. In the distance rushing waters crash down into pools. One valley is only just accessible: Waipi'o.

WAIPI'O VALLEY

For generations the pristine beauty of Waipi'o (Curved Water) Valley has inspired Hawaiian legend and song. The largest valley on the island, its sheer 2,000-foot

Richard Smart, sixth generation owner of Parker Ranch, the largest family-owned cattle ranch in the United States, at the family home.

(opposite) View of Parker Ranch, which reaches from the mountains to the sea. (Reg Morrison)

THE MANGO TREE

"One old Chinese man told me," he said, "that he like for trim his tree so the thing is hollow like one umbrella, and the mangoes all stay hanging underneath. Then you can see where all the mangoes stay, and you know if ripe. If the branches stay growing all over the place, then no can see the mango, and the thing get ripe, and fall on the ground."

And us guys, we no eat mango that fall down. Going get soft spots. And always get plenty, so can be choosy. But sometimes, by the end of mango season when hardly get all ready, and sometimes the wind blow em down, my mother, sometimes she put the fall down kind in the house with the others.

I was thinking about that as I was climbing up the tree. The wind was coming down from the pali, and I gotta lean into the wind every time she blow hard. My feet get the tingles cause sometimes the thing slip when I try for grip the bark with my toes. How long I never go up the tree! I stay scared the branch going broke cause too small for hold me, and when the wind blow, just like being on one see-saw. And when I start sawing that branch he told me for cut, the thing start for jerk, and hard for hold on with my feet. Plus I holding on to one branch above my head with one hand, and the fingers getting all cramp. My legs getting stiff and every few strokes my sawing arm all tired already, so when the wind blow strong again, I rest. I ride the branch just like one wave. One time when I wen look down I saw him with one big smile on his face. Can tell he trying not for laugh.

He getting old but he spend plenty time in that tree. Sometimes he climb up for cut one branch and he stay up for one hour, just looking around, figuring out the shape of the tree, what branches for cut and what not for cut. And from up there can see the whole valley. Can see the trees and the blue mountains. I used to have nightmares that the thing was going erupt and flood us out with lava, and I used to run around looking for my girlfriend so she could go with our family in our '50 Dodge when we run away to the ocean. But I never find her and I got lost. Only could see smoke, and people screaming, and the lava coming down.

The nightmare everytime end the same. I stay trapped on one trail in mountains, right on one cliff. Me and some guys. The trail was narrow so we walking single file. Some people carrying stuff, and my mother in front of me, she carrying some things wrapped in one cloth. One time she slip, and I grab for her, and she starting for fall and I scream "Oh no!" and then I wake up. And I look out my window at the mango tree and the blue mountains up the valley. The first time I wen dream this dream I was nine.

Since that time I wen dream plenty guys falling off the trail. And plenty times I wen grab for my mother's hand when she start for fall. But I never fall. I still stay lost on the cliff with the other guys. I still alive.

And my father still sitting in the mango tree just like one lookout, watching for me and my mother to come walking out of the mountain. Or maybe he stay listening to the pali wind for the sound one lady make if she falls. Or maybe he just sitting in his mango tree umbrella, rocking like one baby in the breeze, getting ripe where we can see him. And he's making sure no more extra branches getting in the way.

—Eric Chock, *The Best of Bamboo Ridge,* 1986

Small Hawaiian towns have an easy, friendly ambience.

(600-m) lava walls are blanketed in green and ribboned with waterfalls. The valley stretches back six miles to the double falls of Hi'ilawe, dropping 1,200 feet (365 m) to a stream that wanders down the lush flat valley floor and meets a mile-wide black sand shore fronting perilous surf over a sandbar.

Rich in tradition, the Valley of the Kings once was the religious and political center of Hawai'i: Here Kamehameha received the blessing of his war god and defeated his cousin and rival, Keoua. Thousands lived here, cultivating Hawai'i's staple crop, taro, fishing, and harvesting breadfruit. Many were lured from Waipi'o by western lifestyles and driven off by devastating inundations from *tsunamis*. Today, a few remaining families still cultivate smaller patches of taro and lotus.

To visit the Waipi'o Valley lookout, from Honoka'a town take the secondary paved road (HI 24) nine miles north to its end. The only way into Waipi'o is little changed from Isabella Bird's time: "We were at the top of the Waipi'o *pali* and our barefooted horses, used to the soft pastures of Waimea, refused to carry us down its rocky steep, so we had to walk." That was 1873; today the bumpy, very steep track with its hairpin turns is passable only with four-wheel drive; downhill vehicles must yield to uphill. The walk down is arduous and takes about 25 minutes, or you can ride one of the shuttle tours based at the top. One is by mule-drawn wagon.

Through rainforests, spanning deep green gorges, the belt road to Hilo passes small sugar towns and unmarked turnoffs to isolated beaches. If you just zoom through, at the least take time for the majestic Waipi'o Valley lookout. The other route between the Kona Coast and Hilo, the very steep Saddle Road (HI 200), heads over the 6,600-foot (2,000-m) pass between Mauna Loa and Mauna Kea volcanoes. Rental cars are not permitted.

■ MAUNA KEA

Mauna Kea stretches up into the island heartland behind Kamuela, rising to a snow-capped 13,796 feet (4,207 m). Winter skiers come with rented four-wheel drive vehicles to drive up and then ski down the immense treeless slopes of the volcano. Observatories cluster on the chill summit, in flawless clear air that makes it the world's premier location for astronomers. Nations from around the world have come to build some of the boldest telescopes in the world: infrared from

Lushly vegetated pali *capture the moist tradewinds on the windward side of the islands, converting the rainfall into thousands of streaming waterfalls.*

NASA (U.S.), Canada, the U.K. and France; sub-millimeter from the U.K. and Cal Tech; optical from the University of Hawai'i; and Uncle Sam's new generation Keck, a superscope with a unique segmented mirror system that makes it look like the sci-fi eye of a giant bug.

On the eastern face of Mauna Kea, above the rugged Laupahoehoe area, a cairn protected by Douglas fir trees surrounds the **Doctor's Pit.** The trees are named for David Douglas, a noted Scottish botanist who discovered more than 200 species of plants in the Pacific Northwest and Hawai'i, and whose name is a part of many scientific names. Mystery haunts the grounds of the Doctor's Pit, originally dug for trapping wild cattle. In 1834, Douglas's body was found here and to this day his death remains shrouded in doubt. One theory has it that he fell in and was trampled by a trapped bull; another, that he was murdered by an escaped English convict. Douglas was buried in the graveyard of Kawaiahao Church in Honolulu (precise location unknown), and inside the church, a plaque rather oddly describes Douglas as a *victima scientiae,* a victim of science.

MARK TWAIN AT KILAUEA VOLCANO, 1866

We bought horses and bent our way over the summer-clad mountain terraces, toward the great volcano of Kilauea. We made nearly a two days' journey of it, but that was on account of laziness. Toward sunset on the second day, we reached an elevation of some four thousand feet above sea level, and as we picked our careful way through billowy wastes of lava long generations ago stricken dead and cold in the climax of its tossing fury, we began to come upon signs of the near presence of the volcano—signs in the nature of ragged fissures that discharged jets of sulphurous vapor into the air, hot from the molten ocean down in the bowels of the mountain.

Shortly the crater came into view. I have seen Vesuvius since, but it was a mere toy, a child's volcano, a soup kettle, compared to this. . . . Here was a yawning pit upon whose floor the armies of Russia could camp, and have room to spare.

After a hearty supper we waited until it was thoroughly dark and then started to the crater. The first glance in that direction revealed a scene of wild beauty. There was a heavy fog over the crater and it was splendidly illuminated by the glare from the fires below. The illumination was two miles wide and a mile high, perhaps; and if you ever, on a dark night and at a distance beheld the light from thirty or forty blocks of distant buildings all on fire at once, reflected strongly against overhanging clouds, you can form an fair idea of what this looked like.

A colossal column of cloud towered to a great height in the air immediately above the crater, and the outer swell of every one of its vast folds was dyed with a rich crimson luster, which was subdued to a pale rose tint in the depressions between. It glowed like a muffled torch and stretched upward to a dizzy height toward the zenith. I thought it just possible that its like had not been seen since the children of Israel wandered on their long march through the desert so many centuries ago over a path illuminated by the mysterious "pillar of fire." And I was sure that I now had a vivid conception of what the majestic "pillar of fire" was like, which almost amounted to a revelation. . . .

I turned my eyes upon the volcano again. The "cellar" was tolerably well lighted up. For a mile and a half in front of us and half a mile on either side, the floor of the abyss was magnificently illuminated; beyond these limits the mists hung down their gauzy curtains and cast a deceptive gloom over all that made the twinkling fires in the remote corners of the crater seem countless leagues removed—made them seem like the campfires of a great army far away.

—Mark Twain, *Roughing It,* 1872

(following pages) Snow-capped Mauna Kea rises to 13,796 feet.

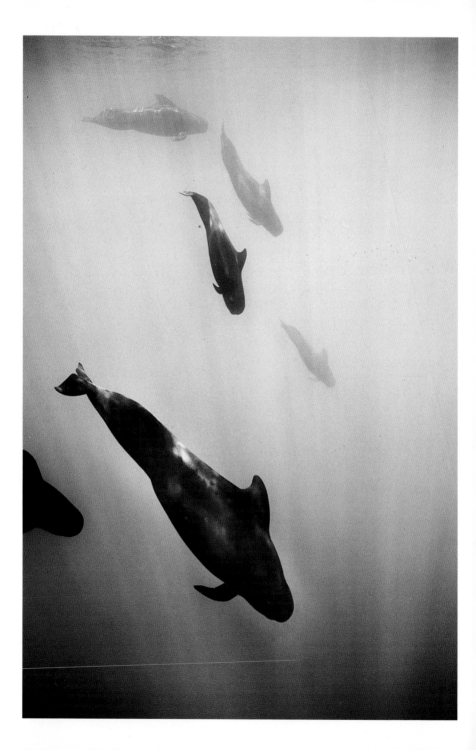

M   A   U   I
V A L L E Y   I S L A N D

MAUI IS NAMED AFTER THE PRANKSTER SON of Hinaakeahi (Hina of the Fire), a demigod revered through the Pacific for his superhuman feats, including lifting the sky so people no longer had to crawl on all fours, and lengthening the day by lassoing the sun. Maui enjoyed wrapping his good deeds in trickery, and when he sought the gift of fire for mankind, he employed his usual tactics. First, Maui captured the mud hen, who knew the secret of fire, and told her he'd wring her neck until she told him how to make it. After he'd wrung her neck a few times, the mud hen directed him to rub sticks together, and tricky herself, she advised him to use the wrong kind of sticks. Maui kept on wringing her neck, and when at last she told him how to make fire, Maui said he had one more thing to rub. Grabbing the bird once more, Maui rubbed the top of her head with a fire stick until all the feathers fell off. To this day the Hawaiian mud hen has a bald head—and Hawaiians have the secret of making fire.

From the air, Maui the island seems to have a human shape—a head, neck, and torso floating on the blue waters of the Pacific. In fact, Maui is two dormant volcanoes joined by an isthmus, and it is on this neck that you're most likely to arrive, at Kahului airport. The mountainous center of the head is cloaked in tropical rainforest, and on the torso an immense brown and green volcano, Haleakala, rises into cloud cover. Ringed by more swimming beaches than any other island, Maui's cream-colored sandy bays curve before sapphire blue and indigo waters.

Leaving the airport, the majority of visitors cross the neck of Maui, passing through flatland where bright green sugar cane ripples in soft wind. To the northeast, on the nape of Maui's neck, are the two towns of Kahului and Wailuku (the county seat) where residents conduct everyday business. To the west is picture-postcard Maui, where coco palms line gleaming white sand beaches, humpback whales breech and sing, and touring sailboats ply the waters of Lahaina Roads. Here, beneath the surface of seas colored pink and purple by the setting sun, bright red and butter-yellow reef fish drift in the currents, much as do the sea birds floating on air currents of the sky. Inevitably, this also is where the bulk of Maui's mega-resorts, condos, restaurants, and nightlife are concentrated. At

These pilot whales were photographed about 30 feet under water five miles off the Kona Coast of the Big Island. Growing from 15-18 feet long, pilot whales live in pods of up to 50 individuals and cruise the islands of Hawai'i all year long.

Kapalua, Ka'anapali and Lahaina, at Kihe'i, Wailea, and Makena, where Hawaiian villages once thrived, tourism now is an exploding, almost devouring force.

Yet there is another Maui, and it doesn't take long to find. Seventeen miles (27 km) by road from busy Lahaina, on the highest peak of the West Maui Mountains, 400 inches (10 m) of rain fall each year and waterfalls cascade down the verdant 'Iao Valley. The road up the windward northern side of Maui's torso brings you to the laid-back ambience of nineteenth-century tropical Hana. Along the way, you meet head-on the astonishing diversity of Maui, passing through lush coastal rainforest high above the turquoise sea.

At the heart of the island, clothed in brown desert at its soaring summit, Haleakala, the largest dormant volcano in the world, reaches into the clouds. Flanked on the west by "Upcountry" cattle ranches and flower farms, the barren crater and Haleakala's lush eastern valleys offer a phenomenal variety of flora, fauna, and spectacular scenery.

Although there is concern about over-development, tourist areas hugging the western shores stay clear, so far, of an island mass that is 75 percent wilderness. Still, old-timers worry, as tourism outpaces the once-thriving industries of sugar and cattle. Fortunately, large areas are protected in one kind of preserve or another, residents understand the fragility of tourist destinations, and the golden goose is unlikely to die of over-feeding. At its best, which is to say almost anywhere you go, Maui is a haven from modern stress, enameled with enough sophisticated glamor to delight rather than overwhelm.

■ HISTORY

Maui the demigod pulled up the island from the sea with his fishing hook. Delighted, he hauled up the other islands and claimed Maui for his own.

In the fourteenth century, high chief Pi'ilani of Hana built the largest temple on Maui—Pi'ilanihale He'iau. It still stands. He built a royal road around Maui, in itself an engineering feat, and today, half the island's highways are still called Pi'ilani.

It was a time of battling kings and war canoes, as wars raged until nearly the end of the eighteenth century. Strict *kapu* (taboos) were enforced, and the penalty of death fell on any commoner unfortunate enough to cast his shadow on the king. The last ruling chief of Maui was Kahekili, lifelong enemy of Kamehameha the Great (and probably his father). Ruthless and powerful, in the 1780s Kahekili brought O'ahu and Moloka'i under his rule.

While Kahekili was on O'ahu in 1790, Kamehameha sailed a fleet of double war canoes to attack Maui. Making use of cannon acquired from a British ship, and the mastery of two British seamen, John Young and Isaac Davis, Kamehameha massacred Kahekili's forces at 'Iao Valley. Returning to confront battles on his home island of Hawai'i, Kamehameha fought on-again, off-again battles for Maui that continued for another three years. In 1793, Kahekili died on O'ahu and his realm was divided. In a master stroke of strategy, Kamehameha landed a fleet of war canoes at Lahaina, and brought Maui under his rule in 1795. About 1800, he transferred the royal court to Lahaina, a favored residence of Maui chiefs, and made it his capital.

Two very different forces originating in New England arrived on Maui soon after Kamehameha's death and the demise of the *kapu* system on the Big Island in 1819. (See "History" in the "HAWAI'I "chapter.) By this time, European ships had reported whales in the Pacific, and as whales in the Atlantic were nearly depleted, hundreds of ships headed around Cape Horn and into the then little-known Pacific Ocean. Many of them dropped anchor in the little port of Lahaina on the northwest shore. At the same time that rowdy whalers arrived, another group of New Englanders disembarked: Protestant missionaries—a moral bunch eager to mend the Hawaiians' sensual ways. They wanted to protect the Hawaiians from themselves, and from the whalers who were infecting Hawaiians with syphilis, precipitating a radical decline in fertility.

Missionary strictures destroyed a way of life. After Chief Hoapili, governor of Maui, was converted to Christianity, new laws were instituted against drinking and womanizing, engulfing the capital in dissent. Whalemen rioted and missionaries sermonized. Native Hawaiians found their traditional way of life threatened by opposing forces from New England.

King Kamehameha III grew to manhood under the influence of missionaries, and to their dismay, he was fond of drinking, gambling, and carousing with women. Reared under the regency of Queen Ka'ahumanu, when he took the throne at age 18, Kamehameha III declared guerrilla war on Christian morality. The king and his clique opened the first sally by drinking 32 barrels of liquor in a single week, and urged a return to the hula, surfing, gambling, and racing. Big, vibrant Hawaiian women, who traditionally had surfed and taken lovers, found few attractions in following the example set by the missionary wives, and many thought Kamehameha III was on the right track. Schools and churches emptied.

The king and his sister Princess Nahi'ena'ena presented the missionaries with a dilemma. Reared in the old ways, in which it was normal practice, if not a duty, for a royal brother and sister to marry in order to produce a high-caste heir, they were forbidden by the Christians from doing so. The king's sister, struggling between a lifelong love for her brother and her adopted Christian conscience, lived a double life, marrying a prince from the Big Island while continuing to sleep with her brother. In 1836, Nahi'ena'ena gave birth to a son who died within hours, and she herself died a few months later. Chastened, Kamehameha III conceded defeat, shut down his distilleries, and turned to kingly duties.

CANE CUTTER'S JOURNEY

In the early 1900s, Hawaiian sugar companies posted handbills in Spanish, Portuguese, and Italian towns near Mediterranean ports, advertising for sugarcane workers. In exchange for working a certain number of years for very low wages, they would receive free passage to Hawai'i and the New World. This account was written in 1992 by California attorney, Manuel Abascal.

My mother's family knew of the opportunity because my grandmother was able to read and write, a rare ability for a woman at that time. In Spain, schools admitted only boys. However, my great-grandmother, a truly wise woman, had traded the only teacher in town, "El Professor," all the goat milk his family could ever use in exchange for teaching her daughter. So, in 1911, when my mother was five years old, her family decided to make the journey to Hawai'i. They walked for many days along the beach, from Malaga to Gibraltar, carrying all of their belongings. They were not too sad to leave the soil they had tilled for landowners.

Everyone on the ship was filled with hope for a better life even though they traveled in cramped, squalid quarters, headed for soil to till for others. Whenever my mother recounted the journey she became sad that she saw many people take ill not long after it began. Some suffered from frailty and the strain of the voyage, others from a measles epidemic for which there was nothing, not so much as an aspirin, to ease the pain. My mother and her three-year-old sister were kept under their mother's long petticoats for most of the trip, in hopes that they would offer protection from the epidemic. It worked. Those large ships came to be known as "coffin boats," although the travelers that perished were buried at sea.

continues

The moment everyone, including the brave young ones, most feared was not the discovery that one or another malady was "in their cards." Rather, it was that moment when their very large ship suddenly seemed to become so very small in the raging seas of Cape Horn at the tip of South America. Everyone on board prayed like they never had before. Once they passed Cape Horn, my mother remembered smooth sailing to the Islands.

After they landed in Lahaina, Maui, families from the same country who had come at different times were grouped together, because of common language and culture, as well as for the convenience of the landowners in organizing work crews. There were different villages for the Italians, Portuguese, and Spanish who had shared the same large ship and different villages for the Chinese and Japanese. Not far away were the villages of the native Hawaiians.

The house assigned to my mother's family is still standing, one of several which have been preserved in Lahaina. In the back is the earthen oven that she, her younger sister, and many other children from their camp anxiously watched as her grandmother baked the bread for the family and the treats for little ones. It was also in the backyard that my mother's lifelong appetite for fruit was born. Every fruit she ever ate started her talking about how good it was as a child on Maui, when she quenched her thirst with mangos, papayas, and pineapples.

The work was very hard. The people got along. For the first time for each of them, there was not only hard work, but also housing, enough food, even a doctor to see if need be. There was a school not far from the work camps, one tiny room under a huge tree. Both the school and the tree are still standing. Such close living conditions brought the mutual understanding that everyone should cooperate. There was competition between the best workers, but not to discourage one another.

Sundays were the days they did not have to work, and the villages became crowded by all of the adults who were in the fields during the week. Young men courted blossoming women, my mother's elder sisters among them. They were watched very closely, not only by their mother's stern eyes, but also by the children who were trying to understand. Getting away meant a walk, followed by others. Sundays also meant that many people came to my grandmother's house to have their letters written, or to have read what was written to them.

The hard work, long hours, and low pay did not make life in Maui worse than the life they had left behind. None of the adults regretted the decision to till the soil on Maui rather than till the soil of the Old Country. All the children attended school, boys and girls together.

By mid-century, Lahaina was the whaling capital of the Pacific. In 1846, nearly 400 whalers laid anchor at the little seaport and brought prosperity to Maui. By the 1860s, the whale oil was being replaced by petroleum, fewer and fewer whaling ships were dropping anchor in Lahaina, and it reverted to a sleepy town.

Sugar, first planted at Haiku in 1870, began to flourish after 1876, when an irrigation ditch was dug to channel water onto the dry, central Wailuku plains. As the neck of Maui turned green with fields of cane, sugar led Maui's economy until tourism blossomed at Ka'anapali in the 1960s. Today, as more than two million visitors a year flock to Maui, both locals and the more responsible developers struggle to preserve Maui's beauty.

■ CENTRAL MAUI

A narrow, flat neck blanketed in green stalks of sugarcane joins the mountainous head and torso of Maui. Kahului and Wailuku towns hug the north shores and slopes at the nape of Maui's neck, at Maui's center. Serving as the island's urban center, the twin towns are good spots for local-style plate lunches or *saimin* (noodle soup).

KAHULUI

During World War II, the U.S. Navy built the Air Station Kahului to serve as a supply and maintenance depot for the Pacific fleet. Today, it is the site of the airport—and for some visitors not much more than a place to alight before rushing off to east or west.

A part of the Navy area included a park with a mile of sandy beach. Now called **Kanaha Beach Park,** the sands are white and separated by rock groins built to reduce erosion. The bottom is shallow and it's the best place in the town areas for swimming. Although the waters are smoke-colored, windsurfers congregate here and locals consider it one of the best spots on the island for beginning and advanced board-sailing. Dirt roads used by shore fishermen cross the park. Kanaha Beach has picnic facilities and is directly behind the airport; take Keolani Road to reach it.

Kanaha Pond Wildlife Refuge is a birdland, where Hawaiian stilts and gallinules breed and wintering birds fly in from Alaska. You can watch the pond's birdlife from an observation pavilion at the junction of highways 36 and 396 where there's a parking lot. In 1971, the refuge was registered as a National Natural History Landmark.

Alexander and Baldwin Sugar Museum takes its name from the sugar company founded by Samuel Alexander and Henry Baldwin in 1869. The former plantation manager's home, built in 1902, is filled with period artifacts and exhibits which describe the history of sugar on Maui—including A&B's battles with Claus Spreckels, the so-called "king" of sugar, over water development for the irrigation of cane fields. There are old photographs of immigrant Japanese laborers, and a typical contract: $15 a month for 10-hour work days, 26 days a month, $2.50 banked toward return passage. The planters were innovative, constantly experimenting with new methods of growing, harvesting, and milling the cane. On the museum grounds, you can watch a working scale model of a cane crushing plant. The museum is near the airport, off the intersection of Pu'unene Avenue and Hansen Road.

WAILUKU

The county seat of Wailuku, with its hilly streets, wooden storefronts, and easy-going atmosphere, deserves a bit of attention. For those interested in the island's

Interior of an abandoned sugar mill.

history, touring the little town is a quiet pleasure, and unlike West Maui, certain to be uncrowded.

In the foothills of Wailuku overlooking the harbor, a missionary complex is laid out in tartuffian splendor: **Bailey House Museum,** standing on land given to the American Board of Commissioners for Foreign Missions by King Kamehameha III and the governor of Maui. Built in 1840 and maintained by the Maui Historical Society, it was the home of Edward and Caroline Bailey for 45 years. The house is stuffed with quilts, dolls, and china that came out of Boston and around Cape Horn to the Sandwich Islands, and its Hawaiian collection is a little treasure. On display are stone and shell implements; *kapa* cloth; wood, feather and bone pieces; gourds; and a hand-hewn *koa* wood canoe. Outside on the grounds lie vestiges of an ancient Hawaiian irrigation system used for taro, and growing among rare plants are some of the original varieties of Hawaiian sugar cane. The museum is on 'Iao Valley Road, one block from the intersection of High and West Main streets.

'IAO VALLEY STATE PARK

Driving south from Wailuku town, you're on flat terrain, the flanks of the West Maui mountains to your right. These hills are the remains of a volcano that

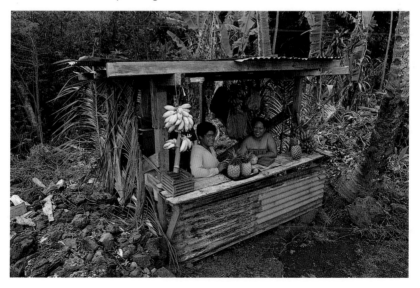

Roadside fruit stand.

spewed up the head of Maui and once towered some 7,000 feet (2,135 m) above the sea. Now eroded down to 5,788 feet (1,765 m), the diminished summit, Pu'u Kukui, is deluged each year with some 400 inches (10 m) of rain, making it the second wettest spot in the island chain. Radiating from the summit, remote, untamed, and inaccessible gorges rip open the mountainside. 'Iao (**Cloud Supreme**) **Valley** is the most well known—and the only one where visitors may drive up to its mouth. The turnoff is seven miles (11 km) west of Wailuku—take 'Iao Valley Road (West Main Street, or HI 320). From the parking lot a well-traveled trail with innumerable steps climbs a loop that opens onto glorious views of the valley. Cloud streams waft through 'Iao, alternately obscuring and revealing misted, steep canyon walls. Punctuating the valley and towering like a stele is **'Iao Needle**, a 2,250-foot (686-m) green-carpeted cinder cone.

It was here in 1790 that Kalanikupule, son of Kamehameha's arch enemy the ruthless Maui king Kahekili, sought to stem the tide of the warrior king's onslaught. At this battle Kamehameha brought over to Maui a weapon new to Hawai'i, a *haole* (foreign) cannon. Kalanikupule put up a fight but was forced, along with his chiefs, to flee through a mountain pass. Victors chased vanquished warriors scrambling up the steep valley walls, and bodies fell mangled into the bloodied waters of 'Iao stream until pyramids of the slaughtered dammed the flow.

Kepaniwai (Damming of the Waters) gives its name to the **Kepaniwai Heritage Gardens**, in 'Iao Valley State Park. Here, a Hawaiian grass shack, a missionary "salt box" house, a Japanese tea house, and a Chinese pagoda stand amidst manicured gardens honoring Hawai'i's multicultural past.

■ WEST MAUI

Across the 14-mile (22-km) neck, three highways, cutting through fields of tall, waving cane, link east Maui to west Maui's famous beaches and hotels. The finest beaches for swimming or sunbathing are along the 18 miles (29 km) from Olowalu to Kapalua. At the south end of the neck, Honoa Pi'ilani Highway (HI 30) splits north and south. To the north it follows the face of Maui through Lahaina, Ka'anapali, and Napili along the west coast, continuing around the crown of the head before dissolving into unpaved track, impassable except by four-wheel-drive vehicles.

This older humpback whale, who was wheezing when she was photographed, has probably migrated from Alaska to Hawai'i and back again for at least 50 years.

If you come in winter stop at Ma'alaea Bay, the throat of Maui, where high-fluked humpback whales calve and spout in somewhat shallow waters. After summering in Alaska, more than half of all humpbacks travel down the Hawaiian island chain to spend the winter in waters between west Maui and Lana'i. As they are sensitive to noise, the whales stay farther out to sea off Lahaina and Ka'anapali. Fortunately, jet-skiing is off-limits in winter, and you may see more than one bumper sticker saying "Save the Whales—Harpoon a Jet Ski." Federal law protects the humpbacks by requiring that swimmers and boats keep a distance of at least 300 yards (274 m). Whales can be seen all along the west coast, and Ma'alaea is a prime spot to watch them breech.

LAHAINA

No other town in the islands preserves the nautical flavor of a mid-nineteenth-century Hawaiian seaport so well as does Lahaina—in fact, the entire town has been declared a National Historic Landmark. The refurbished and energetic little seaport retains much of its lusty whaling past in a tourist mode. Along Front Street, the main artery facing the harbor, old wooden buildings lean over the water, their ships' chandleries and grog shops metamorphosed into clothing, gift, and jewelry boutiques. Interspersed are T-shirt shops and a fistful of art galleries heavy on the marine theme. (You may not want to see another breeching whale on canvas for the next 20 years.) Resident artists attend the galleries on Friday nights.

Adventurous visitors will find a panoply of appealing trips offered by tour companies lining the harbor front. On-the-spot temptations include parasailing, snorkeling at Molokini islet, undersea viewing trips, day tours to Moloka'i, bike rides, helicopter tours, dinner cruises, golf and sport fishing, or a ride on a little steam engine railroad. From December until April, whale-watching excursions sail from the harbor. In Lahaina, you can walk around dressed in shorts and a T-shirt, gobbling fast food, or go out in elegant garb for champagne dining. Night life in the little town dances to a fast beat.

All day long Lahaina manages to bustle and relax at the same time. Yet, somehow, its old charm percolates through. The time to find it is in the early morning—before mobs of sightseers and traffic clog the narrow streets. In the cool hours following dawn, the few people seen walking may actually be residents. To sense the "charming, drowsy, and dreamy village" Charles Warren Stoddard found in 1885, stop beside the sea wall at Front Street. Harbor waters are clear and calm, the air free of diesel bus fumes, and fishermen are out on the breakwater. Bring along a copy of the free booklet *Lahaina: A Walking Tour of Historic and Cultural Sites,* published by the Maui County Historic Commission; old sites in a concentrated area centering along and near Front Street are marked on a small map. The sites are woven through a Lahaina teeming with activity.

Front Street, the main street of Lahaina, follows the shoreline. Beginning at the south-central end of town, two blocks *mauka* (inland) from Front Street at the intersection of Prison and Wainee streets stands Hale Pa'ahao, the **Stuck in Irons House.** Built in 1852, Lahaina's old wooden prison housed Hawaiian inmates who broke missionary moral code, and brawling whalemen who broke the Sabbath, drank, swore, and bolted down Front Street racing horses. The building was restored in 1988, using guidelines from old photographs. Plaques describe prison life; one is taken from the journal of a visitor in 1855: "10 dozen kanakas, male and female, all had the freedom of the prison yard and mingled promiscuously with each other." On Front Street, one block north of Prison Street, stop at the two-story, white-washed **Baldwin House.** Built of coral block between 1834 and 1835 and restored in exacting detail, the oldest standing building in Lahaina was originally the home of Reverend Dwight Baldwin. Its

A view of Lahaina harbor, the Pioneer Inn and an historic schooner which is open to the public.

furnishings include a sextant, a baby crib used for all six Baldwin children, and Mrs. Baldwin's rocking chair. A Harvard-trained physician, Baldwin is credited with curbing a smallpox epidemic in 1853—a disease brought to Hawai'i by westerners. Opening their home to Hawaiian nobility and influential guests, the Baldwins lived in the house from 1836 until 1868. The prime land of the house is the seed that grew into the extensive holdings of Maui's H. P. Baldwin Estate.

The bookstore next door retains something of the building's original purpose. It was the **Masters' and Mates' Reading Room**, a rudimentary library and quiet lair where ships' officers wrote letters. The second floor houses research materials and offices of the Lahaina Restoration Foundation, the town's guiding beacon.

Across the street, walk a few steps to the waterfront. Here is the heart of old Lahaina—the old, two-story **Pioneer Inn**. Built in Victorian style in 1901, with verandas railed in lacy woodwork facing the sea, it still accepts guests in a newer annex and in the old green-and-white-painted frame building. (See "Accommodations" in PRACTICAL INFORMATION.") Eating breakfast on its lanai looking out onto the harbor is a tradition among locals. In the adjacent bars, the nightly din might call to mind a whaling crew embroiled in a drinking bout. At the south side of the hotel, **the largest banyan tree in the U.S.** sprawls across the courthouse square. Planted in 1873, its rooted aerial vines are so huge the tree provides enough shade for over 500 people. On the north side of the hotel and *makai* (seaward), ruins of Hale Piula, the unfinished royal residence of Kamehameha III, face the **Hauola Stone**. An HVB (Hawai'i Visitors Bureau) signpost marks the spot in the breakwater. Large and flat, it is an ancient Hawaiian stone of healing.

Floating on the other side of the breakwater, the steel-hulled brig *Carthaginian II,* now a whaling and merchant ship museum, conjures a vision of another time, when Lahaina Roads was crammed with trading vessels. One of the few square-riggers in Hawai'i, this 97-foot (30-m) trader was built in Germany.

As you walk north on Front Street, the coastline veers seaward at the north end of town. Here the jutland is landscaped in greenery surrounding the largest Japanese Buddha statue outside Japan. Dedicated by the Jodo Mission to the first immigrants to Hawai'i from Japan, its bronze face looks out to sea, toward Japan.

KA'ANAPALI

Five miles (8 km) north of Lahaina is Ka'anapali Bay, where a long curve of wide, white sands faces deep, radiant blue seas, and swimmers can see down to the bottom 30 feet (9 m) below the surface. Soon after statehood in 1959, a single low-rise hotel and golf course arose before the bay—the Royal Lahaina Resort, which still rests regally amid lawn-covered knolls. Separating the bay into halves is a volcanic spatter cone, Puʻu Kekaʻa (Rumbling Hill) also known as Black Rock, said to represent the vanquished form of a demigod who taunted Maui. Not long after the Royal Lahaina was built, another hotel, the Sheraton, put down roots here. It was a unique structure then—its lobby is on the top floor, and the building cascades down the cliff. These two hotels, forerunners of the Kaʻanapali complex, maintain a measure of calm in the eddying swirl of resort tourism.

At the southern end of this bay is the Kaʻanapali complex. Some 30 years ago American Factors, an old sugar company in search of diversification, changed its name to Amfac and pioneered "master-planned tourism" on still out-of-the-way Maui. Along three miles (5 km) of beach extending south of the bay towards Lahaina is a mega-complex of gleaming, manicured hotels, golf courses, and a shopping village named Whalers. A free shuttle service to Lahaina runs all day and most of the night.

Side-by-side highrises line the shore of the Kaʻanapali complex. At this section of shoreline, swimming is dangerous; the reef is near, the sands narrow, and the waters turbulent. On the other hand, if your tastes run to fantasy-land (though not a Hawaiian one), you can remain so occupied that you may never miss the beach. Here is the fantasy-land of a man named Chris Hemmeter, who placed his mark on Kaʻanapali in the seventies. His idea of a Hawaiian Resort is about as Hawaiian as a Roman villa. In fact, that's about it—Greco-Roman cement style and decor on the beach in Maui. With vast pools where you can swim through tunnels, zoom down a snake-like flume, or sit at a bar in the pool, both the Westin Maui and the Hyatt Regency Maui bear the Hemmeter mark. While these resorts may appear to have nothing Hawaiian about them, they *are* in Hawaiʻi, and there is no other place on earth where trade winds caress body and spirit so benignly in the sun.

NAPILI BAY AND KAPALUA

HI 30 and the Lower Honoa Piʻilani shore road run up the coast. The lower road slides past a miles-long string of moderately priced hotels and condominiums following a shore of non-stop beaches, some of them projecting right into a reef. The Napili Bay beach of white sands, crowded with tenants from the chock-a-block

(following pages) Hoʻokipa Beach Park on east Maui is one of the best windsurfing spots in the world.

condos looping the cove, has good swimming and snorkeling. The benign surf makes it a good place for beginning surfers.

Snorkelers drift over warm turquoise waters along this strip, looking down onto a magical kingdom of coral heads and reef. Mushroom corals loll on the white sand bottom. The three-inch (8-cm) brighteye damselfish swims here. Colored golden-olive, the damselfish likes surge areas where it can make a home in the holes and cracks of the reef. Slightly larger and found only in Hawai'i, tight clouds of white-spotted damsels with snub faces and bright white dominoes on their black bodies swim over coral fingerheads. Here are Hawaiian surgeonfish *(palani),* with golden fins and gold-blue tails. You wouldn't want to sniff this beauty out of the water—it's smelly, because, we are told, a goddess being ferried by the fish lost control and urinated on it.

Kapalua Bay, the next cove north, is a beach much like Napili, minus the mob. With white-white sands, fine and soft, the crescent-shaped pocket of Kapalua is protected by rocky side-croppings that subdue the blue-green waves. Sparkling in the northwest curve of the island, the tasteful complex at Kapalua Bay Resort is a golfers' paradise with a championship course and international tournaments, fashionable shops, and elegant surroundings. Developed by a subsidiary of Maui Land & Pineapple, it sits in pleasant contrast to the uninspired condos of the Napili stretch.

Immediately north of Kapalua is **D. T. Fleming Beach Park**, a broad strip of white sand backed by an undulating lawn and dappled with palm and ironwood trees. Picnic there and swim in the summertime. In the winter when waters roil and turn furious, swim instead at **Oneloa Beach** a fraction of a mile north, where one end of the slight cove is protected. Few find this lovely little sand patch rimmed by sea cliffs; the path down to Oneloa is short and steep.

Past Oneloa, curving northeasterly around the top of the island, the Maui coastline leaps and turns like tight curling hair. Surfers' havens slice the shore. Down cliff paths to secluded Honolua Bay or to Pohakupule (Windmill), rocky beaches and bottoms offer up some of the best surfing breaks in the state, with waves curling up to 15 feet (4 m), offering long, sliding rides on winter surf.

Beyond, the road (HI 30) dissolves into a primitive, unpaved track (rental cars not permitted), making a loop around West Maui toward Wailuku at the neck of the island.

■ EAST MAUI

Dominating the torso shape of east Maui is Haleakala volcano. Highway 360 (better known as the Hana Road) twists up the northern (windward) shore and follows the island contour to the eastern slopes. Here lies Hana and the lush, rainforested southeast coast. The western slopes rise from the neck of Maui into Upcountry ranchlands and, higher up, the misted summit. To the southwest, the coast of the torso is lined with beaches and resorts.

KIHE'I AND WAILEA

From the throat of Maui at Ma'alaea Bay, Pi'ilani Highway (HI 31) takes you to the southwest shores where one beach park after another faces the sea. These beaches are most enjoyable before the daily wind rises at noon. At **Kihe'i,** an ancient fishing village that grew into a little town, the beaches run for miles in an unbroken line, a jogger's paradise. Small hotel-condos ranging from luxury to budget cluster near the stretch of open, flat sands. Three beach parks south of Kihe'i at Kama'ole are excellent swimming strands.

Further south, the mega-resort at **Wailea** fronts a mile-and-a-half (2-km) strand of white sand crescents and good swimming. Nearly a billion dollars have been spent at the 1,500-acre resort, where once there was only space and *kiawe* scrub. Now Wailea's upscale establishments total five hotels and four condominium villages, each offering from 250 to 550 rooms, suites, or villas. Designers have gone for the Greek. The hotels neither look nor feel Hawaiian, and the only Hawaiians you'll meet are on hotel staffs. Yet the hotels *are* basking in Maui sunshine, and the tradewinds are kind to the skin—no desert dryness here.

Winter whale-watching, good from vantage points down the length of the leeward shore, is a special treat off the Wailea beaches. Sometimes, just 100 yards (90 m) from shore, a 40-foot (12-m) humpback may be seen breeching in the ocean, perhaps with a newborn beside it. Often an entire family group, or pod, can be seen spouting farther out to sea.

Four miles (6 km) south of Wailea, approaching the end of the paved road, is **Makena,** where the new Maui Prince resort sprawls behind two beaches. Lumped together and often called simply Makena Beach, Little Beach and Big Beach are considered by many to be the most beautiful on Maui.

Little Beach, or Pu'u Ola'i (Earthquake Hill), lies in a little cove at the tip of a cinder cone bulging the shoreline out into the ocean south of Makena Bay. Swim here in lucid turquoise waters lapping over a sandy shallow bottom. Body and board surfers come for the gently breaking waves, and snorkeling is excellent around the point to the south. A popular spot, Little Beach also is known as a nudist sanctuary—its enthusiasts mildly alert to punishment by the law and by the sun.

Big Beach lies directly south of Little Beach. (The proper name of Oneloa [Long Sand] seldom is used because the name is the same as the beach in the northwest.) No development is visible from the long half-moon of smooth white sand, nearly hidden from the road by *kiawe* trees. Green sea turtles laid their eggs in the sands here until the turn of the century. Big Beach really is big—more than 100 feet (30 m) wide and half a mile (1 km) long, all of it open to the ocean with a steep drop-off and heavy waves. If the pounding surf doesn't keep you awake, this makes a good place to camp. In the early seventies, Big Beach was popular with "Maui-Wowie"-smoking counter-culturalists.

You can drive down a dirt road to the beaches. Turn at the highway sign marked "Shoreline Access No. 101," less than a mile past the intersection of Makena Alanui and Makena roads. Or park off the highway and walk through the trees to the beach. The two beaches are linked by a foot trail.

Beyond the paved road, off a dirt track at the point of land where the island curves south, is a deep bay named for Comte de La Perouse, the French navigator who dropped anchor in its calm waters in 1786. La Perouse, who had come to verify Cook's findings on behalf of the French crown, took in a landing party and became the first westerner to step ashore on Maui. After sailing away, he never again was seen and was assumed lost at sea in the South Pacific.

ROAD TO HANA

To reach the wild north shore of east Maui's torso, take HI 36, the Hana Road. Following the north shore, the 52-mile (83-km) road is a rising, dipping, slithering mass of 600 curves through jungle-clad cliffs, past plunging waterfalls and over 54 bridges. This rutted and bumpy, paved road to Hana sometimes is called the "narrow escape to paradise." It's a half-day trip if you allow no stops and that's hard to do—this is one of the most scenic drives in the state. (Start with a full gasoline tank; there are no service stations.) You'll want to stop for picnicking, and for breathtaking views of white-foamed shorelines and of jungled valleys backed with misty cascades, and cold, clear pools. Guavas, mountain apples, passion fruit, and red and fragrant yellow ginger thickets frame the road.

Curving past valleys enclosing old fern and vine-draped villages, roadside views change quickly. At the halfway mark, the road descends near Ke'anae (Mullet) Point and offers a glimpse of an old Hawai'i, when life centered on the sea and soil. Coco palms border wet taro patches behind bungalows. The flatland lies before a rocky shore.

Rising slightly, the road comes to its finest treasure, **Wai'anapanapa (Glistening Water) State Park**, about three miles (5 km) before Hana. A short walk leads to a lava tube, which you can walk straight through to the waters of a black sand beach. The heavy surf is only for powerful swimmers and scuba divers—who think they've reached Nirvana, swimming through lava arches and underwater to a cave believed to be a place where lovers once met secretly.

H A N A

Until the road from Kahului was completed, Hana, at the extreme east end of Maui, remained isolated from the rest of the island. It remains a quiet place where the sounds heard are those of soft wind, of seas crashing or lapping ashore, and the chirps and drips of the rainforest. Frequent rains pelt rich agricultural lands, and rolling hills are verdant pastures. Only about ten people per square mile call Hana home, and of those more than half claim descent from native Hawaiians.

"Heavenly Hana," as it's known, is about a hundred years from the resorts of west Maui. Clinging to the foot of the volcano's eastern slopes that slide gracefully down to the deep curve of Hana Bay, Hana is a pretty ranch town swathed in pandanus and banana trees. Frame homes set amid flowering trees cluster in small lanes. Hasegawa's General Store, an outgrowth of an old plantation store that sold everything, stocks merchandise so varied that someone once wrote a song about it. The one-room **Hana Museum** exhibits an astounding variety of Hawaiian brooms made from coconut fibers, as well as war clubs, carved stone idols, *kapa,* and quilts.

On the outskirts of Hana, just after Wai'anapanapa State Park, lies **Pi'ilanihale He'iau** (House of Pi'ilani), Hawai'i's largest temple, built about A.D.1400. Pi'ilani, a famed Maui chief who managed to wield power for an unprecedented 40 years, built the terraced stone platform giant-size, 415 feet (126 m) long by 340 feet

(103 m) wide. Today, visitors who stand beside a cliff overlooking a vertical plunge to foaming shoreline, often sense otherworldly forces here, the powerful presence of ancient gods eternally inhabiting sacred ground. Permission to visit the *he'iau* is required and may be arranged through the Hotel Hana-Maui (248-8211).

At the foot of town, calm waters lap at the sandy shore in the broad, deep curve of Hana Bay. **Hana Beach Park** lies at the southern end. The beach has an older name—Kapueokahi, the Single Owl. A *kupua,* or ghostly being, he was capable of changing himself from owl to man. The brown sand beach, formed from eroded cinders, is 700 feet (200 m) long and 100 feet (30 m) wide, with gently sloping sands at the water's edge. When heavy surf pounds the coast, this is the safest beach for swimming and snorkeling in the Hana district. (Stay inside the bay. Outside, currents flow out to sea.) The park facilities are popular and local residents often gather here for impromptu music-making.

Hana Bay claims an illustrious history, and a bloody one. Since it was remote, chiefs from Hawai'i gathered fleets of double-hulled war canoes in the bay to assault Maui, and in 1802 when Kamehameha landed, it is believed he dedicated several *he'iau* to Kuka'ilimoku, the war god whose sacred idol was entrusted to his guardianship. Because King Kamehameha the Great succeeded in uniting the islands, he was the last chief to take strategic advantage of Hana Bay.

Marking the south end of the bay, **Ka'uiki Head** is a 386-foot (117-m) eroded cinder cone that once held a cave—the birthplace of Queen Ka'ahumanu in about 1773. Kamehameha first saw her near Hana when she was seven years old. She grew to be six feet tall and imperially beautiful, an ardent surfboarder and swimmer. A lover of battles, she was also partial to intrigue, and to men. When she was sixteen, she was married to Kamehameha and became his favorite wife.

Activities around Hana are oriented to the outdoors. You don't have to be a guest at the town's small inns or hotel to arrange horseback riding at sunrise or sunset, picnics, swimming, and hiking excursions. If you do stay at the luxurious bungalow hotel called Hana-Maui, bring a hefty wallet. Rates start at $360 (with meals). (See "Accommodations" in "PRACTICAL INFORMATION.")

BEYOND HANA

Hana highway, now numbered HI 31, curves southwest around the east flank of Maui to its end at Kipahulu on the south coast. Along the way, overlooked beaches appear to crouch beneath cliffs and can be reached only by risky sea cliff trails where loose volcanic cinder material breaks free. These eroded cinder beaches face roaring seas, and their red, brown, black, and white colors fill up half a rainbow.

A couple of miles before the road's end is **Seven Pools Park,** where 'Ohe'o Stream plummets over seven waterfalls into seven clear and icy pools. Bounding down the southern slopes of Haleakala volcano, like a liquid stairway the stream carves its way through lush greenery into a wide mouth and roiling sea. While slippery boulders require caution, swimmers find the pools hard to resist.

High above the stream the **Haleakala rainforest** is a biological treasure, a realm populated with strange creatures found nowhere else—fish that climb 200-foot (60-m) waterfalls, flightless moths, and carnivorous caterpillars, and giant picture-wing fruit flies. Between the crater and the rainforest, bogs support miniature bonsai-like *o'hia* trees, and floral sprays three feet (1 m) across sprout from native lobelias. Unfortunately, the forest is inaccessible and officially closed to visitors.

A mile beyond Seven Pools, **Kipahulu,** on the southern foot of Haleakala, is where the famed aviator Charles A. Lindbergh (1902-1974) lived out his last years. In the tiny, green, and damp village, **Palapala Ho'omau Congregational Church** stands in lava rock on a headland above the sea. The church was restored by Lindbergh, and now watches over his grave.

The extraordinary beauty of Hawai'i's arid lava zones reaches surreal proportions.

Seven Pools and Kipahulu mark the southern boundary of Haleakala National Park. Beyond here the Hana Road dissolves into a bumpy pot-holed dirt track that crosses the southern limits of Kaupo Gap, an abruptly arid lava zone. Car rental companies do not allow their vehicles to be driven through this area, so to reach the southwest coast, or the Upcountry slopes and the volcano summit, visitors must backtrack to Kahului.

RANCHING ON MAUI, 1905

*M*ost of the stock raised on the ranch was slaughtered locally, but four or five times a year surplus steers were sent to Honolulu to be marketed. Shortly after my fifth birthday Daddy announced that I was old enough to go with him when the next shipment of beeves was made, and not until I went on this expedition did I realize that Daddy and the *paniolos* often risked their lives when they jogged out of my secure world every morning.

For days after I knew I was to go I spent most of my time leaving offerings before *akua* stones, praying to Christ, burning incense before Tatsu's image of Buddha, and lighting candles before the shrines of Portuguese saints to make certain that all the Great Forces would be solidly ranged about me to prevent any possible disaster which might interfere with my going.

The afternoon the steers were due to come down the mountain Makalii took me out to meet them. We spotted the cattle and riders swooping down a green hill. The Herefords reminded me of a swift red river foaming at its edges where their white legs and faces showed. The afternoon shook as they bellowed their fury and bewilderment at being driven from the high grasslands they knew.

Makalii opened the gates into the holding pasture. Daddy galloped ahead of the herd, sitting his saddle in the straight-legged fashion of Hawai'i—a beautiful, poised seat suggesting a winged centaur about to take flight and sail off into space. As he passed he brandished his coiled lasso and smiled. Owing to the steep pitch of the land it was impossible to prevent the wild mountain cattle from running. Daddy raced through the gates, maneuvering so the stock would not collide with the posts and bruise themselves.

When they were safely through, he pulled out of their way. They surged across the pasture, belly-deep in grass, slowed up, wheeled around, and collected in a tight knot facing the riders. Holomalia followed Daddy into the pasture and they conferred for a few moments. The rest of the men halted at the gates which Makalii was closing, slacked girths, and shook saddles to cool their horses' hot backs.

Wind scurried down from Haleakala; the sharp sweet whistle of plover sounded overhead. Across the green isthmus joining the two halves of the island, the West Maui mountains stood out distinctly, golden mists hanging in their deep valleys. A sort of elemental excitement, brewed by animals, wind, grass, and drifting clouds, flowed toward me. Makalii had trained my ears to hear the minute sounds of rocks, soil, and vegetation worked on by changes in the atmosphere, I could listen in the dark, and by the sound of the wind name the point of the compass from which it was blowing. I could sense the imperceptible change of one season sliding into the other: a sort of vast, muted rustle in earth, sky, and sea—an instant of altered vibrations, then a great peace, like a sigh, when the transition was completed. In a dim instinctive way I was conscious now of the majestic rhythm of Nature's machinery moving behind tangible objects and, reaching out, I grabbed Makalii's hand.

"What is it?" he asked in Hawaiian.

I looked at Haleakala, at the men and cattle, listened to the majestic dissonances of the Pacific. How could I express even to my old Makalii what I was feeling? But with the amazing intuition of his race he knew. Wrinkles gathered up the outer corners of his eyes.

"Today you feel like an *akua* walking on earth," he said, smiling.

I nodded. He had it exactly. In that moment, I felt immortal, I was a lesser god with a small niche in the huge swoop of living.

—Armine von Tempski, *Born In Paradise*, 1940

UPCOUNTRY MAUI

The heartland of Maui's torso is "Upcountry Maui," where artists come to live and paint, where sweet Kula onion, potato, and flower farms pattern the hills, and where horses trot in pastel green meadows. No one remembers who coined the label "Upcountry." However it happened, it is *up*, up into the grassy mountainous waistband that girds the central slopes of Haleakala volcano. To get here, take Haleakala Highway (HI 37) from Kahului, beginning at the stoplight intersecting HI 36 on the east side of the airport. (There are only two stoplights in Upcountry. The other one is eight miles [13 km] up.)

Makawao is cowboy country, and it all started in the 1820s, when whaling ships' cooks started asking around for meat. By 1830, Mexican cowboys were brought here to teach Hawaiians cattle ranching. The cattle industry still flourishes, and every year on the Fourth of July the town erupts in a rip-roaring rodeo. Makawao also is home to polo on Maui. The town, two miles (3 km) east of HI 37, has a sort of contrived Old West atmosphere with worn wooden buildings and new galleries and boutiques that retain the nineteenth-century false-front look.

Kula, five miles (8 km) south of the Makawao turnoff, is a vast garden where jacaranda trees take on their lavender plumage and fat blue hydrangeas blossom in the cool mountain air. Flower farms flourish on the undulating landscape. Kula potato farms date from 1840, when the Irish potato was introduced. On the road, the turn-of-the-century octagonal building is the **Church of the Holy Ghost**. Debate continues over Father James Beissel's 1897 design; it generally is agreed he chose an octagon because it was a familiar shape to his Portuguese parishioners. Nearly 100 years later, the carefully restored spire-topped church looks like an elfin pastry in Kula town, and the parishioners still are mainly Portuguese.

South of Kula on HI 37, on the 20,000-acre 'Ulupalakua Ranch, cattle munch

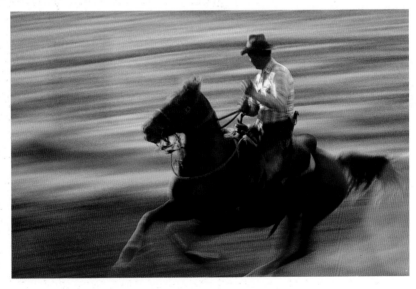

Hawai'i's cowboys (paniolos) *have been overseeing Hawai'i's cattle industry since the mid-nineteenth century (Greg Vaughn). (opposite) Silversword, unique to the Hawaiian islands, thrive on the sunbaked slopes of Haleakala.*

in pastures beside Hawai'i's only vineyard, the 20-acre **Tedeschi Vineyard**. The winery manufactures both conventional wine and a unique wine made from pineapple in a lava jailhouse built in 1857, where a stone-carved rain god stands sentinel. To try these wines, visit the tasting room.

HALEAKALA NATIONAL PARK

Maui's "highway to heaven," rising up into the misty cloud hovering on Haleakala (the House of the Sun), is the world's most rapidly ascending road. It makes you realize that eastern Maui really is a mountain, and you're driving up the slopes of the largest dormant volcano in the world. From Kahului to crater rim, over a distance of 37 miles (60 km), the smooth, well-angled road ascends from sea level to 10,023 feet (3,057 m)—past eucalyptus and cactus plants, above the tree line into an undulating, dry-brown, alpine desert clustered with lava boulders, where wide vistas sweep under passing billows of cloud. Because of the altitude, the temperature (especially at dawn and dusk) can drop to nearly freezing, around 33 degrees F (1° C). Depending upon the weather it also can be in the 80s (25° C). In these rarefied heights, you'll want to be prepared for anything.

To reach Haleakala National Park from Kahului, take the Haleakala Highway (HI 37). Turn onto HI 377 just past the Makawao turnoff, continuing another six miles (10 km) to Haleakala Crater Road (HI 378), which takes you up sharply curving switchbacks to the volcano's crater rim. En route, watch for caravans of helmeted bicycle riders coasting down to sea level, and stop at the Haleakala National Park headquarters, one mile (1.6 km) from the park entrance, for brochures and general information. There are a number of overlooks. At the crater's rim, eleven miles (18 km) farther up, a good place to stop is at the round, glass-panelled **Visitor Center** near the end of the road. It stands to the side of a cinder cone hovering on the rim. This is Pu'u 'Ula'ula (Red Hill), highest point on the mountain and 28,000 feet (8,540 m) above the ocean floor.

When you look down, the immense 3,000-foot (915-m) deep crater of Haleakala lies before you, often swathed in velvety cloud. A moonscape rolls down and away from the rim into a distant veil of fog—coagulating and dissolving like an ephemeral beast. Pink and grey cinder cones, swirled streams of barren red sands, and eerie, windworn lava formations emerge from shadows to fill the horizon. Blobs of lava called bombs, and spatter cones—islets in a mist-sea—are associated with gods and goddesses. Directly below the Visitor Center is Kalu'u O Ka

O'o, home of Pele's brother, a god of mist and steam. The single, powerful presence enfolding all who gaze on the crater is silence. By some unknown force the awesome view seeps soundless into the consciousness, and you feel the power of the gods. Here, at the gods' ancient home, Hawaiian *kahuna* (priests) performed sacred rites of initiation.

The oval-shaped crater, an astounding 27 miles (43 km) in circumference, is 7¹/₂ miles (12 km) across and 2¹/₂ miles (4 km) wide—19 square miles (30 sq. km) formed by the action of rainwater percolating through porous layers of cinders and ash. Hiking and horse trails cross the crater, and three cabins built in 1937 are available through the park superintendent. (See "Parks and Camping" in "PRACTICAL INFORMATION.") Two massive gaps slash the crater rim, formed by an eons-long geological battle of volcanic outpourings versus erosions by wind, torrential rains, and streams. Kaupo Gap cuts south from the crater's eastern end, and on the northern side, Ko'olau Gap opens down onto the Ke'anae flatland.

The best times to see the crater are early morning, when dawn slips over the rim, and at sunset. During these moments you can visualize the demigod Maui slowing the path of the sun to make the day longer by lassoing it "with the loop of Maui's snaring rope." According to the creation chant, *The Kumulipo,* Maui harnessed each ray of the sun. When he released the fiery ball, Maui left some of the ropes dangling, and every evening at sunset you may see them slipping off into darkening sky. If clouds cooperate, you too may gaze at a glimmering horizon of pink, red, gold, and orange colors, that has awed writers for nearly two centuries. In 1866, Mark Twain described the crater's dawn:

> A growing warmth suffused the horizon, and soon the sun emerged and looked out over the cloud-waste, flinging bars of ruddy light across it; staining its folds and billow-caps with blushes, purpling the shaded troughs between, and glorifying the massy vapor-palaces and cathedrals with a wasteful splendor of all blendings and combinations of rich coloring. It was the sublimest spectacle I ever witnessed, and I think the memory of it will remain with me always.

Protecting and preserving Haleakala occupies the prime efforts of park authorities, and with more than one and a half million visitors each year, it is a formidable goal. The enormous preserve stretches from the summit area down the slopes eastward to the coast, joining the volcano crater with the rainforests of the Kipahulu coastal area. In order to protect fragile ecosystems, no road has been built to connect the two sections, and most of the area in between is closed to the public. In 1980, Haleakala National Park was given the status of an International Biosphere Reserve by UNESCO.

The complexity of resources in Haleakala National Park requires careful management. Dry forests, considered the richest in plant species of all Hawaiian forests, once rimmed the lower mountain flanks. Rainforest flourished on the eastern slopes. Arriving in Hawai'i in their voyaging canoes, colonizing Polynesians brought pigs that soon multiplied and roamed the wet forests. Later came European goats and pigs, the gifts of Captain Cook and Captain Vancouver some 200 years ago. These, added to the existing feral population, ravaged the dry forest and turned vast areas into weed-strewn rocky pastures. Only a few patches of native trees and shrubs survive, and in the diminishing rainforest, tender flowers are smothered by muddy pig wallows. As plant cover is eaten away, irrevocable erosion of the mountain slopes progresses rapidly, and some scientists say that the silt carried into the ocean by rain and wind is responsible for killing fish and coral.

By 1986, the nearly impossible goal of fencing in part of Haleakala was completed. A 32-mile (51-km) perimeter fence now controls animals within the park and keeps feral goats and pigs from the crater. A massive removal program of thousands of animals was undertaken by park authorities, and today no feral goats remain inside the barrier section of the park.

Perhaps the most well-known examples of conservation on Haleakala are the native silversword *('ahinahina)* plant and the Hawaiian *nene* goose. Some 50 years ago, less than a hundred plants grew on the western rim of the crater. Today, more than 50,000 delicately rooted silverswords stand tall on the mountain. The *nene* population, once down to 30 birds, now numbers in the hundreds.

L A N A ʻ I
P I N E A P P L E   I S L A N D

SHAPED LIKE AN OYSTER SHELL AND FORMED BY A SINGLE VOLCANO, tiny Lanaʻi is rugged, wild, and austere. Steep, eroded gorges and red lava mountains fall away to the east from a central rolling tableland, and to the west, 2,000-foot (600-m) cliffs drop to the sea. Remote beaches nestle untrammeled on northern shores, and in the northwest, eerie piles of red earth and ancient lava mold a barren moonscape. From a trail winding up through Norfolk pine forests above the only town (Lanaʻi City) five of Hawaii's other islands can be spotted—every island except Kauaʻi.

Nine miles (15 km) across the ʻAuʻau Channel from the glamorous shops and nightlife of west Maui, Lanaʻi remains serene, relaxing, and a fine place to star gaze at night. Until recently there was only one hotel, the ten-room Hotel Lanaʻi, set on a grassy hill overlooking town, where wind ruffles pines on cool evenings, and there's a single TV set in the front lounge. Most travelers, upon

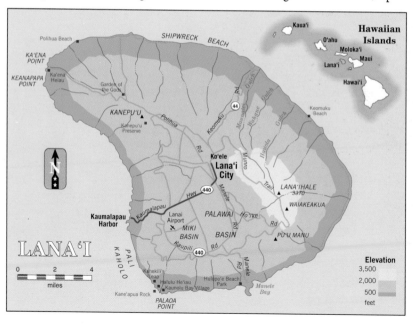

learning that the smallest island was a huge plain of pineapples with few paved roads, left Lana'i to its wild sheep and goats. Today Lana'i has awakened to elegant tourism. Two luxurious and pricey hotels opened in 1990 and 1991 by the real estate arm of the Dole Food conglomerate rise on the island, and things never will be quite the same.

It takes stamina to see the rugged beauty of Lana'i. The best way is to rent a four-wheel-drive vehicle, take a map, and explore. There are 30 miles (50 km) of paved road; many more unpaved roads and jeep trails crisscross the island. Axis deer, mouflon sheep, and goats, partridge, and pheasant all can be seen in the wild. If you go hiking in the mountains, you may see a ram—one of the most beautiful sights on the island—his great horns curving down around his head and standing in silhouette against azure sky. Yet there's a paradox here. Game birds and feral animals, all introduced in the past two centuries, lack natural predators, rapidly reproduce, and ravage the native ecosystem. For this reason, hunting has long been allowed on Lana'i, and the island is popular with sportsmen.

■ HISTORY

Fearing its reef-studded shores, ancient Polynesian and Hawaiian voyagers often bypassed Lana'i. Later it had a reputation as the home of terrifying man-eating spirits, and it remained uninhabited until the son of a great Maui chief was banished there. Named Kaulula'au, he was something of a juvenile delinquent, breaking *kapu* by chopping down breadfruit trees. His father exiled him to Lana'i, and probably expected him to die there, yet people kept seeing his campfires on the shore. Before long, word filtered back to Maui that Kaulula'au had slain the odious spirits, and his father, no doubt rejoicing, declared Lana'i safe for habitation. Controlled by Maui chiefs, it soon supported a population of some 3,000 people who farmed the tableland until the island was decimated by war at the end of the eighteenth century. By the time European mariners were steering clear of the reefs, the rich central tableland lay fallow. While Lana'i played only a small role in Kamehameha the Great's surge to unite the islands, its name means "day of conquest."

In the 1860s, Lana'i was settled by Mormons under the leadership of the charismatic Walter Murray Gibson, who bought the island with Mormon funds and registered it to himself. For this, he was promptly excommunicated. Gibson's followers stayed. They established a sugar plantation, a mill, and cane railroad at Palawai Basin in the south-central part of the island. Crops had to be irrigated, as Lana'i receives scant rainfall—35 inches (90 cm) annually in the highlands and in the lower levels, barely a foot (25 cm). Difficulties increased and the Mormon farming and ranching operations failed. In 1901, they sold the island.

By 1922, businessman James Dole, a descendant of missionaries, envisioned planting Lana'i's rolling fields with pineapple. For $1,100,000, the island was his. Dole planted fruit, brought workers from the Philippines, built a plantation town, and forever changed life on Lana'i. His 15,000 acres represented the agricultural effort of the entire island, and it soon became the world's largest pineapple plantation.

In recent years, Dole (merged with Castle & Cooke, and renamed Dole Food Company) has radically cut the number of acres it plants in pineapple. More and more fields are sown to pasture and experimental forage crops, and the last Lana'i pineapple will soon be shipped aboard a barge from Kaumalapau Harbor on the west coast.

Hawai'i's pineapples are legendary as evidenced by this scene photographed for tourists in 1950. (Oakland Museum)

An island with only one town, dominated by one company, and planted in one crop faces striking changes in the approaching century. On Lana'i where family ties are strong, the 2,400 residents today are 51 percent Filipino, 18 percent Japanese, and 11 percent *haole*. Children of recent generations have gone away from the fields, some to universities. Those who want to return no longer come home to back-breaking jobs planting 6,000 to 10,000 seed sprouts a day.

In the late 1980s Lana'i—and Dole Food—embarked on a new era: tourism. Tourism instead of vast pineapple cultivation. Tourism jobs; elegant tourism, Rockefeller style, for the super-rich.

Built by Dole and operated by Rockresorts (of Caribbean fame), a single hotel altered the gritty soul of Lana'i. Opened in 1990, the Lodge at Koele in the cool 1,700-foot (510-m) central highlands above Lana'i City, marked the dawn of the new era. On its grounds, amid tall, old pines on 21 acres of lawns and gardens, stands Hawai'i's original Norfolk pine tree—the towering shaft that inspired the planting of similar trees and brought a piney atmosphere to Lana'i. Koele has the air of a Victorian country estate, with a broad view over land where decades ago a cattle ranch stood; the hotel's reflecting pool was once a stock watering hole. A major sister hotel, the Manele Bay, above a beach six miles (10 km) south of Lana'i City, is the other luxury enclave for the very wealthy.

There may be irony in trading dirty work in the earth for clean work in the hotels. Yet in the 1990s, residents recognize opportunities for youth in tourism and express confidence in its stability. As Lana'i swaps its main crop of pineapple for tourists, the legacy Dole Food bequeaths the island is controversial—islanders want the old life style, and tourism jobs as well. Whether Dole can make that happen, or eventually will sell off the land to foreign interests, consumes the entire island in debate.

■ LANA'I CITY

A mile from the small airport, the only town, Lana'i City, sits precisely in the center of the island at a cool elevation of 1,645 feet (500 m)—perhaps the most isolated settlement in all the islands. Almost all the residents of this plantation town still live in frame houses clustered near its main street. The town is little changed. Stores still close at lunch time and no traffic light, movie theater, or disco mars its tin-roofed, quiet, ambience. As living accommodations are built

JAPANESE BRIDE

The author of this piece, Clara Jelsma, recorded her mother's memories of being an immigrant homesteader in Hawai'i between 1905 and 1925.

About this time Father's older brother, Soske, received a letter from his half brother, Umetaro, who had emigrated to Hawai'i 16 years before. He had written that he had purchased 200 acres of land there and would like to have Soske find a wife for him and send her to Hawai'i. He specified that she should be a country girl, but educated, and not too ugly.

Soske found this to be a very big order. Country girls were not very educated, and the pretty girls were in the city. Also, it seemed hard to believe that Umetaro, who had always been the black sheep, could really be doing so well that he could have bought 200 acres of land.

Since he was not sure whether it was true or not, he felt he could not ask for a bride from the village or from among strangers. So, he decided that it would be best to find a bride from among the kinfolk.

Thinking over the qualifications which had been specified Soske thought about Umetaro's first cousin, Iku Hayashi. She was not too homely and was a country girl. But she could be considered educated since she had studied in Tokyo and had been travelling around trying to be a nurse.

continues

Japanese sugarcane workers at Spreckelsville, Maui; by Joseph Strong, c. 1885. (Taito Co., Ltd., Tokyo, Japan)

Soske wrote to Umetaro asking what he thought about his choice. Umetaro wrote back that he would trust in Soske's judgment and accept whoever he decided was best. If he considered Iku to be a suitable bride for him, that was fine with him.

So, Mother was notified.

If you want to go to Hawai'i as a bride, come home immediately, she was told in the letter from Soske.

As she read the letter, Mother was not very much excited by the prospect of marriage. But the thought of going to Hawai'i was enough to entice her to head home immediately. No one from her little village had ever travelled abroad.

Soske was only a farmer, but because the government had run a highway through his rice field and rebated him 20,000 yen, he furnished Mother liberally with money for her trousseau.

"If you're going abroad, you should go in good style. Buy the very best," he advised her.

So, Mother went shopping in Nagoya and bought the best of everything she thought she needed. She purchased her kimono, her *montsuki* (bridal garment with the beautiful *obi* or sash, her *haori* or outer garment, and her *jiban* or slip), her gold wedding ring, her Wittnauer gold watch, her umbrella, her *zori* (slippers), and her *geta* (clogs). She had never owned or worn such fine things in Japan. . . .

Finally the day of departure came. It had been about two years since she had decided to go to Hawai'i. She was thirty years old, and felt fully prepared for the life before her. Of course, she envisioned Hawai'i to be a place like Nojiri where you could buy all the things you needed.

She was handed a three pound Crisco can of *ume* by Umezo Kongaki, a well travelled friend of Umetaro. The sour pickled plums were from his trees and were given to soothe the sea sickness en route. "Give the extra ones to Umetaro," he told her.

Umezo accompanied Soske and Mother to Yokohama harbor where she boarded the *Taiho Maru*. Last words were exchanged and a few tears shed. Then the men returned home. Mother was on her way.

The ship was full of other brides on their way to Hawai'i. Most of them were women in their thirties. They were from various places and backgrounds, and all hopeful about a new life in Hawai'i.

❖ ❖ ❖

continues

The disembarking from the *Taiho Maru* in Honolulu was one of relief for the weary, sea sick passengers. The immigration center was a place of confusion and loud activity.

Very prominent there was a large, talkative man of about sixty from Niigata by the name of Katsuno-san who was a sort of manager for the immigrants coming in and had some official position at the immigration office. Katsuno-san was loud and spoke very coarsely, joshing the women with his crude remarks.

The identification time at the immigration center was a joyful time for some and a shocking crisis to others. Some brides who knew their husbands only by the photographs sent them, many of which were very deceptive, were so shocked at seeing their mates that they fled from their husbands.

When Mother's name was called, she was startled to see a tall, ferocious looking man with overgrown hair and an unkempt, bushy beard coming toward her. Could this man really be her cousin, Umetaro, she wondered. She had not seen him for over sixteen years.

—Clara Mitsuko Jelsma, *Teapot Tales*,
from *The Best of Bamboo Ridge*, 1986

for hotel employees, a new mood begins to prevail, and the tired atmosphere is receiving a jolt of energy. Old plantation buildings are being renovated. A couple of brave boutiques have opened. More will follow.

■ MUNRO TRAIL AND MOUNT LANA'IHALE

The seven-mile (11-km) Munro Trail, a jeep road and hiking trail, begins behind Koele Lodge and winds up through pine forests to the summit of Mount Lana'ihale, the island's highest point (3,370 feet/1,027 m). Here is a lookout with a view of the other islands. About a third of the way up the trail a hiking path leads to an overlook above Lana'i's deepest gorge, Ha'uola Gulch, which drops 2,000 feet (600 m) before it meets the sea on the island's east coast.

The trail was developed by George C. Munro, a New Zealand naturalist, who stepped ashore on Lana'i in 1911. For the next three decades, while Dole cultivated pineapple on the rolling mesas, Munro trudged the highlands, planting Norfolk pines to capture moisture and reduce erosion. On the lower slopes of western

Lana'i several unique and scattered patches of dryland forest survive. One of these is **Kanepu'u Preserve** six miles (10 km) northwest of Lana'i City. At this site in 1918, George Munro, by now a ranch manager, erected fences and removed stray cattle to preserve a grove of *lama* (native persimmon) and *olopu'a* (a native olive), together with dozens of less common native plants. For 30 years he worked to protect the site, and his dedication reminds us that long before the modern concept of ecology evolved, visionaries like Munro understood its precepts and tried their best to preserve the land.

In 1935, when the eminent botanist Raymond Fosberg visited Kanepu'u, he described it as "the last place in Hawai'i where one can witness the forests that must have once covered vast areas of the dry lowlands." By the 1970s, several plants were gone; however, the groves and 48 native species remained, including *ili'ahi,* the endangered Lana'i sandalwood, and wild specimens of *nanu,* the Hawaiian gardenia. In 1989, Dole, now owner of 98 percent of the island, made a gift of a conservation easement over 462 acres at Kanepu'u to the Hawai'i chapter of the Nature Conservancy.

In the northwest quadrant of the island, an unpaved road and jeep trail lead to the **Garden of the Gods.** Here, boulders are piled in eerie, tottering, eroded heaps permeated with earthy colors, which change hues at dawn and sunset. The boulders are set upon red sand hills that sweep down to the north shore, and the scent of sage hovers in the wind.

Ka'ena Point, at the foot of a jeep track on the northwest corner of Lana'i, was once a penal colony where, between 1837 and 1843, women subsisted in misery. "Thou shalt not sleep mischievously" wrote the missionaries in their translation of the Seventh Commandment in 1825. Baffled by the new concept of adultery, astonished Hawaiian women found themselves shipped off to Lana'i on the schooner *Ho'okaika,* out of Maui. At Ka'ena they were confined to a sort of environmental prison—without walls or guards, and with little food. Furious winds and perilous currents kept them isolated within sight of their homes on Maui or Moloka'i.

■ NORTH LANA'I

Ten miles (16 km) from Lana'i City, an eight-mile long (13-km) stretch of sandy areas punctuated by points of rock stretches along the north coast from Polihua in the west, to Kahokunui in the east. "Shipwreck" is the name for the entire stretch of north shore beach.

Shipwreck Beach is a thread of sandy plots fine for beach combing and shore fishing. Swimming is dangerous, as the waters are murky, the seabed rocky and shallow. The section most easily accessible is reached from the end of HI 440 (Keomuku Road). Take the north branch dirt track to the lighthouse ruins at Po'aiwa.

Hulks of ships torn by sharp, wave-shrouded coral lie rotting on the reef off Shipwreck, scourge to mariners since the days of whalers. Beside the beach lies the rusting wreck of a World War II Liberty Ship. Islanders and sculptors track the sands for mangled shapes of driftwood or old hand-blown glass balls used by Japanese fishermen as floats.

Wide, windy, and remote **Polihua (Egg Nest) Beach,** a mile and a half (2 km) long and the largest white sand beach on Lana'i, follows the island's contour at the

Shipwreck Beach on Lana'i.

west end of the north coast. Once this was a green sea turtle *(honu)* nesting beach. Tragically, this endangered, federally protected species has not been seen since 1954. The beach can be reached only by four-wheel drive. Check with the rental agency for road conditions before taking the dirt tracks northwest from the end of the inland paved road at the Garden of the Gods. At the edge of planted fields, a sign points the way to the shore.

Although it is possible to hike the north shore all the way from Shipwreck west to Polihua, not even a jeep track connects the two. Each is reached by widely separated tracks.

■ SOUTH LANA'I

Six miles (10 km) south of Lana'i City by paved road (HI 441), the second of Dole's new luxury hotels, the Manele Bay, opened in 1991. This elegant pile of concrete stands on a low cliff above the island's best and most accessible beach. The resort is pricey: up to $600 per night, and there are butlers to draw your bath water for you.

Hulopo'e (White) Beach is a quarter-mile (400-m) crescent of smooth sands framed in *kiawe* trees, fronting waters locally famed for snorkeling. You can plunge into the scuba site called Cathedrals, where coral pinnacles rise from 70-foot (21-m) depths, creating chasms alive with slipper lobsters, striped convict fish, and three-foot (90-cm) zebra moray eels *(puhi)*.

With good deep-water swimming, a picnic area, and the island's only beach park with facilities, Hulopo'e has been a traditional favorite of residents. Years ago, a wide tidal pool was blasted out of shoreline rock to make a safe swimming section for children in the east arm of the bay. A resident pod of spinner dolphins is known to make regular morning visits. Now that a luxury hotel rises on the unspoiled and largely unknown shore, the easy-going atmosphere of Hulopo'e and the pleasure of the locals are fated to be joined by the sleeker sophistication of wealthy pleasure-seekers.

At the far end of Hulopo'e Beach, a volcanic spatter cone rears up like an eroded sculpture. On its far side is **Manele Bay,** a small inlet beneath lava cliffs. Manele once held a curve of black sand. Then in 1965, construction of a small boat harbor engulfed the west end of the beach. On the shore, ruins of old native Hawaiian houses stand like a painted backdrop to yachts anchored in waters of the harbor. Boat anchoring is not permitted outside the designated harbor, and the types of fishing allowed, or not allowed, are clearly posted.

Harbor construction left a patch of white sand at the eastern corner of Manele Bay, where calm waters offer fine snorkeling and diving. It is wise to watch for small boat traffic. A Marine Life Conservation Area since 1979, the two crescents of Hulopo'e and Manele beaches teem with sea life.

A sunset stop at Palawai Basin on Manele Road (441), halfway between Lana'i City and the south shore, rewards visitors with fiery red earth caught in the evening light. You can hike in to **Luahiwa** from Hoiki Road to the west side of the basin where 20 boulders on the hillside are carved with some 400 petroglyphs. Most are linear and triangular human figures, others dogs, or horses.

A passenger ferry shuttle operates across the 'Au'au Channel from the town of Lahaina in Maui, to Manele Bay.

At Kaunolu where cliffs descend to the southwest tip of the island, the ruins of ancient **Kaunolu Bay Village** stand like silent sentinels in the wind. Halulu He'iau stood on the west side of the small bay. Inland from the *he'iau*, petroglyphs are etched on boulders above the west side of a stream bed. The figures are triangular muscled humans, and goats. At the eastern side of the bay Kamehameha the Great built a home and fishing retreat. A jeep track off the Kaumalapau Harbor paved road bumps and bounces south to the ancient village, a National Historic Landmark archaeologists consider to be one of the finest preserved Hawaiian ruins in the island chain. Grave markings, 86 houses, and 35 stone shelters have been identified.

In 1868, Kamehameha V visited his grandfather's fishing retreat here, and it is said he hid a stone image of Ku'ula, god of fishermen, somewhere nearby. A plaque set into a stone in 1963 tells this story.

To the west of the bay at **Kane'apua Rock**, warriors of Kamehameha the Great courted death to prove their loyalty to the king. From a patch of lava 60 feet (18 m) above the sea, they plunged out as far as possible to clear a 15-foot (4.5-m) outcropping before dropping into 12 feet (3.6 m) of water. It is known as **Kahekili's Leap**, and perhaps Kamehameha bestowed the name to honor an old foe. In his youth Kamehameha had fought Kahekili on Lana'i—and lost.

North of Kaunolu at more than 1,000 feet (305 m) is **Pali Kaholo** the highest sea cliff on Lana'i. It is unusual to find a sea cliff on a southwest shore in Hawai'i —normally they rise on north coasts, where wind and waves batter and erode them. Lana'i, shielded on the north by West Maui, is an exception, and here it is the south shore that is most vulnerable to wind and waves.

In ancient songs the island of Lana'i was noted for its *kauna'oa*, a strange ground-running plant that thrives on leeward beaches. A parasite rooted in the sand above the high water mark, *kauna'oa's* thread-like stems rest on the sand and reach out to attach themselves to host plants. The smooth, peach-colored tendrils are gathered in handfuls and twisted or braided to make a thick lei. Small pieces of greenery add contrasting color. The lei requires no tie; after a few hours the tendrils bind themselves together.

Hawaiian woman in white holoku; *by Cornelia Foley, 1937. (courtesy of Cornelia Foley)*

WATER BORN

Mo'omomi Beach, narrow and hooked like a horseshoe
From centuries of wear, is reefless. Seas pound it
And strong currents often cut through
Carving pockets and cleaning stations out
Of the lava. I brought you there to dive,
To spear ulua, fish with an approach like a spaceship.
We moved easy, consumed,
Flippers never breaking the surface,
Drawn into an unnoticed current, and carried
Out to deep, purpling water.
Alerted by the color I turned to you
But you knew, your mottled eyes filled the window
Of your mask like a single bruise.
We pumped hard for shore
Burning our lungs up, making no headway,
I turned again, you'd fallen far behind,
All timing gone from your stroke.
I felt death by drowning
And went to hold you, taste the last water in your hair,
To slip under with you, and await the coming sharks,
Their fins dipped, bodies arched,
The beautiful pewter of their tails,
To accept death and be finally brave for us,
Bellow like an old hero
Into a deafening white mouth.
It lasted less than seconds
And I remembered about a current,
Go with it, ride till it slows and lets you off.
Panic lifted, order rose out of my chest
Like smoke, we breathed and were limp.
We hadn't gone far, and a steady swim brought us in
East of the beach. Through it all you'd held on
To your 3-prong and stringer of poked fish.
We rested on a pile of warm stones
One of many that speckles Mo'omomi
And marks the ancient fallen.
You asked about them, their weapons and deaths,
Putting our scrape into perspective.
Picking up the spear and fish
We headed back,
Renewed, heroic, or as close as we'd ever get.

—Norman Hindley, *Water Born, The Best of Bamboo Ridge*, 1986

KAHO'OLAWE

Kaho'olawe, the smallest, driest, windiest island in the Hawaiian chain, is uninhabited. Brown and brooding and without natural barriers, it lies in the shadow of Maui's great volcano, Haleakala. By the time tradewinds have raced around that immense volcano, they have spilled their rain and hit nearby Kaho'olawe bone dry and at near-gale force.

Kaho'olawe probably was settled later than the other islands. Archaeologists date the earliest known site around A.D.1000, some four to six centuries after the settlement of O'ahu and Moloka'i. At inland sites, amid evidence of sweet potato cultivation, fishing artifacts have been found. It is thought these early Hawaiians lived inland and visited the coast, making offerings to the fish god 'Ai'ai at Haki'oawa, where an altar faced the sea on a rise above the northeast shore. At an inland basalt quarry, they hacked out a fine quality of adze stones that were traded across the channels to other islands. In traditional migration chants, Keala'ikahiki on the island's western tip, is mentioned as a place where ancient navigators set out on voyages to Tahiti.

No archaeological evidence of settlement on the island after the early 1600s has been found, suggesting Kaho'olawe's population may have been radically reduced in the mid-seventeenth century—a time of inter-island warfare and environmental degeneration.

For a brief time in the mid-1800s Kaho'olawe served as a penal colony established by missionaries. Ranching followed—a move that brought dire consequences to the land as sheep and cattle destroyed most of the vegetation, and up to 15 feet (4.5 m) of topsoil blew off in the wind.

In 1941, after the Japanese attacked Pearl Harbor, the War Department leased the island for target bombing and shelling practice. When World War II ended in 1945, the war-time status lingered, and in 1953 an executive order transferred jurisdiction of Kaho'olawe to the Navy. It is now strewn with unexploded and dangerous ordnance, and civilians are not allowed on the island.

For years the fate of Kaho'olawe simmered on a back burner. With the renaissance of Hawaiian culture in the 1970s, protesters began to demand the return of the island to the Hawaiian people. Civil suits followed, and soon the Navy was required to submit environmental impact statements—an almost laughable requirement for land so impacted with ordnance that some military experts believe it never can be cleared.

No one can live on bomb- and projectile-strewn Kaho'olawe. Military representatives continue to claim that the island is the only viable site in the Pacific for conducting necessary international air, land, and sea maneuvers.

In 1976, an agreement between the Navy and the State permitted a group of Hawaiians to step ashore at Haki'oawa, but the effect could be no more than symbolic. In 1990, a presidential directive halted bombing practice on Kaho'olawe. A joint body of the Department of Defense-State of Hawai'i, the Kaho'olawe Island Conveyance Commission, mandated "to examine the future status of Kaho'olawe," plugs away at compiling findings and recommendations. The next step will be cleanup, but where the money will come from to make the island safe again after 50 years of bombing and shelling practice, is anybody's guess. To activists, Kaho'olawe is an unhealed wound. Until the island is returned to the State and Maui County, or to an official Hawaiian body, the legacy of Kaho'olawe is clouded in anger, frustration, and cynicism.

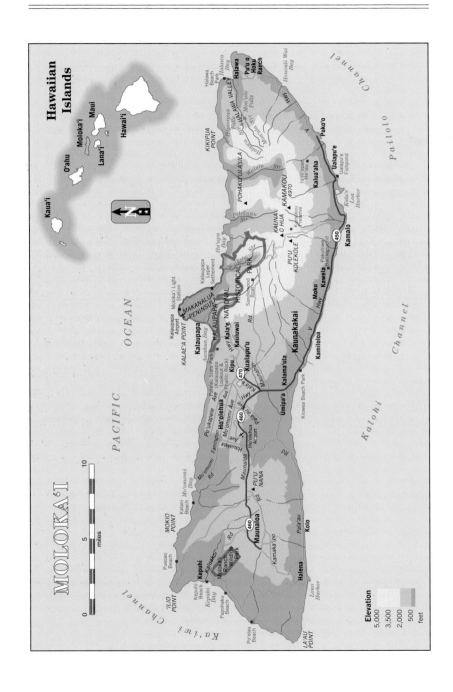

M O L O K A ' I
L O N E L Y , F R I E N D L Y I S L E

Moloka'i lay like a homely sway-backed whale on the water.
—Mark Twain

RURAL MOLOKA'I RETAINS A DISTINCTIVE, nineteenth-century charm, perhaps because nearly 50 percent of its population is native Hawaiian and keeps alive the real Hawai'i's mood and culture. Living in tiny towns studded with fruit-packed, flowering gardens, the island's 7,000 residents see few tourists, and because Moloka'i has dangerous reefs and no natural harbors, development has come slowly. Though the glamorous hotels lighting up west Maui can be seen just eight miles (13 km) away across the Pailolo Channel from Moloka'i's rugged eastern shore, visitors who prefer a natural Hawai'i rather than the mega-resorts of larger islands are in the right place.

In geographically diverse Moloka'i, lush tropical preserves flourish on the eastern shore. Most of the north shore is a line of soaring valley-slashed sea cliffs, among the tallest in the world, falling 2,000 feet (600 m) to meet wild ocean waters below. The western section of the north shore tapers down to remote fishing beaches, and the western interior is a dry plain clad in the bright green color of seed corn fields growing in rich red earth, and scrub plains that drop into shallow ravines where brown-green *kiawe* trees grow tall. At the western end, Hawai'i's largest beach, Papohaku, stretches along the Kaiwi Channel. Outlined in the shallow waters of southern shores are ancient fish ponds, some restored and used as they were long ago, for farming fish.

A twice-daily ferry from Lahaina, Maui, arrives at Kaunakakai, Moloka'i's main town, from which a single highway travels the length of the island. It follows the south shore up into the highlands and curves along the eastern flank of the island to end at the north shore sea cliffs. In the west it ends at Kaluako'i, the island's only large resort. There is no public transportation on Moloka'i, and car rental agencies are located only at Ho'olehua Airport, eight miles (13 km) west of Kaunakakai.

■ HISTORY

In ancient chants, Moloka'i is the child of Hina in her embodiment as goddess of the moon. It has always been something of an outpost. Called the Lonely Isle in olden times, it was a haven for *kapu*-breakers and the vanquished, and associated with mystical practices of the *kahuna* (priests) and sorcery. The power of the *kahuna* was feared throughout the archipelago, for it was believed they could pray a person to death. The sacred hula associated with ceremonial rites was born on this island.

In 1786, eight years after Captain Cook first saw the islands, the British sailor George Dixon anchored off south Moloka'i, and Hawaiians on the island took their first look at foreigners.

Four years later Kamehameha the Great came here to negotiate a marriage, then sailed from south Moloka'i to the Big Island in a double war canoe, accompanied by the young bride-to-be, Keopuolani, her mother, and her sister. The little girl was the daughter of a chieftess and her brother—the prescribed marriage if its issue were to be a child of the highest caste *(Niau'pio)*. This caste was so exalted that if the shadow of a *Niau'pio* caste member fell on someone of inferior caste, that person had to be killed and the body burned. By the age of eleven, Keopuolani was betrothed to Kamehameha, who already had a roster of wives, including his favorite—the beloved, wise, and childless Ka'ahumanu. As young Keopuolani was capable of bearing Kamehameha a *Naiu'pio* son, and because this was a religious and political necessity, she became his "sacred wife."

The strategy of the warrior king called for conquest of his most important targets—the largest islands and populations—before he mopped up the smaller isles. In his final year of conquest, 1795, a line of war canoes four miles (7 km) long appeared in waters off Moloka'i's southern shore, and soon the island was his. In the same year Kamehameha married Keopuolani, now 16 years old, in Waikiki.

When explorers, whalers, and sandalwood traders arrived in the islands they found no natural harbor at Moloka'i and steered clear of its reef-strewn muddy south shores. British Captain George Vancouver lowered his anchor there in 1792. Though he remained aboard, he estimated the population at 10,000, including large numbers of people in the remote and lush north shore valleys.

By the 1830s, missionaries had arrived, and cattle and sheep ranches began to flourish on the island. In 1848, during the reign of Kamehameha II, the Great *Mahele* became law. The greatest land revolution Hawai'i had ever known, it divided and reallocated the king's land, with the intent of giving native Hawaiians an opportunity to possess land. (Also see "HISTORY AND CULTURE.") In the 1850s, Kamehameha V acquired nearly 40 percent of the island and formed the 60,000-acre Moloka'i Ranch, which was, for a time, the second largest cattle station in the islands. Sold after his death, it was acquired by Honolulu businessmen in 1897.

In the 1860s, a gift arrived with consequences no one could foresee: axis deer, from the emperor of Japan to Kamehameha V. From the point of view of the deer, this must have seemed like a fine, predator-free environment. They began to propagate rapidly, and were soon a blight on native plant and birdlife. Feral cattle and sheep added to the ravage of the ecosystem.

In 1866, the nickname Lonely Isle took on a new meaning for Moloka'i. The dreaded disease **leprosy**, believed to have entered Hawai'i with the immigrant waves from China, had spread throughout the islands, and Kamehameha V decided to isolate lepers on Moloka'i. He established a leper colony at Kalawao on the island's lonely north peninsula. Lepers were wrenched from their homes, taken by

Father Damien with girls of the Moloka'i's leper settlement, c. 1880. (Hawaii State Archives)

ship to Moloka'i, and tossed into the seas near the windy peninsula—doomed to survive, if they could, without support on a wave-lashed projection of land.

To this broken-hearted, lawless scrubland, Father Damien (Joseph Damien de Veuster), a Belgian priest, came in 1873. For the next 16 years, the "Martyr of Moloka'i" worked and lived among the tormented, wrapping superating sores, banging coffins together, and praying over graves. During Damien's last days the colony was moved to the western (and more protected) side of the peninsula, called **Kalaupapa** (Flat Plain). In 1889, at the age of 49, Father Damien died of leprosy, contracted from the people he'd strived so hard to help. He was buried at the settlement. In 1937, his remains were exhumed and reburied at Louvain in Belgium where he had trained for the priesthood. Today, the process of canonization for Father Damien grinds slowly forward.

By 1921, a significant number of Hawaiians were settling on 40-acre Moloka'i homesteads acquired under the Hawaiian Homestead Act. With them came a gracious heritage and the spirit of aloha—and Moloka'i acquired its present label: the Friendly Isle. When pineapple was introduced in the twenties, the companies imported laborers from the Philippines and Japan to work the fields. Many homesteaders leased their lands to the pineapple companies. While that put them in a position of dependency, it offered a measure of security. Some 60 years later, in the late 1980s, Dole and Del Monte closed their pineapple operations on Moloka'i, and the realities of lost lease rent and unemployment dealt residents a mighty blow. While diversified agriculture and labor-intensive seed corn may someday replace the single crop, a majority of Moloka'i residents prefer limited tourism—confined to "master-planned" beaches on the western coast. There are about the same number of hotel rooms on the island (700) as might be found in a single medium-sized Waikiki hotel.

■ CENTRAL MOLOKA'I

Moloka'i's small airport lies at the island's narrow mid-point, eight miles (13 km) from Kaunakakai, which hugs the south-central shore. In addition to regularly scheduled inter-island flights, there is quite a lot of private plane traffic. One time when we landed here, my husband asked the tower where to park and was told to head for an apron vaguely located under the tower. Taxiing there, he asked if we were in the right spot. The tower voice replied: "Tarreefick!" The car rental agencies were closed. No one was around. When a pickup truck drove in, we asked for a lift. No problem. We climbed into the open truck and were taken straight into town. The Friendly Isle really is *friendly.*

Moloka'i's largest town, flat and treeless **Kaunakakai,** looks like an Old West movie set, with false-front buildings lining the single street. Its three commercial blocks offer a couple of old-fashioned general stores, two grocery markets, an all-purpose drug store, and a bakery-restaurant. No traffic light, movie house, or elevator; no disco or boutique, bus line, or fast-food emporium intrudes in the sleepy port town. The one hotel is within walking distance of the main street. Called the Pau Hana Inn, it has a cowboy flavor, and if you like impromptu Hawaiian music-making, this local hangout is good fun at night.

Kaunakakai, an abbreviated form of Kaunakahakai, means "beach landing." If you stroll down to the shore of the tiny port town, you'll see a concrete wharf extending out over coral and mud into deep ocean. This modern pier, which is also where the ferry from Lahaina arrives, replaced an old coconut log pier onto which, in early days, passengers disembarked from ships. They then boarded a rail car which was pulled by a mule up to the beach.

As Moloka'i lacks a natural deep-water harbor, the Army Corps of Engineers dredged a channel adjacent to the pier in 1934. It can only service barges, and even today deep-draft ships cannot be accommodated at Moloka'i. In a corner of the man-made harbor is a marina that provides the only public boat ramp on the island. (At other areas of the island, residents launch over the beach.) On the west side of the wharf, behind the thatched canoe club, lie the ruins of Malama, a vacation home and compound built by Kamehameha V. Today only a stone platform remains of the royal residence.

A couple of miles (3 km) to the west of Kaunakakai is **Kiowea Park,** famed for its coconut grove named in honor of the island's high chief, Kapua'iwa. In 1863, Kapua'iwa (Prince Lot) became Kamehameha V, and it is said he planted the trees himself here at his place of birth. Due to erosion of the soil by the ocean, some of them now lean directly over the water, and at low tide you can see freshwater springs that once were on land, burbling in the ocean. (Watch for coconuts plummeting to the ground without warning. If there's strong wind, it's not advisable to walk here.) With its muddy waters and a rock-strewn beach, Kiowea is better for picnics than swimming.

Across the highway from Kiowea, marching in line like a band of troops, are seven small chapels belonging to seven different denominations. Known as **Church**

THE DAMIEN LETTER

Few people have inspired such admiration as Father Damien, the Belgian priest who in 1873 went to care for Moloka'i's lepers. Perhaps inevitably, less saintly humans soon were itching to point out his flaws. One of these was a Dr. C.M. Hyde who wrote this letter about Damien to a fellow minister and allowed it to be reprinted in several newspapers.

Honolulu
August 2, 1889
Rev. H.B. Gage.

Dear Brother,—In answer to your inquiries about Father Damien, I can only reply that we who knew the man are surprised at the extravagant newspaper laudations, as if he was a most saintly philanthropist. The simple truth is, he was a coarse, dirty man, headstrong and bigoted. He was not sent to Moloka'i, but went there without orders; did not stay at the leper settlement (before he became one himself), but circulated freely over the whole island (less than half the island is devoted to the lepers), and he came often to Honolulu. He had no hand in the reforms and improvements inaugurated, which were the work of our Board of Health, as occasion required and means were provided. He was not a pure man in his relations with women, and the leprosy of which he died should be attributed to his vices and carelessness. Others have done much for the lepers, our own ministers, the government physicians, and so forth, but never with the Catholic idea of meriting eternal life.—Yours, etc.,

C. M. Hyde

Hyde's letter was reprinted in Australia in the Sydney *Presbyterian, where Robert Louis Stevenson, author of* Kidnapped *and* Treasure Island *happened to read it. Stevenson had only recently left Hawai'i and had spent a week at the Moloka'i leper colony just a few days after Damien's death. His reply, also published in the newspapers, was as follows:*

An Open Letter to the Reverend Dr. Hyde of Honolulu
Sydney,
February 25, 1890
Sir

. . . Your Church and Damien's were in Hawaii upon a rivalry to do well: to help, to edify, to set divine examples. You having (in one huge instance) failed, and Damien succeeded . . .

. . . Of Damien I begin to have an idea. He seems to have been a man of the peasant class, certainly of the peasant type: shrewd, ignorant, and bigoted, yet with an open mind, and capable of receiving and digesting a reproof if it were bluntly administered; superbly generous in the least thing as well as in the greatest, and as ready to give his last shirt (although not without human grumbling) as he had been to sacrifice his life . . .

. . . [You say] Damien was *coarse*. It is very possible. You make us sorry for the lepers, who had only a coarse old peasant for their friend and father. But you, who were so refined, why were you not there, to cheer them with the lights of culture? Or may I remind you that we have some reason to doubt if John the Baptist were genteel; and in the case of Peter, on whose career you doubtless dwell approvingly in the pulpit, no doubt at all he was a "coarse, headstrong" fisherman! Yet even in our Protestant Bibles Peter is called Saint . . .

. . . [You say] Damien was *dirty*. He was. Think of the poor lepers annoyed with this dirty comrade! But the clean Dr. Hyde was at his food in a fine house.

. . . [You say] Damien *was not a pure man in his relations with women*. How do you know that? Is this the nature of the conversation in that house on Beretania Street which the cabman envied, driving past?—racy details of the misconduct of the poor peasant priest, toiling under the cliffs of Moloka'i.

Many have visited the station before me; they seem not to have heard the rumour.

But I fear you scarce appreciate how you appear to your fellow-men; and to bring it home to you, I will suppose your story to be true. I will suppose—and God forgive me for supposing it—that Damien faltered and stumbled in his narrow path of duty; I will suppose that, in the horror of his isolation, perhaps in the fever of incipient disease, he, who was doing so much more than he had sworn, failed in the letter of his priestly oath—he, who was so much a better than either you or me, who did what we have never dreamed of daring—he too tasted of our common frailty.

—Robert Louis Stevenson, *Scots Observer*, 1890

Row, it stands in silent testimony to the arrival of fervent Protestant missionaries upon the sacred ground of ancient Hawaiians.

Beyond Kiowea, travel north and *mauka* (inland) from Kaunakakai on Route 460 and turn onto Route 470 (Maunaloa Highway) just before the rural village of Kualapu'u. The land rises gently up to its highest point where there is a parking lot. A quarter-mile (400-m) walk through a pine wood brings you to **Kalaupapa Lookout.** Here, atop 1,664 feet (507 m) of sheer cliff, an incomparable view of the sheer north coast *pali* stretches before you—14 miles (22 km) of the highest sea cliffs in the world, 1,000 feet (300 m) or more, weeping with waterfalls, and another 15 miles (23 km) of lesser heights. Directly below lies a sweeping view of a fin-shaped projection jutting out from beneath the wall of *pali*—the Makanalua Peninsula (also known as the Kalaupapa Peninsula), site of the Kalaupapa leper settlement.

About a quarter-mile (400 m) walk from Kalaupapa Lookout, **Phallic Rock** protrudes immodestly from the pine-needled floor of a dense ironwood grove. It is said that if a woman strokes this worn six-foot (2 m) outgrowth reverently, she'll become more fertile.

Mule train down to Kalaupapa leper settlement, north Moloka'i.

KALAUPAPA LEPER COLONY

Jutting out mid-way on the north coast lies the fin-shaped Makanalua (Kalaupapa) Peninsula, site of the **Kalaupapa Leper Colony**. The isolated flatland, belted with wind-whipped waves on three sides and cut off at its back by the sheer bulkhead of ominous cliff, seems laden with melancholy. Lepers, once forcibly banished to this desolate flatland, lived here in despair and violence until the arrival of Joseph Damien de Veuster—Father Damien, in 1873. (See "History" and literary excerpts in this chapter for more.)

Since Father Damien's time, great strides in medicine and support have come to Kalaupapa. With the introduction of sulfone and other antibiotic drug therapies, the disease can now be arrested and those taking the drugs are no longer contagious. In the 1960s, some 100 years after the first shipload of lepers stood off the eastern side, admission of new residents at Kalaupapa ended. The settlement is destined for gradual phase-out, although Kalaupapa will continue to operate so long as any resident wishes to stay. Today some 50 elderly people still choose to live in the drowsy compound. In 1980, Kalaupapa became a National Historical Park, including a modern hospital, historic sites, wooden churches, and dusty lanes with small and tidy homes.

Unless you visit the colony on a guided tour, visitors must hire local guides and make arrangements in advance. (Call 567-6171.) Starting from "topside," you can walk or ride a mule (riders must weigh in under 225 pounds) down the Kalaupapa Mule Trail, descending 1,664 feet (505 m) in three tortuous, breathtaking miles (5 km) through 26 switchbacks; your guide will meet you at the bottom. Kalaupapa also can be visited by air.

Most tours stop at Kalawao, the first settlement on the east side; Father Damien's church, St. Philomena; and the monument and grave of Mother Marianne who spent 30 years at Kalaupapa. Artifacts collected by patient (and tour operator) Richard Marks include specialized tools for everyday living such as a spoon that wraps around the wrist for patients who had lost fingers. While some of the tour is on foot, you'll also ride in a car—it will be an old car; there are no new ones at Kalaupapa. Unless you are on the mule train tour, bring a pack lunch; no meal facilities are available. Photography is permitted of everything you see except patients. While the peninsula is a tourist attraction, its residents are not.

Built in 1909, **Moloka'i Light Station** stands above ferocious seas on the northern tip of the peninsula, and acts as a critical navigational guide through the narrow and perilous Kaiwi Channel between Moloka'i and O'ahu. Its 138-foot (43-m) concrete tower remains unchanged since its construction and is one of the few original structures still in use in Hawai'i. The light atop the tower is visible 28 miles (45 km) out to sea and serves vessels bound from the west coast of the United States and the Panama Canal. For 57 years the isolated tower was operated by lighthouse keepers. When automation came in 1966, the colorful history of their tenancy came to an end. The lighthouse residence, rebuilt in 1950, is leased to a

LEPER GIRL

This story was inspired when Robert Louis Stevenson witnessed a group of lepers leaving their home of Kona, on the island of Hawai'i, to join Moloka'i's leper colony.

*B*etween nine and ten of the same morning, the schooner lay-to off Hookena and a whaleboat came ashore. The village clustered on the rocks for the farewell: a grief perhaps—a performance certainly. We miss in our modern life these operatic consolations of the past. The lepers came singly and unattended; the elder first; the girl a little after, tricked out in a red dress and with a fine red feather in her hat. In this bravery, it was the more affecting to see her move apart on the rocks and crouch in her accustomed attitude. But this time I had seen her face; it was scarce horribly affected, but had a haunting look of an unfinished wooden doll, at once expressionless and disproportioned; doubtless a sore spectacle in the mirror of youth. Next there appeared a woman of the middle life, of a swaggering gait, a gallant figure, and a bold, handsome face. She came, swinging her hat, rolling her eyes and shoulders, visibly working herself up; the crowd stirred and murmured on her passage; and I knew, without being told, this was the mother and protagonist. Close by the sea, in the midst of the spectators, she sat down, and raised immediately the notes of the lament. One after another of her friends approached her. To one after the other she reached out an arm, embraced them down, rocked awhile with them embraced, and passionately kissed them in the island fashion, with the pressed face. The leper girl at last, as at some signal, rose from her seat apart, drew near, was inarmed like the rest, and with a small knot (I suppose of the most intimate) held some while in a general clasp. Through all, the wail continued, rising into words and a sort of passionate declamatory recitation as each friend approached, sinking again, as the pair rocked together, into the tremolo drone.

—Robert Louis Stevenson, *The Eight Islands*, 1893

Kalaupapa patient who will rent it to you for a night, if you make arrangements in advance (See "Accommodations" in "PRACTICAL INFORMATION.")

■ EAST MOLOKA'I

The words *makai* (toward the ocean) and *mauka* (toward the uplands) apply as they do on all the islands, and on Moloka'i there is another: *mana'e*, meaning toward the east end. Here, especially on the northern shore, remote rainforested valleys undulate down to the sea, like great green cracks in the sea cliffs. They are accessible only in calm seas of the summer months, when small boats can run up close to the wide sandy beaches that fill the valley mouths. Only the easternmost Halawa Valley can be reached by road. This district lies apart in wilderness, untouched, or barely so, by civilization.

From Kaunakakai, a single road (HI 450) runs east along the southern shoreline. About three miles out from town, a few small hotels, wreathed in red and yellow hibiscus trees hug the shore. The fringe of the south shore, studded with coco and mango groves (some with picnic facilities), fronts muddy waters silted by the run-off of rainforest streams. No swimming beaches here. Occasionally, surfers may be seen far offshore standing on their boards in low waves. Along the way, ancient fishponds, piled with lava boulders in semicircles of varying size, can be seen in the shoreline waters.

Just before the four-mile marker, a turnoff leads up ten miles (16 km) to **Kamokou Preserve** and the highest point on Moloka'i—Kamokou, at 4,970 feet (1,515 m). The road rapidly dissolves into a muddy and dangerous jeep track. The 2,774-acre sanctuary, managed by the Nature Conservancy, is a boggy rainforest where 219 species of endemic plants and endangered native forest birds are protected. Among tree ferns, *'ohi'a* trees, and wild orchids, live two bird species found nowhere else: the *'olomao* (Moloka'i thrush) and the *kakawahi'e* (Moloka'i creeper). Hawaiian owls (*pueo*) and brilliant red *'apapane* flash in the forest. Hiking trails here are very muddy, and the best way to go into the preserve is under the guidance of the Nature Conservancy, which conducts hikes once each month. (For details see "Hiking" in "PRACTICAL INFORMATION.")

Further along the crest is the **Moloka'i Forest Reserve**. Here lies Lua Na Moku Iliahi—the **Sandalwood Boat**. In the 1830s, Hawaiians sought a way to gauge the quantity of sandalwood required to fill the hold of a trader. To do this, they sized

and shaped an earthen pit in the shape of a sailing ship's hull and heaved in cut sandalwood until the pit was filled. Within just a few years the fragrant sandalwood forests were wiped out; some say the workers ripped out saplings so that their children would be spared the backbreaking labor. Now you find dark green cypress and eucalyptus, *kuku'i* (candlenut) trees, and wild berries to pick—as well as a lot of mud.

Back on the highway, eight miles (13 km) east of Kaunakakai, at Kawela village a Hawai'i Visitors Bureau sign marks **Pakuhiwa,** an early battleground and canoe-launching site used by Kamehameha the Great. Near the 10-mile marker stands **St. Joseph's,** a tiny, Gothic, white-frame chapel built by Father Damien in 1876.

Kamalo Village marks the southern point of Moloka'i. Just beyond, a monument locates the Smith & Bronte Landing—a bleak spot where the first civilian aircraft to fly the Pacific crash-landed in 1927, the same year Lindbergh flew across the Atlantic.

As the road curves slightly eastward, three miles (5 km) past Kamalo, the 18-acre **'Ualapu'e Fish Pond** has been restored and restocked with *'ama'ama* (mullet).

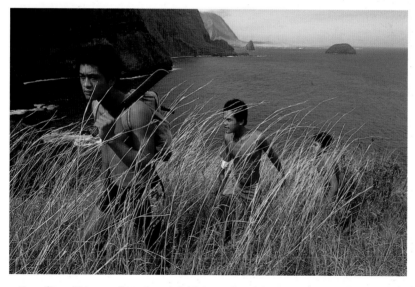

Sons of Joyce Kainoa walking through fields on north Moloka'i. (opposite) Conch blower in traditional ti *leaf rain cloak; north shore of Moloka'i at the mouth of Wailau Valley.*

Reopened in 1991, it is designated a National Historic Landmark.

A mile and a half (2 km) further, on the far side of Mapulehu stream, a roadside gate beside the highway leads to the largest and oldest *he'iau* (temple) on Moloka'i, the **Ili'ili'opae He'iau.** It is an short easy walk into **Mapulehu Valley.** The ancient, mossy stone platform—dated to between 1100 to 1300—is immense: up to 22 feet (7 m) high, 87 feet (26 m) wide, and 286 feet (87 m) long. Legend says it was built in a single night by *menehune*—mythical elves who carried stones in the dark from a valley across the island. Here, where gods demanded human sacrifice and the *kahuna* trained novices, visitors sense their power. It is said the *kahuna* of Moloka'i possessed a force and mastery of power far surpassing the *kahuna* of other islands. The *he'iau* is on private land; visitors take a wagon-ride tour to the site. (See "Special Tours" in "PRACTICAL INFORMATION.")

As you continue *mana'e* (east) on HI 450, you'll see that the land becomes more lush, and the road begins an easterly climb with hairpin turns above cliffs, passing Whispering Stone, where fishermen once prayed for a good catch. The road then curves inland at the eastern tip of the island, through rolling cattle lands to reach an overlook above the white sands of **Halawa Bay.** Halawa is the most easterly valley on Moloka'i, and the only one accessible by car.

As you approach Halawa Valley the *pali* backdrop seems part of a vivid watercolor painting, framing a tiny green-painted wooden church. At a sharp bend, stop to look down onto the beach before hairpinning down to the valley floor. A wandering stream wends through pastel shades of green to the beach. You may wish to swim at Halawa beach; take care, the sea can be treacherous. The left cove is somewhat protected. The sea here was a favorite surfing spot of Moloka'i chiefs and still is locally popular. Opposite the valley mouth lie two rocky islets where booby birds gather.

You can take the two-mile (3-km) hike to the head of the valley to dip in an icy mountain pool fed by the 250-foot (75-m) cascade of **Moa'ula Falls.** This well-traveled trail is not steep, though it is often muddy, and it takes about an hour to traverse. As you pass mango trees, bananas, and wild taro, don't tarry or the mosquitoes will descend in a hungry cloud. The trail starts at the old church; where it forks, look for a white plastic water pipe across the path. Take the right fork and continue to follow the pipe—it appears, disappears, and reappears. Stream crossings are very slippery and depths vary; take care. When you hear the falling water there's still a way to go. The wide, deep pool is reached soon after the stream crossing. (Hang onto the metal water pipes to climb down.)

Myth has it that these idyllic surroundings are guarded by a *mo'o*, a lizard acclaimed in ancient chants who occasionally swallows swimmers. Place a *ti* leaf on the water before entering the pool: If it floats, you can swim; if it sinks, the *mo'o* would rather you didn't. Nearby, **Hipuapua Falls** tumbles 500 feet (150 m) down the sheer *pali*.

Halawa means "curve," and in the curve of the valley taro, staple of the Hawaiian diet, once was heavily cultivated. The area was settled as early as A.D. 650 and by the 1800s some 500 people still lived here, supplying the entire island with taro. In 1946, a *tsunami* destroyed the homes and fields of the few remaining commercial taro farmers and fishermen in Halawa, and waves of another *tsunami* again flooded the valley in 1957. While the old taro fields now are sunk under rampant tropical growth, a few residents still choose to live in the isolated valley.

■ WEST MOLOKA'I

West of Kaunakakai, the Maunaloa Highway (HI 460) bisects western Moloka'i. Past lands where pineapple once flourished, the road twists and rises gently through dry grassy plains. At the 15-mile marker from town the road forks. The northern route heads west to the plush resort of Kaluako'i; the southern one winds upward for two miles (3 km) to **Maunaloa (Long Mountain)** village, where bright bougainvillea bushes and mango trees front frame and stucco homes, dogs sleep on the front steps, and a *mo'a* (chicken) may scratch at the ground near a fishing dory parked on a trailer.

Like Tombstone after the West was won, this old plantation town has revived to become the island's version of trendy craft shops and art galleries. One is unique —the Big Wind Kite Shop. In windy Maunaloa at Hawai'i's only kite factory, designer-owner Jonathan Socher flies hula dancers in the wind; heavenly palm trees sway, painted clouds ruffle by, and mythical beasts gallop the skies.

HALENA BEACH

Down the narrow road that continues south from Maunaloa town, the undeveloped southwest shores of Moloka'i are only slightly touched by civilization. **Halena (Pale Yellow) Beach** is rocky; a place to cast a line and fish for blue crevally or *pa'u'u* (ulua fishes) and grey mullet (*'ama'ama*). Backed by wide sand dunes lined with *kiawe* trees, the surrounding rock at Halena is a creamy yellow color. This area is known as Camp Halena for the cabins available to the public from Moloka'i Ranch. (Call 552-2767.)

To reach it, near the bottom of the road take the east branch: This is Halena Road, which can be driven down to a point near shore. There is a gate one mile (1.6 km) east of the beach. It is sometimes open; if Moloka'i Ranch is running cattle, the gate will be locked. Call in advance to the number above in order to get the key.

To visit **Lono Barge Harbor,** take the western branch off Halena Road. At a rocky point on the west side of the harbor lies narrow, sandy **Hale o Lono (House of Lono) Beach.** From this patch of sand every year in October, the Moloka'i to O'ahu outrigger canoe race starts. Canoe paddling clubs throughout Hawai'i, and from California, practice year-round for this race. The crossing of the perilous Kaiwi Channel is considered one of the most challenging open ocean competitions in the world. Spectators gather at Hale o Lono the morning of the race, the only time the beach is open to visitors.

KALUAKO'I AND KEPUHI BEACH
About five miles (8 km) west from the main fork above Maunaloa Village, HI 460 reaches the western shore. Far from everywhere, the Kaluako'i Hotel and Villas sprawls on part of a 6,800-acre resort with miles of beach. The luxurious facility, opened in 1977 at a cost of $15.5 million, includes an 18-hole, par-72 golf course. Fronting the hotel is **Kepuhi Beach,** whose long, wide, and white sands drop off sharply into deep water. Swimming here is safe only on the calmest of days; otherwise it's treacherous. This beach is best enjoyed for sunbathing and its profile of O'ahu, which rises in brown and purple colors across sparkling blue white-capped waters.

PAPOHAKU BEACH
Separated from Kepuhi by a hill, **Papohaku (Stone Fence) Beach** is three miles (5 km) long and 100 yards (90 m) wide, the largest, whitest beach on the island. Backed with sand dunes and *kiawe* trees, it is beckoning and picturesque, and like Kephui, it is best as a viewing beach. Powerful currents of Kaiwi Channel thunder onto the shore unbroken by a protecting reef, and the strong backwash is perilous to beach strollers. From the early 1960s until 1972, the beach sands were mined to feed O'ahu's construction boom.

Hairy little plants called *'ena'ena,* found only in western Moloka'i, grow on the hot coastal sand dunes behind the beaches. This Hawaiian cudweed differs from other cudweeds in its thick covering of delicate hair that casts the leaves in a silvery blue color. *'Ena'ena* (hot) grows about a foot (30 cm) high and bears tight clusters of tiny muted yellow flowers.

MOLOKA'I RANCH WILDLIFE PARK

The plains of Africa, somehow, have escaped onto Moloka'i. In the hills *mauka* (inland) from Kepuhi Beach, giraffe, oryx and kudu, ostrich, eland and ibex—1,000 animals from the African plains and India—roam **Moloka'i Ranch Wildlife Park,** a 1,500-acre game preserve on lands of Moloka'i Ranch. In a habitat of ravines and dry scrub plains quite like their ancestral homes, zebras trot in the sun, their white stripes stained by the red Moloka'i earth. The sudden sight of African and Indian animals munching grass in Hawai'i is startling. Luckily, there aren't any oversized cats.

In the late 1960s, the ranch imported antelope to feed on the *kiawe* trees infringing onto pastures. The control worked so well the ranch added other animals and began a breeding program for zoos and game reserves. Pheasant, quail, and

African surprise at Moloka'i Wildlife Park.

wild turkeys took up residence on their own; they flew in, liked what they found, and stayed. Tours began when the Kaluako'i resort opened.

The animals can be observed on two-hour tours in four-wheel-drive vans. The photo opportunities when visitors feed giraffes are wonderful; a special food is doled out from oversized coffee-can-like tins provided by the park. Reservations are required; call Moloka'i Ranch; 552-2767.

MO'OMOMI BEACH

The northern coast of western Moloka'i is all but inaccessible. One place, **Mo'omomi Beach**, is well worth the effort. Long ago Hawaiians came by canoe to catch and dry fish at a place on the shoreline called Mo'omomi (pearl lizard). Bashed by wind and pounding surf, this stretch is known as the **Desert Strip**, or Keonelele (Wind-Blown Sands). It is a storm beach. Sands are steep at the water line, the ocean bottom abruptly deep. At the eastern side, called Kawa'aloa (Long Canoe), a shattered reef gives mild protection and experienced surfers sometimes paddle over from Mo'omomi Bay. This area is exposed to almost constant wind that picks up shoreline sand and carries it inland, sometimes as far as four miles (6 km), to form sand dunes that continually pile up, reform, and evolve into weirdly shaped wind-carved stone. The fragile native ecosystems thriving at Mo'omomi are managed and protected by the Nature Conservancy. Driving in is not permitted, and the gate is locked. Under special circumstances, you can arrange to drive in. Call the Moloka'i offices of the Nature Conservancy at 524-0779.

To reach Mo'omomi Bay Beach take Route 470 (Maunaloa Highway) from central Moloka'i. At Kualapu'u turn northwest onto Route 482. After a few minutes turn west on Route 480, a narrow paved road passing through Ho'olehua village and continuing for a couple of miles to the bay. Here the Hawaiian Home Lands Recreation Center fronts a tiny, protected, white sand beach on the east side of the bay that is popular and safe for swimming.

ULTIMATE MOVIE BACKDROP

Hawai'i is the kind of lush, polychromatic backdrop that film and television direc-tors call "paint"—usually because they waste buckets of it trying to reproduce such ripe beauty inside a soundstage.

But there have been scores of moving image artists who have refused to settle for anything but the real thing. Hollywood's love affair with Hawai'i began with 1925's *Dangerous Innocence,* and reached a high-water mark with World War II classics like *From Here to Eternity* and *The Caine Mutiny.*

On the small screen, Hawai'i has been even more successful. For over 20 years, through the back-to-back hits of "Hawaii Five-O" and "Magnum, P. I.," the is-lands were never off the air. Modern films use the island's spectacular scenery for a location but not necessarily a setting: *Raiders of the Lost Ark* and *Point Break,* to name just two. In all, over 140 American productions have splashed on the Hawai-ian "paint" to enhance their visual appeal.

Dangerous Innocence—featuring one of gossip columnist Hedda Hopper's excru-ciating film appearances—has gone the way of all film stock, but 1932's *Bird of Paradise* has proved more durable. The video is worth a rent to see the gorgeous stretches of unspoiled beach that have long since been transformed into beach-front. The plot—a native daughter marrying a colonial—was good for another go-round in the fifties, with Louis Jourdan and Debra Paget stepping into the grass sandals of the original's Joel McCrae and Dolores Del Rio.

The beauty of Hawai'i has often caused Hollywood imports to break into song, as witnessed by such musical fluff as 1942's *Song of the Islands.* The story, such as it was, put a spin on the "islander versus interloper" plot by making the "native" into a Caucasian. Watching Betty Grable (as the local girl) trade tunes with Victor Ma-ture (as the mainland arriviste) makes you wonder if there was really a war going on.

No such doubts intrude upon *From Here to Eternity,* made by director Fred Zin-neman in 1953 from James Jones's steamy novel. This movie, bowdlerized, melo-dramatic, determinedly middle-brow, is perhaps the Hawaiian classic, if a movie made in black-and-white deserves the honor. Frank Sinatra's callow Maggio is great, as is the re-creation of the attack on Pearl Harbor. But the scene which put more sand in more swimsuits than any other is Burt Lancaster and Deborah Kerr on the beach, making littoral—if not literal—love.

Frank returned to Hawai'i for his directorial debut in *None But the Brave* (1965),

Crooner Danny Kaleikini from the Kahala Hilton.

a strange but finally effective new hybrid—a macho anti-war drama. The Japanese have returned to Pearl Harbor repeatedly in film, most notably in the bloated docu-epic, *Tora! Tora! Tora!* (1970), the place to go if you want drama, Oscar-winning special effects, and the "real" story of the attack.

Gunning for the Technicolor honors are *South Pacific* (filmed on Kauaʻi in 1958), James Michener's *Hawaii* (1966), and, yes, Elvis Presley's *Blue Hawaii* (1961). In the latter, Elvis sang "Can't Help Falling in Love" to an island queen. Elvis came back less successfully with *Girls, Girls, Girls* and *Paradise, Hawaiian Style* (1966). Hollywood Hemingway adaptors also loved the locale, using it as a Caribbean stand-in for *The Old Man and the Sea* (the Spencer Tracy film version, made in 1958), and the underrated *Islands in the Stream* (1977).

Cramming the superabundant Hawaiian landscape into the confines of a television tube might seem a difficult task, but Hollywood has managed rather well. "Hawaii Five-O's" Jack Lord was so identified with the island that even today he receives a handful of write-in votes for governor (during the series heyday, it was hundreds). In such mini-series as the "Thorn Birds" (1982) and "War and Remembrance" (1987), producers had high hopes the high-carat setting of Hawaiʻi would show off their paste jewels to good effect.

—Gil Reavill, author of this piece, wrote Compass American Guides' Los Angeles, a guide to that city through the lens of the movies.

Hawaiian sunsets have been a staple of Hollywood kitsch for decades.

HONOLULU AND WAIKIKI
DIAMOND HEAD / PEARL HARBOR

WAIKIKI, THE HAWAIIAN ISLANDS' MOST FAMOUS beach resort, lies at the base of an O'ahu landmark known the world round—the volcanic profile of Diamond Head, or Le'ahi (brow), shaped some 400,000 years ago. In downtown Honolulu, an important business and economic hub of the Pacific, stands the symbol of the only monarchy in the United States—'Iolani Palace; its history is the history of the last days of Hawaiian royalty.

Highrises stab the skylines of Waikiki and downtown Honolulu, and their detractors bemoan the island's commercialism—its ostentatious homes, glitzy boutiques, and clogged freeways. Honolulu's admirers tell you to use your *maka* (eyes) and look around you. Waikiki Beach is one and one-half miles (2.4 km) of exquisite white sands, and nearby Ko'olau mountain waterfalls, hiking trails, and forest reserves are only minutes from Honolulu's urban centers. At the same time, Honolulu offers gourmet dining and a glamorous nightlife, Japanese Noh theater, and Broadway plays, performances of ancient and modern hula, ballet, and symphony concerts. Then there is the shopping—spacious open plazas brimming with shops and designer boutiques straight from Paris, Milan, London, and New York.

Honolulu (Protected Bay) is the mid-Pacific's business and economic center, Hawai'i's state capital, and the eleventh-most populous metropolitan area in the United States.

■ WAIKIKI

Nine miles (14 km) east of O'ahu's main airport, skirting downtown Honolulu on the Nimitz Highway, lies Waikiki, undeniably among the most exquisite, lively, and overdeveloped tropical beaches in the world.

HOW IT ALL BEGAN

In 1907, when the Great Lady of Waikiki, the Moana Hotel, was just six years old, the shortest way from Honolulu to the beach was the King Street electric trolley. With open-sided cars and flop-over seat-backs, it trundled along McCully Street and out onto a wooden trestle mounted over a swamp. Passing over rock and soil mounds, the trolley ran through small, mosquito-infested, malodorous islands with Chinese-owned duck farms and an assortment of chickens, cows, mules, and horses, before it turned onto Waikiki Road (now Kalakaua Avenue).

The trolley rolled past a dense growth of trees and shrubs on the ocean side. Landward from the Moana was Ainahau (Cool Place), where the young Princess Kaʻiulani (1875-1899) once lived. Nearby, the palms of the Royal Grove enclosed the summer homes of royalty—up Keʻalohilani (Glow of Heaven) Street, were the homes of King Kalakaua and his Queen, Kapiʻolani. Kamehameha V built his summer place where the Princess Kaʻiulani Hotel now stands. The summer home Queen Liliʻuokalani described as her "pretty seaside cottage" faced onto Ohua Street, and her own pier reached out into the water along the shore of the present Kuhio/Queen's surf beaches.

Beside the open ocean, past long white threads of breaking surf, the trolley line ended near the base of Diamond Head. Spectator stands for the race track and polo field of Kapiʻolani Park stood on the plain nearby.

At the beginning of the century the beach at Waikiki (Spouting Water) was a narrow strand of sand that ran from the Moana pier to the western end of the present Royal Hawaiian Hotel. In those days, every time a heavy rain fell, swollen streams sped down nearby valleys, flooding the Royal Grove, Ainahau, and parts of Waikiki Road. Inundated swamps spewed water through a culvert under the road, and water settled into a pond next to the Moana Hotel, cutting overflows across the beach. Often, it took as long as a week for the water to abate.

The accessibility to Waikiki brought by the trolley line gained popularity for the Moana, and soon more seaside hotels and homes of influential or wealthy families were built along the shore. Concrete sea walls spread in both directions from the little beach—built by landowners in a time before people realized that, rather than preserving the beaches, walls can cause their erosion. Access to the beach and surf grew increasingly limited for common folk. One person who noticed this was the writer Jack London, who sailed into Honolulu in 1907 aboard his barely seaworthy though celebrated ketch, the *Snark*.

An apocryphal story relates that London was walking on the beach one day with an acquaintance, concerned that Waikiki was less accessible to ordinary Hawaiians than previously. Remarked London, "It's a damn shame that the royal sport of surfriding is dying out." The other gentlemen replied, "Something can be done and we will do it." The outcome of this was the Outrigger Canoe Club,

founded in 1908. It continues to thrive as a haven on the beach for surfers, ca-
noers, and swimmers. The haven works wonderfully for those who can afford it,
though many water enthusiasts are discouraged when Club membership swells
and a moratorium is put on new members.

By the mid-1920s the marshes and duck ponds around Waikiki were soon to
become history. In 1930, the 250-foot wide Ala Wai Canal was completed. Built
to channel speeding rainwaters from the valleys, it runs the length of Waikiki several blocks inland from the main road. Its brackish, tidal canal waters now undulate into the Ala Wai Yacht Harbor fronting the Ilikai and Prince hotels.

CONTEMPORARY WAIKIKI
Under the modern assault of concrete and glass, the mile-and-a-half resort strip
moves to a fast beat. About 25,000 permanent residents call Waikiki home, and
some 70,000 visitors converge on Waikiki every day, strolling along its stretch of
white sands and through the shops of Kalakaua Avenue. With about half the accommodations for visitors in the state, Waikiki hosts plane-loads of convention-
eers, package tourists, and honeymooners from the U.S. mainland, Japan, and

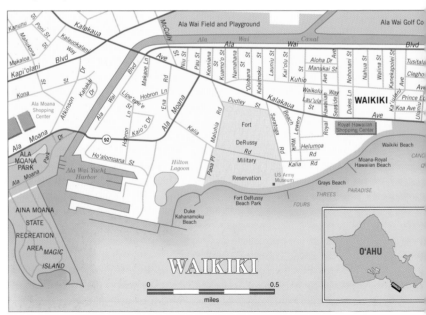

Europe. In its roughly 450 restaurants you can taste many of the world's cuisines. There are hundreds of bars and as many or more shops and designer boutiques than can be found on New York's Fifth Avenue. It's a vibrant crowd scene, and despite the noise of construction and rebuilding, people smile in the benign climate, and you hear laughter in the street.

If the beaches draw tourists all day long, the streets come alive at night as discos boom, bars blare, and ladies of the night parade. The more exclusive hotels provide another side to Waikiki, where gourmet dining, Hawaiian music and the hula, and popular dance music are featured.

Waikiki sunsets are an antidote to the clatter and clutter. Great orange balls surrounded in brilliant pink sink into a sea studded with sailboats, leaving crimson and rust-colored skies that dim to smoky blue. Twilight lasts but a moment in these climes, so look quickly, and don't miss the high-rises glowing like sheets of gold in the fading light.

Holding the whole show together are the fabled white sands and surf of Waikiki. With its gradually sloping seabed and softly lapping waves, Waikiki can be enjoyed by every level of swimmer or surfer. Recent construction of groins

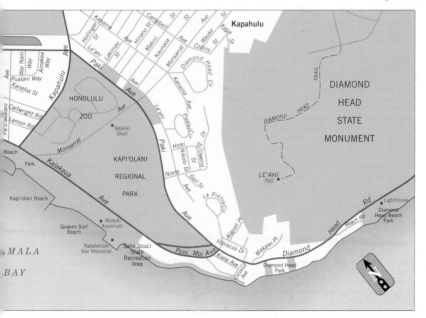

SURFING WAIKIKI

*C*all me Queequeg. Out once more to surf at Tongg's, the lineup perhaps two hundred and fifty yards offshore. Storm clouds above the Koolaus and over past the cathedral-like mass of Diamond Head, rain beards—gray, grayer—dropping from the low sky, and then suddenly a squall is on us, boards and riders blown down wind, paddling hard into the chop and spray just to hold position. A simultaneous abrupt absence of light: furrows, folds, flanks, buttresses, and crevices of Diamond Head obliterated, waves almost black. *Wai* and *kai,* fresh and salt water, rain and sea. Son of the water planet (Earth-the misnomer). But then, faster than we can adjust to the change, the sun's reappeared, the water's jade green, and saying he has to get home, Wendell paddles *ewa* towards Sans Souci beach.

Wendell. "Local" Chinese, in his late fifties/early sixties. Former airline mechanic, grew up in Honolulu. The year before, Wendell arrived one morning—spontaneously generated as if summoned by the waves—out at Tongg's riding high on his massive ten footer, paddling easily, surgical tubing around his waist as a leash. Unorthodox, but effective. No one else there that day, we sat bobbing on the swell, shafts of the boards erect before us, thick plume of smoke rising from the cane fields down on the Wai'anae peninsula. Watches and clocks irrelevant mechanisms of measure here, time organizing itself into sets and lulls, sets and lulls, Wendell speaking of the change in the color of the water since he was a kid, the loss of clarity/kelp/shellfish. We sat silent for a while, gently rising and falling, Diamond Head always again compelling our attention, like the landform obsessing Richard Dreyfuss in *Close Encounters.* Sometimes, clouds scudding behind the volcano's vast bulk as we lifted and dropped, sometimes it seemed we were the fixed point, Diamond Head that must be moving.

Glassy, that state of grace: no wind, no noise, board shooting along, waves perfectly defined, absolutely themselves, their shape not affected by any other force, a realm of clarity and ease. Water thick as milk, as cream. As porridge.

A windless winter day, after a month of cold. Very heavy rain, each drop making a small crater on the ocean surface, but despite the cumulative impact of so many minute explosions the net effect is to calm the water, to eliminate all other normal movement or pattern—ripple, chip, groove, rill. In the torrential downpour, each successive incoming wave seems smooth, sheer, immaculate, pure as the formula of the textbook curve.

Poet Philip Larkin: "If I were called in/To construct a religion/I should make use of water." Not to think of believing in the Almighty or not believing in the Almighty one way or the other, but then to hear the words on one's lips after two hours in the surf: "Thank you, God."

For what? Oh, for this pulsing, undulating, shimmering, sighing, breathing plasma of an ocean. For the miracle of warm water. For readable waves and no wind.

—Thomas Farber, *On Water*, 1991

and seawalls has altered the offshore sea bottom, and the lines of breaking surf are somewhat different than when royalty surfed here. Fortunately for Waikiki's visitors and residents, jet skis and other thrillcraft are prohibited.

Each section of Waikiki—from the Colony Surf Hotel west to Duke Kahanamoku Beach at the Hawaiian Village Hotel—has its own name, often that of the facing hotel. At the east toward Diamond Head, the beach is fronted by an arbor grown thick with gnarled branches of *hau*. Tall coconut trees grow amid open lawns. These same trees, now sheltering visitors, were planted in the 1870s by the Scotsman Archibald Cleghorn, father of Princess Ka'iulani. Known as Honolulu's "father of parks," Cleghorn also planted two banyan trees that have grown large in front of the zoo across the street.

At this east end, **Sans Souci Beach** takes its name from a beach bungalow named the Manuia Lanai, where Robert Louis Stevenson stayed in January of 1889. Eventually, a small hotel was built here—the Sans Souci. Prior to the overthrow of the monarchy in 1893, loyalists met there, and the Sans Souci became infamous after arrests made on the premises, including that of Prince Jonah Kuhio Kalaniana'ole. In a later five-week stay at the hotel, Stevenson extolled its delights in his writings. Today, the Kaimana Beach Hotel stands on the site, and its patch of sand still is known as Sans Souci. Safe and shallow with a sandy bottom, the beach is a good spot for children to swim.

It was at the **Waikiki Aquarium,** west of the Kaimana, that Jack London was heard to exclaim, "I never dreamed of so wonderful an orgy of color and form." It is the only aquarium in the U.S. located on a live coral reef, and the first facility to breed and maintain living coral in captivity. It pioneered methods of raising large quantities of *mahimahi* (dolphin fish, or dorado), whose snubnosed male resembles a small iridescent sperm whale. Unlike reef fish, *mahi* are fast swimmers accustomed to open ocean and are kept in a specially designed tank.

(following pages) Moonrise over Waikiki.

The aquarium is the world center for information on the chambered nautilus and was the first in the U.S. to display the living creatures, as well as holding the record for successfully breeding them. Although deep-sea mollusks have existed for more than 500 million years, the chambered nautilus has never been reared outside its natural environment; it lives only in deep water—at depths up to 2,000 feet. No one has found baby nautilus or their eggs in nature.

Here also are the endangered Hawaiian monk seals, giant 100-pound clams, and galleries of Hawaiian and South Pacific sea life. Established under the aegis of the University of Hawai'i in 1919, and operated by the School of Ocean and Earth Science Technology, the present facility dates from 1955.

If you move west to **Kapi'olani Beach Park**, you can swim, board-surf, snorkel, and dive. The best swimming area here is **Queen's Surf**, named for a nightclub and restaurant that once stood on the site of a former private home. Today the area is all beach, backed by lawns. At the eastern side in front of the aquarium, residents often pole-fish for tiny goat fish called *'oama*. These waters are laced with a shallow reef that drops off abruptly. Snorkelers should come in high tide, to see red- or yellow-striped goatfish poking in the coral for small crustaceans and worms. At the opposite end, near a groin called "the wall," beginning

An otherworldly-looking manta ray with a seven-foot (2-m) wingspan glides over a coral reef.

surfers practice in the small surf, and swimmers should be on the lookout for lost boards flopping in the waves.

The next beach west is **Kuhio Beach Park,** named for Prince Kuhio, Hawai'i's second delegate (non-voting) to Congress at the turn of the century. Here you can dive, snorkel, body- and board-surf. Swimming at Kuhio is wonderful. With a sandy bottom inside a parallel groin, it's like a deep pool. The sea pours into the pool over the groin known as "slippery wall." Don't jump off into the sea side—there is shallow reef below.

Even now if you look *mauka* from this beach, straight up Pa'o'akalani (Perfume of Heaven) Street, the view Queen Lili'uokalani once had of the Ko'olau mountains from her summer home remains unobstructed. On the Kuhio sands facing Kalakaua Avenue, stands the statue of a man who in his quiet way spread the name of Hawai'i

Duke Kahanamoku (1890-1968), winner of Olympic gold medals in swimming in 1912, became an international celebrity who introduced surfing to the world. (Hawaii State Archives)

worldwide. His Olympic feats introduced the Hawaiian Crawl to international swimming. Unveiled in 1990, one hundred years after his birth, the statue of Duke Paoa Kahanamoku (1890-1968) stands with a bronze version of his 24-foot (7-m) *koa*-wood surfboard. Swimmer, surfer, and sheriff of Honolulu for 26 years, Duke is still held dear in the memory of Hawai'i's people.

Beside the statue are four huge volcanic boulders. A plaque in these **Stones of Kapaemahu** describes a legend of four *kahuna* who long ago came to Hawai'i from Tahiti. The four priests, famed for their healing powers, transferred their powers to these stones, and then vanished.

Next to Kuhio Beach Park is the **Moana-Royal Hawaiian Beach,** the heart of Waikiki Beach. Wide, soft, and white, the sands front coral-free ocean. The beach is packed with sun-worshippers slathered in sun oil, introverts with their heads in books, children building sandcastles, honeymooners gazing at each other, eye-roving singles, swimmers, and surfers. Here you can ride an outrigger canoe, sail on a catamaran, board-surf, snorkel, and swim in clear, turquoise waters that deepen gradually. The highest concentration of beach rental concessions along the length of Waikiki is in this area.

Offshore are the two most famous surfing lines in Waikiki: Queen's (not to be confused with the patch of beach with the same name) and Canoes. The waves at **Queen's,** named for Queen Lili'uokalani's beach home, are steep. Canoes, which has a longer roll and was well-suited to the old canoes of heavy koa-wood, joins Queen's at its *'ewa* side. (*"'Ewa"* is a term peculiar to O'ahu meaning west toward the 'Ewa Plain.) **Canoes** is also popular with board surfers. Sometimes in summer, when there are many beginners in the water, together with outriggers and swimmers, it can be frantic, and lifeguards are busy untangling the mix.

Waikiki even now hides glimpses of her past. On the lawns of the **Royal Hawaiian Hotel** are tall coconut palms, descendants of those growing in the old Royal Grove. It was from this beach that Kamehameha the Great once paddled out to surf the long white-foaming ocean crests. And it was here that he married his sacred wife, Keopuolani, chieftess of the highest rank, who later gave birth to the sons who became Kamehameha II and III.

The famous and classic (Sheraton) Royal Hawaiian Hotel on Waikiki Beach.

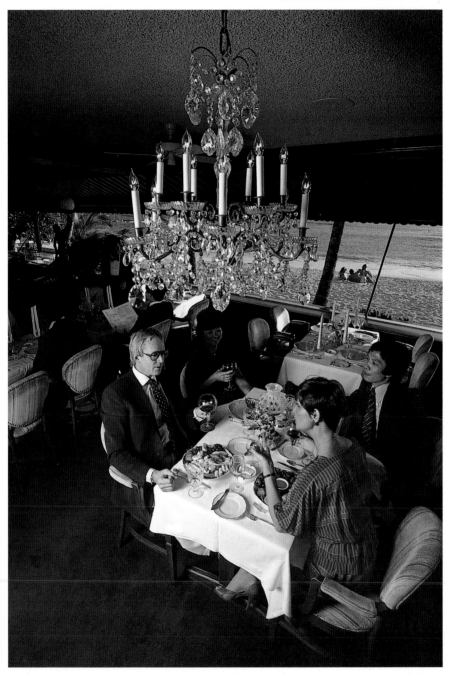

Elegantly dressed diners contrast with scantily clad sunbathers along Waikiki Beach.

On the Royal's sands, Kamehameha presided over Hawai'i's version of the Olympic games—great competitions called the *Makahiki*. They were held between September and January, a sacred time of the year when temples closed, crops were planted, taxes collected, and war put on hold. The *Makahiki* was the high point of this period, when Hawaiians stopped everything to compete in sports, various types of chants spoken or sung, and specialized thanksgiving hula. The king's sacred altar dedicated to Lono, God of the *Makahiki*, lay approximately in front of what is now the Sheraton-Waikiki Hotel. The sacred status of this *he'iau* (Po'okanaka) was removed in 1860, when the site was dismantled and returned to crown land. The sands adjacent to the *he'iau* on the west side were a healing area where *kahuna* practiced Hawaiian sports medicine on injured *Makahiki* participants.

Old-timers still call the next patch of sand in front of the Halekulani Hotel **Gray's Beach,** as it was once the site of Mrs. Gray's by the Sea Teahouse. The original building was a hut owned by Robert Lewers who allowed fishermen to beach their canoes in front of his hut at a time when access to Waikiki was limited for the common folk. Grateful fishermen named Lewers' house Halekulani (House Befitting Heaven). The property later became an estate and was acquired by Clifford Kimball, who converted the home into a hotel and named it the Halekulani.

Princess of Mauoa float parades through Honolulu in March of 1909. (Library of Congress)

In the 1930s, author Earl Derr Biggers stayed here and wrote a murder mystery called *The House Without a Key*, at a time when Honoluluans never locked their doors—a time long gone. The main character was the detective Charlie Chan. In honor of Biggers and his novel, Kimball named the hotel terrace "The House Without a Key." The terrace and lawns facing the sea at the hotel still are known by this name.

Residents and distance swimmers migrate to Gray's for its water—a long and wide, warm and calm channel running from the beach out a quarter of a mile to a protruding rock. The seabed is soft white sand, fresh water springs bubble beneath it, and no coral grows. Swim two round-trips and you've done your daily mile. On either side of the channel are the surfing breaks called **Paradise** and **Number Threes.**

Fort DeRussy Beach is next. Fronting the Hale Koa Hotel, a military facility, this safe, wide, sandy strand has unlimited public access. On the spacious lawns of the Hale Koa is the **U.S. Army Museum.** It is under-visited and deserves better. The dioramas of American soldiers in war are life-like and its memorabilia heart-wrenching. Exhibits describe Hawaiians in early warfare and their modern partici-pation in the nation's defense.

The museum is housed in **Battery Randolph,** one of six coastal implacements built on O'ahu between 1908 and 1915 by the U.S. Army Corps of Engineers.

Honolulu Harbor, 1869. (Library of Congress)

Made of steel-reinforced concrete and designed in low silhouette, it contained its own ammunition magazines and powder rooms. By 1969, Battery Randolph lay on the Army's demolition list, and a wrecking ball was sent to knock it down; however, the battery was built to withstand direct hits, and its concrete sides broke the ball. As a consequence, impregnable Battery Randolph opened as a museum on December 7, 1976.

A walkway between the Hale Koa Hotel's lawns and sands reaches **Kahanamoku Beach and Lagoon** fronting the extensive Hilton Hawaiian Village Hotel. Both beach and lagoon are man-made extensions of Waikiki beach constructed by Henry J. Kaiser in 1955 when he built the original Hawaiian Village hotel. Before that time the area was known as Kalia, family home of the Kahanamoku clan where the fabled Duke learned to swim. (Referring to swimming power, Duke once said to me, "It's all in the legs.")

■ DIAMOND HEAD

Diamond Head, Hawai'i's volcanic profile recognized around the world, lifts its face at the eastern end of Waikiki. Named Le'ahi (Brow) by Hawaiians, it was first

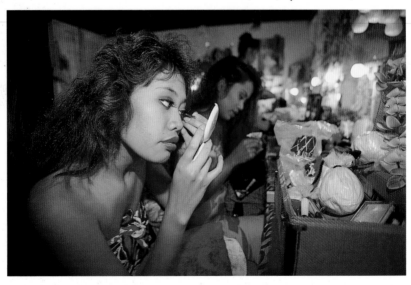

Women applying makeup before a dance performance.

(opposite) Ride operator at state fair.

MARK TWAIN'S HONOLULU

Mark Twain sailed into Honolulu in 1866 as a correspondent for a California newspaper, the Sacramento Union—*his assignment to write 25 articles about the Sandwich Islands.*

*P*assing through the market place we saw that feature of Honolulu under its most favorable auspices—that is, in the full glory of Saturday afternoon, which is a festive day with the natives. The native girls by twos and threes and parties of a dozen, and sometimes in whole platoons and companies, went cantering up and down the neighboring streets astride of fleet but homely horses, and with their gaudy riding habits streaming like banners behind them. Such a troop of free and easy riders, in their natural home, the saddle, makes a gay and graceful spectacle. The riding habit I speak of is simply a long, broad scarf, like a tavern table cloth brilliantly colored, wrapped around the loins once, then apparently passed between the limbs and each end thrown backward over the same, and floating and flapping behind on both sides beyond the horse's tail like a couple of fancy flags; then, slipping the stirrup-irons between her toes, the girl throws her chest forward, sits up like a Major General and goes sweeping by like the wind.

Moving among the stirring crowds, you come to the poi merchants, squatting in the shade on their hams, in true native fashion, and surrounded by purchasers. (The Sandwich Islanders always squat on their hams, and who knows but they may be the old original "ham sandwiches?" The thought is pregnant with interest.) The poi looks like common flour paste, and is kept in large bowls formed of a species of gourd, and capable of holding from one to three or four gallons. Poi is the chief article of food among the natives, and is prepared from the taro plant. The poi root looks like a thick, or, if you please, a corpulent sweet potato, in shape, but is of a light purple color when boiled. When boiled it answers as a passable substitute for bread. The buck Kanakas bake it under ground, then mash it up well with a heavy lava pestle, mix water with it until it becomes a paste, set it aside and let it ferment, and then it is poi—and an unseductive mixture it is, almost tasteless before it ferments and too sour for a luxury afterward. But nothing is more nutritious. When solely used, however, it produces acrid humors, a fact which sufficiently accounts for the humorous character of the Kanakas. I think there must be as much of a knack in handling poi as there is in eating with chopsticks. The forefinger is thrust into the mess and stirred quickly round several times and drawn quickly out, thickly coated, just as if it were poulticed; the head is thrown back, the finger inserted in the mouth and the delicacy stripped off and swallowed—the eye closing gently, meanwhile, in a languid sort of ecstasy. Many a different finger goes into the same bowl and many a different kind of dirt and shade and quality of flavor is added to the virtues of its contents.

In old times here Saturday was a grand gala day indeed. All the native population of the town forsook their labors, and those of the surrounding country journeyed to the city. Then the white folks had to stay indoors, for every street was so packed with charging cavaliers and cavalieresses that it was next to impossible to thread one's way through the cavalcades without getting crippled.

At night they feasted and the girls danced the lascivious *hula hula*—a dance that is said to exhibit the very perfection of educated motion of limb and arm, hand, head and body, and the exactest uniformity of movement and accuracy of "time." It was performed by a circle of girls with no raiment on them to speak of, who went through an infinite variety of motions and figures without prompting, and yet so true was their "time," and in such perfect concert did they move that when they were placed in a straight line, hands, arms, bodies, limbs and heads waved, swayed, gesticulated, bowed, stopped, whirled, squirmed, twisted and undulated as if they were part and parcel of a single individual; and it was difficult to believe they were not moved in a body by some exquisite piece of mechanism.

Of late years, however, Saturday has lost most of its quondam gala features. This weekly stampede of the natives interfered too much with labor and the interests of the white folks, and by sticking in a law here, and preaching a sermon there, and by various other means, they gradually broke it up. The demoralizing *hula hula* was forbidden to be performed, save at night, with closed doors, in presence of few spectators, and only by permission duly procured from the authorities and the payment of ten dollars for the same. There are few girls now-a-days able to dance this ancient national dance in the highest perfection of the art.

—Mark Twain, *Roughing It*, 1872

called Diamond Head in 1825, when British seamen saw calcite crystals twinkling in sunlight and thought they'd found gems. At the base of the cone on the inland side are the film studios that played home to "Hawaii Five-O" and "Magnum P. I." Also on this side of Diamond Head is the small Army facility of Fort Ruger, built in 1909. From it, a web of bunkers and tunnels penetrates into the crater. In World War II cannon were placed on the volcano's rim. They were never fired.

The best way to see Diamond Head is to climb it. If you stop by the New Otani Hotel in the shadow of Diamond Head to buy a small hiker's kit, they'll issue a certificate on your return, proof that you trudged to the summit. To get there, take Diamond Head Road to the trailhead marker. The trail to the 760-foot crater rim is steep though less than a mile in length; plan on a 45-minute climb. It's a good idea to bring water for the open, hot part of the trail, and a flashlight for the long curving tunnel. Once you're through the tunnel, there are 99 stairs to climb, another short tunnel, and some more steps. The 360-degree view is worth it—you can see the entire leeward coast, below to Kapi'olani Park, and out along the blue Pacific east to Koko Head.

The bowl-shaped crater is dry, its vegetation scrub *kiawe* trees and tiny orange *ilima* flowers. The crater houses the Federal Aviation Administration's air traffic control facility. At the brow of Diamond Head facing the sea, a small temple once stood. It was dedicated to the fish god Ku'ula and received offerings from fishermen. Near the base stood a *he'iau* piled with bodies of the dead at the time of Kamehameha's onslaught. Below, a ribbon of sand beach is accessible by foot.

■ HONOLULU

Physically only six miles (10 km) west of Waikiki, downtown Honolulu is about as far from the hum of tourism as you can get on southern O'ahu. Bounded by Beretania, South, Nimitz, and River streets, its restored older buildings retain much of Honolulu's early merchant spirit. Beside them rise graceful glass and concrete office towers, and cumbersome great piles of government buildings. Winding through its core of historic structures is open space—greenery protected in a "mountains to the sea" concept—which affords views of historic buildings from the top of Punchbowl crater down to Honolulu Harbor.

Honolulu's **Chinatown**, designated a National Historic Landmark in 1973, is one of the more appealing parts of downtown. Located between Maunakea and

Robert Louis Stevenson (seated in background), famed author of Kidnapped *and* Treasure Island, *sailed into Honolulu on January 24, 1889. The following week a luau was given in honor of the Stevenson family, and Hawai'i's last king, David Kalakaua, and Princess Lili'uokalani were in attendance. Stevenson's wife Fanny presented the king with a gold-filmed double oyster shell cradling an attached gold pearl, given to her in the Tuamotu Islands, and Stevenson read aloud an accompanying sonnet dedicated to the king. On this occasion the Stevensons were served roast dog, which they had the good grace to eat and apparently found delicious.*

During the next five months Stevenson became a popular figure in Honolulu, befriending the king, and frequently walking to the estate of Archibald Cleghorn, fellow Edinburgh Scotsman and widowed father of Princess Victoria Ka'iulani. When the princess, then 13 years old, greeted Stevenson, she'd often ask him to sit with her beneath a tall banyan or in a little grass shack and tell her tales of Scotland and the South Pacific.

Stevenson's stories of Hawai'i include a journal and story of the Kona Coast, a tale of Queen Ka'ahumanu, the "lazaretto" stories of Moloka'i, a steady stream of letters and poems and one of the most furious denouncements in the English language. (See "The Damien Letters" in "MOLOKA'I.")

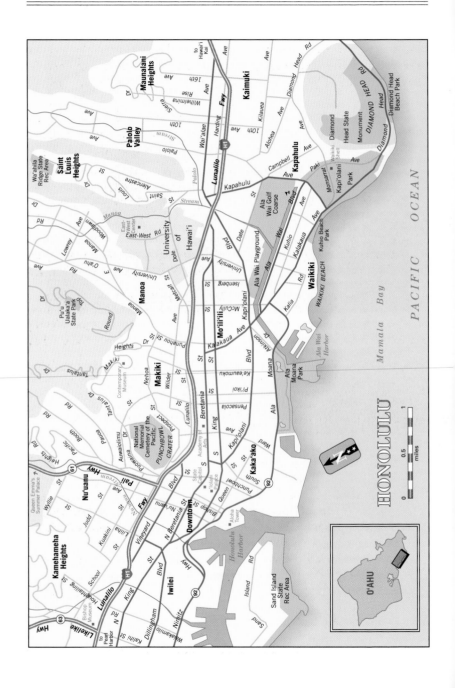

River streets, its herbal stores, contemporary art galleries, and noodle shops are reminiscent of central Hong Kong—a crammed jumble of the old and new. Its restaurants serve excellent Cantonese food, and its customers tend to be Honolulu professionals.

There was a time when rabble-rousers, rogues, and drunkards ruled the streets. Whaling ships dropped anchor and sailors hurried ashore, looking for grog and women. Central downtown's Fid Street area was named Fid after the carrot-shaped, six-inch steel or wooden tool used to open strands of rope when splicing lines. Three hotels dedicated to drinking and prostitution, all named Blonde, operated in Fid Street. (They took their name from the HMS *Blonde* which in 1825 carried back to Hawai'i the bodies of Kamehameha II and his queen, Kamamalu, both of whom had died of measles in London.)

Soon after their arrival in 1820, missionaries built a church right in the middle of saloonville—and the church gave its name, Bethel, to another street of bars and bawdy houses.

At the O'ahu Follies, Honolulu's wildest bar, drinkers swilled down 33 barrels of whiskey every week, while the missionary Hiram Bingham stood outside loudly praying for the sinful guzzlers. Among them may have been the author of *Moby*

Honolulu peeks through a clearing between clouds and pali.

Dick, Herman Melville, who found temporary employment setting pins at the Globe Hotel.

While sailors brought venereal disease, the missionaries brought the concept of sexual sin and instituted laws requiring adulterers to pay for their sins in road-work. Consequently, the streets of Honolulu rapidly improved.

If anyone symbolized the contradictions of Honolulu's culture at this time it was Princess Victoria Kamamalu (1838-1866), younger sister of Kamehameha IV. She became involved in a love affair with the photographer Charles Monsarrat. When they were discovered, Monsarrat was banished by the king. The princess, however, went on to become the monarchy's last *kuhina nui,* a position akin to prime minister and perhaps even more powerful. When Victoria Kamamalu died, the black-clad missionaries who attended her Christian royal funeral found themselves listening to chants praising her amorous escapades.

Central downtown's **Fort Street Mall,** the main cross street, now meets Nimitz Highway where the Hawaii Tower rears skyward. The fort built here by Kamehameha the Great in 1816 was used by the missionaries as a prison. The mission had decreed that no divorced person could remarry as long as the original spouse remained alive. Reasoning that the way around that law was to dispose of the former spouse, a Hawaiian named Hamanawa poisoned his wife. His was the first murder trial held in the Hawaiian Islands. After being found guilty, Hamanawa was hanged by the neck over the side of the fort. The hanging was watched by Hamanawa's young nephew, David Kalakaua, who later became king. Kalakaua never forgave the mission.

By 1870, in the reign of Kamehameha V, the fort was torn down to fill in a new section of the harbor. If you cross the highway and look over the edge of Pier 12, you can see the blocks that were once part of Kamehameha's fort poking out of the water.

'IOLANI PALACE

'Iolani Palace, built for King Kalakaua in 1879-1881, stands at the eastern end of downtown Honolulu on South King Street. Now lovingly returned to its former dignity and grandeur by a volunteer society and the state, the palace is Hawai'i's paean to, and museum of, its monarchy. Missing pieces of art and furniture have been tracked down and recovered from around the world. The Grand Hall staircase is a gleaming spiral of *koa* wood with *kamani* and walnut trim. In the State

Dining Room a table is laid with china from France, crystal from Bohemia, and silver from England, France, and the U.S. In the Throne Room are escutcheons showing the orders of the Crown of Hawai'i, the Order of Kamehameha, and other Hawaiian, European, and Asian honorific orders.

On the second floor, the king's bedroom, library, music room, upper hall, and queen's apartments contain chandeliers, draperies, and furniture either meticulously restored or duplicated. Photographs and gifts from royal European houses decorate walls and tables. Queen Lili'uokalani's chamber recreates the sparse furnishings of her nine-month imprisonment after the overthrow of the monarchy in 1893. In that lonely time she wrote music:

> Though I was still not allowed to have newspapers or general literature to read, writing-paper and lead-pencils were not denied; and I was thereby able to write music, after drawing for myself the lines of the staff . . . I found great consolation in composing . . . " During this anguished time she composed "Aloha Oe."

Although trappings of royalty and Christian mores had been brought by Europeans to the Hawaiian court, the heart and spirit of what it meant to be Hawaiian remained clear in the minds of all Hawaiians. The spirit of aloha, which is love, never was damaged. The Palace tour is perhaps the best way to understand later Hawaiian royalty. (Reservations required. Call 522-0832)

Today the restored grounds of the Palace and 'Iolani Barracks (built in 1870) are public areas where office workers picnic at lunchtime. The Royal Hawaiian Band regularly performs in King Kalakaua's 1883 coronation pavilion.

KAWAIAHAO CHURCH

Across South King Street from the Palace at the corner of Punchbowl Street, is **Kawaiahao Church**, where Hawai'i's later monarchs were baptized, wed, eulogized, and interred. Three thatched churches preceded the present stone church, which was designed in 1837 by the Reverend Hiram Bingham (1789-1869), in New England colonial style complete with Gothic embellishments. Deeded to the people and the mission by King Kamehameha III in 1842, Kawaiahao, or Water of Ha'o, takes its name from a spring at the site.

Kawaiahao's construction is an epic tale of mountains climbed, wood hewn, and logs hauled. Hawaiians dived, dragged ashore, chopped, shaped, and smoothed coral into stone blocks to build the church. They burned broken coral pieces to make lime for mortar. A corner stone of Wai'anae sandstone, laid in 1839, arrived at the site as a great uncut slab, brought by sea, lashed to canoes.

In 1865, when the royal graveyard was moved from what is now the grounds of 'Iolani Palace to a new royal mausoleum in Nu'uanu Valley, a controversy arose over one of the graves. The result is a tomb at Kawaiahao. The tale of how this came about is a haunted one:

Kamehameha V, who ruled from 1863 to 1872, refused to allow the bones of High Chieftess Kekaulei'ohi, mother of Prince William Charles Lunalilo, to be re-buried at Nu'uanu when the royal graveyard was moved. Her indignant son, who in 1873 became the first elected king, vowed that he would have no part of the new royal mausoleum. Four days before his death in 1874, he approved a codicil to his will, providing for a tomb at Kawaiahao for himself and his father Charles Kana'ina. There is some question whether the bones of Lunalilo's mother re-mained in the old 'Iolani burial place. According to some accounts, the family se-cretly carried them away for burial at sea many miles off Diamond Head.

On the night Lunalilo's casket was carried into the tomb at Kawaiahao, a loud clap of thunder startled the retinue. Hawaiians claimed it a heavenly royal salute—the salute denied Lunalilo by the new King Kalakaua on the premise that 21 guns could not be fired for a man who was no longer king. Each year on January 31,

Kawaiahao Church in 1867; painting by George Burgess. (Mission Houses Museum Library)

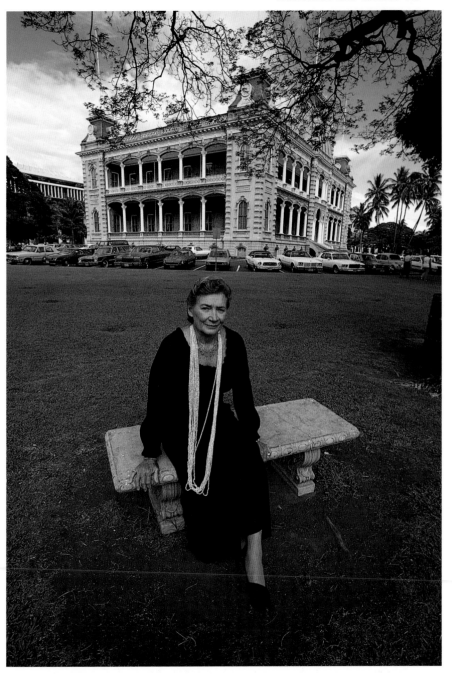

Princess Kawawanakoa, here seated before the 'Iolani Palace, is one of the few remaining collateral descendants of Hawaiian royalty.

Lunalilo's birthday, the tomb is opened ceremonially to the public. The royal crypt, shaped in the form of a Greek cross, stands regally fenced and in need of a good scrubbing at the main entrance to Kawaiahao.

Behind the church an arched gate and sign at the end of a walkway marks the **Alanui** (Pathway), which "since ancient times . . . had been trodden by feet entering the village from the Waikiki area." Kawaiahao, a member of the United Church of Christ Congregational, the largest Protestant denomination in the islands, was designated a National Historic Landmark in 1962.

MISSION HOUSES MUSEUM

Directly across Punchbowl Street from Kawaiahao is the **Mission Houses Museum** on South King Street. Here the missionary incursion that forever changed the islands began in earnest when a small band of American Protestants armed with the Bible, a printing press, and the stiff-necked spirit of their Lord, came face to face with Hawai'i's native people.

Three buildings served as headquarters for the Sandwich Islands Mission—the Mission frame house built in 1821, the Levi Chamberlain House (1831), and the smaller Printing House (1841). These houses make clear that the missionaries intended to cast the destiny of the island people in a New England mold. Islanders were meant to become Christians clothed in stiff New England garb, to pray in a building of colonial architecture, and to sit on New England furnishings. Lumber for the main house, cut in Massachusetts, was shipped from Boston in 1819—the same year the missionaries departed on their hardship voyage around Cape Horn. Only the Printing House, originally a storage vault, is built of coral block.

The restored mission houses, complete with original furnishings and curios, contain the antique rocking chair of Queen Ka'ahumanu and a *koa*-wood crib for missionary infants. A living history program recreates the Honolulu of 1831—with missionaries, Hawaiians, merchants, and even rowdy seamen. The museum also sponsors a walking tour of Honolulu's historic core.

A few steps from the museum stands the bronze and gold **statue of Kamehameha the Great,** in front of Ali'iolani Hale (the judiciary building). Surrounded by stately trees, it is a popular attraction and on Kamehameha Day (June 11), Hawaiians place hundreds of long, long leis on the statue, covering Kamehameha with flowers from neck to toe. This statue, installed in 1883, is the replica of the original statue positioned near his birthplace in Kohala on the Big Island. Another copy of the statue represents Hawai'i in Statuary Hall on Capitol Hill in Washington, D. C.

Street scene in Honolulu, 1874. (Library of Congress)

STATE CAPITOL

Across a broad walk lined with flowering purple bougainvillea, just *mauka* (inland) of 'Iolani Palace facing Beretania Street, stands **Hawai'i's State Capitol Building**. State law keeps this downtown area green and open so that the vista from mountains to sea remains unhampered. The Capitol building, designed by architect Carl Warnecke, is open-roofed at its center, and curves outward like the rim of a volcano's crater. The building soars above a central courtyard, and sun and rain fall on its reef-like mosaic. From a distance the open roof resembles a crown.

Two-story-high, rounded-glass legislative chambers rise like smaller cones on two sides of the courtyard. The House of Representatives is decorated in the blue of sea and sky, and earthen hues complete the Senate chamber. Sixty-foot (18-m) columns suggesting tall royal palm trees gird the five-story Capitol building. Surrounding ponds evoke tropical lagoons.

The Capitol was closed in 1992 for asbestos removal. When it reopens, brochures describing it will be available from the governor's reception room on the top floor.

On the seaward side of the building, facing the palace where she was imprisoned, stands the stately bronze figure of **Lydia Kamaka'eha**, Queen Lili'uokalani

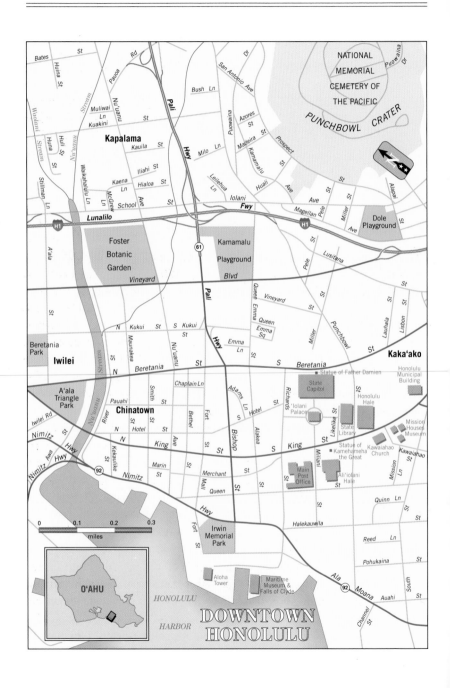

(1838-1917), last ruling monarch of the Hawaiian kingdom. Greatly esteemed by the people in her time, she is revered to this day. The statue, unveiled in 1982, is always adorned with a lei or flowers placed there by admirers.

At the opposite side of the Capitol, facing Beretania Street, stands the bronze statue of Father Damien (1840-1889), the Belgian priest who devoted his life to the care of lepers confined on Moloka'i. The statue, which depicts Damien with a cane, priest's hat, and eye glasses on his leprous face, is an angular, modern impression by the Venezuelan sculptress Marisol (Escobar).

ALOHA TOWER AND HONOLULU HARBOR

Landmark of downtown and beacon for arriving ships, the Aloha Tower stands at the foot of Fort Street, at the entrance to Honolulu Harbor (Pier 8). Once the tallest building in Honolulu, it is now dwarfed by the sleek pillars of business.

Next to the tower at Pier 7 is the Maritime Museum—the Kalakaua Boat House, which takes its name from a sailing club captained by King Kalakaua. Here he played poker, drank whiskey, and swapped stories with Robert Louis Stevenson. Museum exhibits describe voyages of early Polynesians and Hawai'i's relationships with other island groups in the Pacific. An enormous whale skeleton, Hawaiian objects carried at sea, and ocean-going canoes also are displayed. Riding at the end of the pier is the *Hokule'a*—modern replica of an ancient voyaging canoe—that sailed with a crew of 16 for more than two years in the mid-1980s, navigating by the stars from Hawai'i to New Zealand.

Also tied to the pier, is the Falls of Clyde, a 266-foot, iron-hulled, four-masted sailing ship. Built in Glasgow in 1878, she plied the Pacific trade for many years. Her restoration has now made her a showpiece. Even though she's clean and gleaming, a tour of the crew's and officer's quarters make evident the cramped and practical lifestyle aboard traders.

UPLAND VALLEYS
AND PUNCHBOWL CRATER

Located in the lower reaches of Honolulu's Manoa Valley, the East-West Center is Uncle Sam's only federal institution of higher learning. To reach the campus, which is shared with the University of Hawai'i, drive up University Avenue and turn right on East-West Road. Dreamchild of Lyndon B. Johnson and designed by architect I. M. Pei, the center is a place of cultural and technological exchange for

A Japanese store in Honolulu, c. 1900. (Library of Congress)

graduate students from Pacific and Asian nations and the U.S. There are on-going programs for senior and visiting fellows, advanced in their careers. Unusual campus attractions are a teak pavilion brought from Thailand, the Japanese garden, and the university's Korean Studies Center.

Straight inland from downtown lies the valley of Nu'uanu and **Tenrikyo Mission,** a fine example of a Japanese temple. To reach it, take Pali Highway from Beretania Street to 2236 Nu'uanu Pali Highway—about a ten-minute drive. This serene, red-painted, wood-frame pagoda was moved here from Japan in sections and put up without nails. As the building is off the tourist route, it rarely is crowded.

A few minutes drive farther up the valley, at 2913 Pali Highway, is **Queen Emma's Summer Palace,** Hanai'akamalama, named for a demi-goddess who was foster child of the moon. This airy, colonnaded, whiteframe summer home of Kamehameha IV's queen is surrounded by extensive gardens. Inside are paintings of royalty, a room dedicated to a visit by the Duke of Edinburgh (second son of Victoria) with fine Victorian furniture, and *kahili,* the feather staff symbols of royalty. Probably built in 1847, the house was inherited by Queen Emma, who turned it into a social salon. After her death, it was bought by the Hawaiian government (1890), renovated by the Daughters of Hawai'i, and opened to the public.

Queen Emma (1836-1885) was a blood relative of Kamehameha I and a devout Christian, who, with her husband Kamehameha IV, established the Episcopal (Anglican) Church in Hawai'i. She also founded Honolulu's largest hospital, Queen Emma Hospital, usually known as Queen's. After the deaths of her husband and son, she took the name Kalele'onalani. In 1874, as Dowager Queen, she ran against High Chief David La'amea Kalakaua in the second election to the Hawaiian throne. The race was close and emotional; Kalakaua won, and the defeated queen never forgave him.

If you continue up the Pali Highway, you'll see a turn off for the **Nu'uanu Pali Overlook.** It's well worth a visit. From the overlook, at an altitude just under 2,000 feet (600 m), you can see the windward Ko'olau mountains stretching northwest in a panorama of sheer, stream-eroded cliffs *(pali).* Clouds hover over sharp pinnacles and blow away in a spectrum of ever-changing muted colors. It was here, atop the mountain pass, that Kamehameha the Great struck the decisive blow that defeated O'ahu's forces. (See "History" in "GREATER O'AHU.") The conclusion of the Pali battle in 1795 assured the king a realm of all the islands except Kaua'i.

Directly above downtown Honolulu in the foothills of the Ko'olau mountains, is **Punchbowl Crater,** which encloses the **National Memorial Cemetery of the Pacific.** The entrance is off Puowaina Drive. From an overlook at the crater rim, you can see Honolulu stretching down the slopes to the sea. Diamond Head, Waikiki, and Pearl Harbor curve against the horizon, like a view through the fisheye lens of a camera. In 1990, more than six million people climbed the road into Punchbowl, making it the most frequently visited attraction in the state.

During World War II, when Punchbowl served as a fire-control post for defense of the harbor, the Territory of Hawai'i offered Punchbowl to the federal government for a military cemetery. Many of America's heroes lie here, as well as a memorial to Hawai'i's astronaut Ellison Onizuka (who perished aboard the *Challenger* space shuttle). Inside the memorial building there is a chapel, mural maps of battles, and marble walls inscribed with the names of 18,000 military personnel missing in action.

Below the eastern slopes of Punchbowl lies the **Honolulu Academy of Arts** (900 South Beretania Street). Chinese marble horses flank the entrance walkway of this airy, quasi-Spanish building, with its central court and six garden patios.

In its 30 galleries, the Academy presents a solid collection, particularly in Chinese and Japanese art, including the James A. Michener Collection of 5,400 Japanese prints, the Kress Collection of Italian Renaissance paintings, and decorative and graphic arts. The eclectic collection runs from Gauguin and van Gogh to Alexander Calder; from Korean celadon bowls to Persian tiles and New Guinea wood carvings. On view are Hawaiian *kapa* cloth; Japanese bronze, and Chinese jade; Delacroix, Homer, Picasso, and Flemish tapestry. Contemporary art holds forth at the Clare Booth Luce pavilion. In addition, there is a library, theater, and the Garden Cafe.

The museum collection was begun by Anna Rice, descendant of missionaries and Kaua'i plantation owners, who in 1874 married Charles Montague Cooke, also a descendant of the mission. Financial success led to European travel and gave Anna the means and opportunity to begin collecting—at first just a few pieces for her parlor. Back in Honolulu, Anna bought Chinese ceramics, then Japanese art, and the paintings of local artists.

By 1920, when the Cooke home no longer could hold her burgeoning collection, Anna and her family planned a museum, which

Kuka'ilimoku, a war god, made of wood and feathers appears in the Bishop Museum.

opened in 1927 on land of the former Cooke home. It was built of materials that are a part of Hawai'i's history. Its Chinese paving blocks originally arrived as ballast in vessels of the sandalwood trade. The tiles in the Chinese court had come to Honolulu 80 years earlier, and the lava rock in walls was quarried from a Honolulu suburb. The slabs of shell-rock cut into flagstone that paves the entry and patios came from Moloka'i.

Up a quiet, forested mountain slope directly *mauka* (inland) from the crush and din of shopping centers in central Honolulu, is the **Contemporary Museum,** installed in what was once another home of Anna Rice Cooke (2411 Makiki Heights Drive). Its many additions combine western, oriental, and island styles of architecture. The museum is set in three acres of secluded oriental gardens in the Makiki hills, its terraces unfolding like a Japanese scroll.

Exhibits feature international contemporary art of the last four decades, and of twentieth-century Hawaiian artists. A separate pavilion houses David Hockney's environmental installation, "L'Enfant et les Sortileges" (The Bewitched Child), based on the sets and costumes conceived for a revival of Maurice Ravel's 1925 opera. Hockney created six new works for an exhibit of his theater designs in Minneapolis in 1983. "L"Enfant" was the largest and most complex. Permanently installed in Honolulu, it is considered the museum's most important acquisition.

West of central Honolulu on H-1, off the Houghtailing Street exit is the **Bishop Museum** (1525 Bernice Street). Set within a compound of buildings that includes a library and planetarium, the museum is a treasure trove of human history and

Manoa Valley from Waikiki; painting by Enoch Perry, 1865. (Bishop Museum)

art in the Pacific, and includes a selection from the maps of Captain Cook to Duke Kahanamoku's surfboard. Its research, exhibitions, and Polynesian collections are exceptional.

The birth of the Bishop Museum stems from an affair of the heart. Princess Bernice Pauahi (1831-1884), great-granddaughter of Kamehameha the Great and betrothed by royal decree to Prince Lot, fell in love with an American banker, Charles Reed Bishop. As the last direct descendant of the Kamehameha line, the Princess inherited massive tracts of royal lands and the collected Hawaiian treasures of the Kamehamehas. The childless Bishops recognized the need to preserve the cultural heritage of Hawai'i and agreed that the princess's invaluable personal belongings would become the nucleus of a museum. When the princess died at the age of 53, Charles Bishop fulfilled their plan and built the museum, which was opened in 1892.

■ PEARL HARBOR

West of Honolulu on Kamehameha Highway (HI-99), is Pearl Harbor, a splendid natural harbor with a narrow entrance and two expansive inner lochs. Once oysters grew abundantly here, and it was called Wai Momi, or "Pearl Waters." Its development as a U.S. naval base began at the time of the Spanish-American war in 1898, the same year the U.S. annexed the Republic of Hawai'i.

A legend stalled Pearl Harbor's early development. In 1909, work was underway to build a drydock over caves believed by Hawaiians to be home to the shark goddess. Hawaiians predicted tragedy. When the drydock was nearly finished, it collapsed, the seas poured in, and four years of work crumbled. Workmen clearing the debris found the skeleton of a huge shark in the foundation. Hawaiians advised that a *kahuna* (priest) should be asked to placate the angry goddess. After chants and ritual offerings, she apparently relented in her hostility, for no further mishaps befell the drydock.

In a surprise attack at 7:55 A.M. on December 7, 1941, the forces of Imperial Japan bombed Pearl Harbor. During the next two hours, 19 ships were sunk or damaged and 2,300 Americans died. President Roosevelt addressed Congress, declaring December 7th a "day which will live in infamy," concluding his speech with a request to Congress to declare war. It came the following day.

The USS *Arizona,* sunk with 1,102 men entombed in her metal hull is now the **Arizona Memorial and Visitor Center.** To reach it from Kamehameha Highway (HI-99), follow the signs for the *Arizona;* the entrance is west of the naval base gate. The Visitor Center is ashore, and looks out to the Memorial. Brief talks by National Park Service rangers precede documentary films shown in twin theaters and narrated in several languages. Visitors then board the U.S. Navy shuttle boat and disembark at the Memorial.

The Memorial, an expansive, airy, 184-foot concrete structure, is built onto the sunken ship. On a wall of Vermont marble are engraved the names of 1,178 sailors and marines killed aboard the battleship. The American flag flies daily from a pole attached to the *Arizona's* severed mainmast.

Pearl Harbor, designated a National Historic Landmark in 1965, is the only U.S. naval base so honored.

USS Arizona *Memorial, built atop the sunken ship at Pearl Harbor. (Reg Morrison)*

BOMBING PEARL HARBOR

*O*n carrier flight decks readied fighter and attack planes were lined up. The flying crews, also primed for the operation, were gathered in the briefing room. The ships pitched and rolled in the rough sea, kicking up white surf from the pre-dawn blackness of the water. At times wave spray came over the flight deck, and crews clung desperately to their planes to keep them from going into the sea. . . . On a blackboard were written the positions of the ships in Pearl Harbor as of 0600, 7 December. We were 230 miles due north of Oahu. . . .

On the flight deck a green lamp was waved in a circle to signal "Take off!" The engine of the foremost fighter plane began to roar. With the ship still pitching and rolling, the plane started its run, slowly at first but with steadily increasing speed. Men lining the flight deck held their breath as the first plane took off successfully just before the ship took a downward pitch. The next plane was already moving forward. There were loud cheers as each plane rose into the air.

Thus did the first wave of 183 fighters, bombers and torpedo planes take off from the six carriers. Within fifteen minutes they had all been launched and were forming up in the still-dark sky, guided only by the signal lights of the lead planes. After one great circling over the fleet formation, the planes set course due south for Oahu Island and Pearl Harbor. It was 0615.

. . . All of a sudden the clouds broke, and a long white line of coast appeared. We were over Kahuku Point, the northern tip of the island, and now it was time for our deployment.

. . . I saw clouds of black smoke rising from Hickam [Field] and soon thereafter from Ford Island. This bothered me and I wondered what had happened. It was not long before I saw waterspouts rising alongside the battleships, followed by more and more waterspouts. It was time to launch our level bombing attacks so I ordered my pilot to bank sharply, which was the attack signal for the planes following us. All ten of my squadrons then formed in to a single column with intervals of 200 meters. It was indeed a gorgeous formation.

. . . Suddenly a colossal explosion occurred in battleship row. A huge column of dark red smoke rose to 1000 feet and a stiff shock wave reached our plane. I called the pilot's attention to the spectacle, and he observed, "Yes, Commander, the powder magazine must have exploded. Terrible indeed!" The attack was in full swing, and smoke from fires and explosions filled most of the sky over Pearl Harbor.

My group now entered on a bombing course again. Studying battleship row through binoculars, I saw that the big explosion had been on the *Arizona*. She was still flaming fiercely and her smoke was covering *Nevada,* the target of my group. Since the heavy smoke would hinder our bomber accuracy, I looked for some other ship to attack. *Tennessee,* third in the left row was already on fire; but next in row was *Maryland,* which had not yet been attacked. I gave an order changing our target to this ship, and once again we headed into the anti-aircraft fire. Then came the "ready" signal, and I took a firm grip on the bomb release handle, holding my breath and staring at the bomb of the lead plane.

Pilots, observers, and radio men all shouted, "Release!" on seeing the bomb drop from the lead plane, and all the others let go their bombs. I immediately lay flat on the floor to watch the fall of bombs through a peephole. Four bombs in perfect pattern plummeted like devils of doom. The target was so far away that I wondered for a moment if they would reach it. The bombs grew smaller and smaller until I was holding my breath for fear of losing them. I forgot everything in the thrill of watching them fall toward the target. They became small as poppy seeds and finally disappeared just as tiny white flashes of smoke appeared on and near the ship.

continues

. . . After our bomb run I ordered my pilot to fly over each of the air bases, where our fighters were strafing, before returning over Pearl Harbor to observe the result of our attacks on the warships. Pearl Harbor and vicinity had been turned into complete chaos in a very short time.

Target ship *Utah*, on the western side of Ford Island, had already capsized. On the other side of the island *West Virginia* and *Oklahoma* had received concentrated torpedo attacks as a result of their exposed positions in the outer row. Their sides were almost blasted off, and they listed steeply in a flood of heavy oil. *Arizona* was in miserable shape, her magazine apparently having blown up; she was listing badly and burning furiously.

Two other battleships, *Maryland* and *Tennessee*, were on fire; especially the latter whose smoke emerged in a heavy black column which towered into the sky. *Pennsylvania*, unscathed in the drydock, seemed to be the only battleship that had not been attacked.

As I observed the damage done by the first attack wave, the effectiveness of the torpedoes seemed remarkable, and I was struck with the shortsightedness of the United States in being so generally unprepared and in not using torpedo nets. I also thought of our long hard training in Kagoshima Bay and the efforts of those who had labored to accomplish a seemingly impossible task. A warm feeling came with the realization that the reward of those efforts was unfolded here before my eyes.

—Captain Mitsuo Fuchida, Imperial Japanese Navy, *I Led the Air Attack on Pearl Harbor, United States Naval Institute Proceedings*, September 1952

"The Day of Infamy." (Naval Archives)

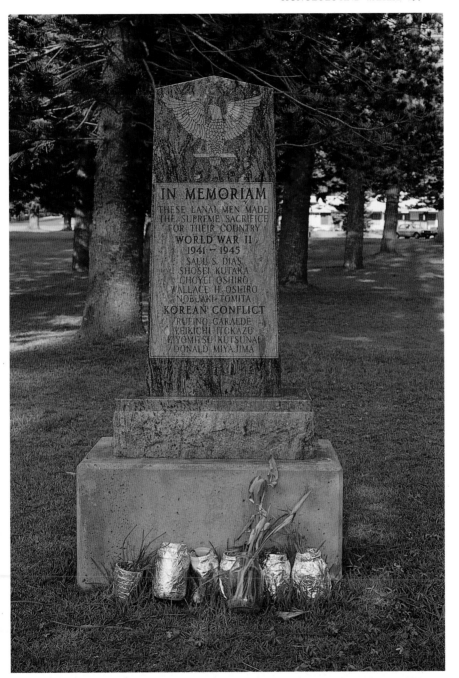

Monument to soldiers from Lanaʻi who died in World War II and Korea; Lanaʻi City Park.

Music of Hawai'i

The ancient Hawaiians were a poetic people who chanted epic tales of gods and goddesses, genealogy, battles, and escapades of the nobility. The Hawaiian word for poetry, *mele,* also described the ancient poet—the *haku mele,* an arranger of words. Chanters specialized in a single form—perhaps in the unaccompanied *mele oli,* a joyful chant, or the *mele ho'aeae,* passionate poems of love. When dance and the sounds of percussion instruments fashioned from nature accompanied the two or three chanting tones, the chanting form was *mele hula.* While stylized chanting related to religious life and lineage, impromptu chanting was entertainment—sometimes funny and explicit, sometimes bitingly sarcastic. Adept at simile, trained and skillful chanters commanded the respect from Hawaiian chiefs and their retinues.

In the early nineteenth century, when sailing ships began to drop anchor in the islands, their crews sang sea chanties, introducing the concept of melody, as the modern world understands it, to the islands.

By the late 1800s, missionary ardor and imported sounds had thrust aside the old music, and the few practitioners of the old chanting forms passed on their knowledge secretively within their families.

If Hawaiian chants faded into the background, Hawaiians soon were adapting the old to new musical forms. In 1898, Hawai'i became a U.S. territory and by 1914, half the people on the mainland were singing "On the Beach at Waikiki," popularized by islander Sonny Cunha and composed by Henry Ka'ilimai. Cunha created a new, appealing style with ragtime rhythms and harmonies, called *hapa-haole*—a song in English with perhaps a few Hawaiian words.

The heyday of Tin Pan Alley in the 1920s brought about dreadful mainland compositions like "Yacka Hula Hicky Dula" with a chorus of "Aloha Oe" sung backwards. The trend was redeemed by the work of part-Hawaiian musicians such as Johnny Noble ("Aloha Means I Love You" and "Pretty Red Hibiscus"), Johnny K. Almeida ("The Beauty Hula," with Johnny Noble), and Charles E. King ("Kuu Lei Mokihana").

Hawaiian musicians rapidly developed new styles and adapted popular rhythmic trends. They composed the *mele hula ku'i:* a part-western chant and dance style evolved from the early *mele hula.* Falsetto singing gained popularity. American trends filtered into *hapa-haole* music—in the 1930s, jazz and blues, and the big band sounds of the 1940s and 50s. In the late 1950s, the close triad-harmonies of Tahiti and Samoa were highlights of "Don the Beachcomber" shows, and music of New Zealand's Maori people completed the musical range. If anything defined Hawaiian music, it was the sound of slack key guitar, which meant strings were tuned down and "slack" compared to those tightened up to match mainland tuning.

In the mid-1970s, Hawaiian music underwent a renaissance which has grown with increasing fervor, and includes rediscovery of the *mele* forms of the ancients, even the *mele hula ku'i* chants and songs of nearly one hundred years ago. With the rediscovery of the ancient, there is also a rebounding of the modern, as a newly vital, distinctly Hawaiian, world-class music has emerged.

Among the greatest musicians who spearheaded the Hawaiian musical renaissance were Sonny Chillingworth, Sonny Kamahele, "Atta" Isaacs, and the inimitable Gabby Pahinui, who would finger-pick cascades of notes on his 12-string guitar and sing in a mesmerizing, raspy falsetto. Today, three of Gabby's sons, Cyril, Bla, and Martin, carry on his tradition and have produced some of the finest of modern Hawaiian music.

A favorite in Hawai'i is Don Ho, who in the early seventies joined the movement with "Tiny Bubbles" and his version of "I Remember You." Although Ho doesn't go outside the islands to perform, he's extremely popular with audiences in Hawai'i, beginning his shows in a slow, genial way and becoming more and more witty and ebullient as his performances progress. One of his gifts is to involve the audience by explaining what the song's words mean.

What is the elusive ingredient of fine Hawaiian music? Perhaps it is a sweetness and a rhythm so connected to nature that it literally pulls on the heart strings of its listeners. Rena Kalehua Nelson, producer and host of a mainland Hawaiian music program, says listeners are constantly calling her to say they find themselves crying when they hear the music on her program—not because it makes them sad, and not because it makes them sentimental, but because it's so gentle and forgiving and that it seems to carry with it aloha, the tenderness of life. "Sometimes I worry about it," says Rena Kalehua. "I worry about people driving along the road and then pulling off the road to cry. It's not because of the words. Most people don't understand the words. It's something in the sounds. They're like Hawai'i."

Gabby Pahinui, premier musician of the renaissance of Hawaiian music.

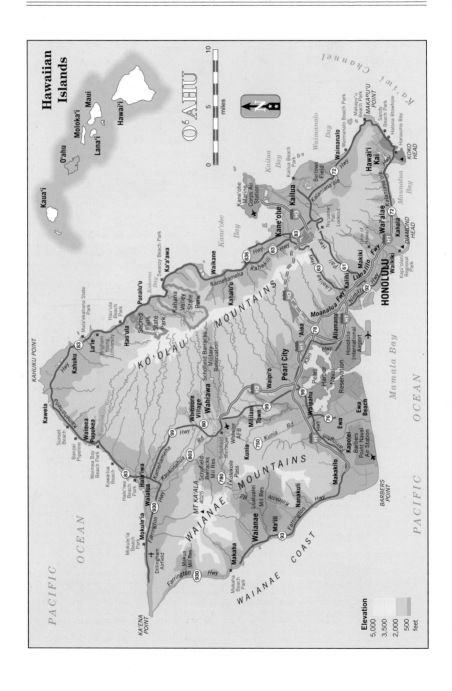

GREATER O'AHU
GATHERING PLACE

FROM YOUR AIRCRAFT, YOU'VE HAD A SMALL GLIMPSE of approaching islands. Now, in descent, O'ahu looms up, the southern tail of this manta-ray-shaped island slashed by a half-sunken volcanic crater filled with a lagoon—its waters sparkling in shades of aquamarine and bright sapphire that edge out into the purple-blue of deep ocean. As your aircraft flies along the southeast coast to turn and make its landing approach, you'll see green residential valleys lined up one after another between forested ridges, each cleft running down to the shoreline where the tall towers of Waikiki and downtown Honolulu face the sea. The two lochs of historic Pearl Harbor come into view as you slip down to the airstrip. (Also see the "HONOLULU AND WAIKIKI" chapter.)

O'ahu, the *Gathering Place,* is an island that offers an amazing array of life's more bucolic pleasures. Here sunbathers stretch out on golden beaches, and swimmers glide through serene waters above gently sloping sea beds. Surfers ride enormous curls of waves that rush ashore in a thunderous roar, and picnickers barbecue and sing to the ukelele on quiet beaches under Pacific stars.

O'ahu's geography is one of soaring, knife-sharp, volcanic mountains, pristine and residential tropical valleys, and fields of sugarcane and pineapple—all surrounded by more than 50 miles (80 km) of palmy beach. Driving through rural O'ahu one encounters the lifestyle of an earlier Hawai'i, and between the small towns hugging white sandy beaches, nothing intrudes on nature and her creations.

In addition to *makai* (toward the sea) and *mauka* (toward the mountains), directions on O'ahu are given by citing landmarks: If you are directed to go *'ewa,* it means west toward the 'Ewa Plain. If you are sent Diamond Head or Koko Head, it means in their direction, or east.

■ HISTORY

The dominant political force in the Hawaiian Islands before the ascendance of the island of Hawai'i's Kamehameha the Great was the tattooed and bloodthirsty Kahekili, scion of Maui's ruling family and probably Kamehameha's real father. In 1782, Kahekili, ruler of Moloka'i and Lana'i, conquered O'ahu and established a capital at Waikiki. Captain George Vancouver, who had served as a young officer on the Cook voyages, visited Waikiki in 1783 and wrote of Kahekili:

> *He* came boldly alongside, but entered the ship with a sort of partial confidence, accompanied by several chiefs who constantly attended him. His age, I suppose, must have exceeded 60. He was greatly debilitated and emaciated, and from the color of his skin I judged his feebleness to have been brought on by an excessive use of the *ava* [alcoholic drink].

Kahekili died at Waikiki in July of 1794 and was succeeded by his son and heir, Kalanikupule. In January of 1795, Kalanikupule commandeered a European brig and tried to sail to the Big Island of Hawai'i to attack the upstart warrior Kamehameha. The assault failed, and before the year ended terrible battles were fought. After conquering Maui and Moloka'i, Kamehameha gathered his fleet of war canoes, and taking with him a few western riflemen, crossed the Kaiwi channel, landing at the sheltered bay of Waikiki in the lee of Diamond Head.

When Kalanikupule withdrew inland, leaving O'ahu's capital undefended, Kamehameha made it his own. Soon Kamehameha's warriors were pushing Kalanikupule's forces up the funnel of Nu'uanu Valley. Unable to regroup in the narrowing valley, many of Kalanikupule's men at the sides of the phalanx scattered up the mountainsides and melted away into forests. Kalanikupule himself slipped away, but his central forces were trapped. Backed to the rim of the sheer cliff at the top of the valley, they were driven over the mountain's knife-sharp edge and died on the jagged lava rocks below. Kamehameha emerged from this battle the monarch of all the islands except Kaua'i. When Kalanikupule reappeared some months later, Kamehameha sacrificed him to Kuka'ilimoku, his god of war. The **Nu'uanu Pali Lookout** is the site of that bloody battle.

■ SOUTHEAST O'AHU

Southeast O'ahu curves around the bottom of the Ko'olau Mountains to form a coast famous for bodysurfing beaches, just 20 minutes from Waikiki. (See "HONOLULU AND WAIKIKI".) To the east, H-1 becomes Kalanianaole Highway (HI-72) and follows the coast around to the windward side of the island. The road winds gently behind Koko Head crater to Makapu'u, passing inland turnoffs into residential areas crouching in rising valleys. On the ocean side of the road, low volcanic cliffs edge the sea.

The turquoise lagoon of **Hanauma Bay** lies in a sunken crater nine miles (15 km) from Waikiki off HI-72. The brightly colored fish in this underwater wildlife preserve are so tame they'll take bits of fish food right from your hand. To visit, walk down the steep road (or take a shuttle ride) from the parking lot at the top of the hill, just off the highway. The bay below is colored in a spectrum of blues, greens, and purples and fronted by a curving swath of sand half a mile long. Hanauma Bay was formed about 6,000 years ago when the sea level rose and a side of Koko Head's crater collapsed, allowing the sea to rush in. On each side of the crater lava shelves cut by wave action run out to each point. The waters on the right side of the bay are called Witches' Brew, because of their roiling when the surf turns rough. The seas on the left are named Toilet Bowl for the swirling waves, flushing and filling a tidal pool. In the middle of the bay is Keyhole, a deep, sandy-bottomed pool in the reef that from the cliff above looks like an enormous piece of brilliant aquamarine gemstone.

The Hanauma reef, stretching across the entire bay and separating shallow bay from deep ocean, may offer the calmest snorkeling in all the islands. Inside the placid lagoon, creatures of the sea (including schools of *ulua* which dart about, their spots or "stars" blinking on their three-foot (1-m) blue-green bodies), flourish and perform for anyone who puts on a mask and floats in the limpid waters.

Hanauma (Hand Wrestling) Bay was once a place to play *uma*, a sport in which two men hand-wrestle from a kneeling position on the beach. It was also one of the most popular places on O'ahu for launching canoes. Mo'okua O Kane'apua Hill, overlooking the bay on the right, is a fine place to take wind directions, and an artful canoer could take a "reading," then scoot down to the water, catching the wind and current to wherever he would go.

Until recently, Hanauma Bay suffered from too many visitors, some 13,000 a day. Tour buses and diving and snorkeling companies hauled people up by the busload and led them down into the ecologically fragile waters. This overuse has been stopped by the city. Bus tours now only pause for views from above. Individuals still may visit, and free tours of Hanauma are led by the city's Department of Parks and Recreation.

As it continues east, Kalanianaole Highway curves past the white sand beaches and rough lava shores that are a part of Koko Head Regional Park. At **Halona (Peering Place) Blowhole**, ten miles (16 km) east of Waikiki, ocean water forced through an irregularly shaped chimney in the lava cliff geysers like a mini-Yellowstone and falls onto a lava shelf at the lookout. If you visit, please stay behind the

A TWO-CENT MISSIONARY

Among the rarest and most famous postage stamp issues ever produced are the "Hawaiian Missionaries." These stamps were first printed in Hawai'i in 1851 and were primarily used on mail that missionaries sent back home to New England. Very few have survived, one reason being the fragile pelure paper on which they were printed. They came in 2-, 5-, and 13-cent denominations, but the 2-cent issue has become the rarest of all with only 15 copies known in existence. *Scott's Stamp Catalogue* values a specimen in mint condition at $350,000. Those that are left seem to be imbued with the island's mystique, and stories centered around them are numerous.

One such story dates from Paris in the 1890s and the collection of a well-known philatelist by the name of Gaston Leroux. Leroux was found murdered in his flat, and the detectives assigned to the case couldn't seem to come up with a suspect or a motive. Leroux didn't have any enemies, and the valuables in his apartment had been left untouched. Eventually, one canny French detective noticed Leroux's stamp collection, turned the pages in his album, and saw that a stamp was missing —what else but a 2-cent Hawaiian Missionary.

The detective's suspicions eventually focused on Hector Giroux, another stamp collector, and an acquaintance of the murdered man. Posing as a stamp collector himself, the detective went for a visit, and before long the two men became quite chummy. One day, the conversation came around to the subject of the Hawaiian Missionaries, and Giroux proudly brought out the 2-center—the same one missing from the murdered man's collection.

After he was arrested and questioned, Giroux finally admitted he'd killed Leroux because he'd refused to part with his 2-cent Missionary.

rail. Accidents happen when unwise visitors climb out on the shelf where the sea can sweep them away. This lookout is a fine spot for whale-watching from December to April when the humpbacks mate and calve.

Wedged between the Blowhole Lookout and Halona Point, is **Halona Cove,** a tiny patch of white sand sometimes called *From Here To Eternity* Beach, because it was the site of the movie's (not the book's) steamy beach scene. A steep path leads down to the sand from the parking lot. The same waves that spout through the Blowhole also surge into the cove, and swimming is safe only when seas are calm.

Further on lies **Sandy Beach,** where, unless you are an experienced surfer, you would be wise to spend your time sunbathing on the broad unshaded strand. Avoided by Hawaiians in early days because of its heavy rip tides and roiled backwash, Sandy was "discovered" by servicemen in World War II, who, ignoring its dangers, suffered many accidents. By 1944, the military designated Sandy off-limits. In the 1960s, however, the beach became popular with local surfers. Only experienced bodysurfers can cope with its murderous shore break, or understand the

House for isolation of a ship's passengers and crew suffering from smallpox. On site of present day Kapi'olani Park below Diamond Head. Painting by Paul Emmert, 1853. (Hawaiian Historical Society)

changes in the ocean bottom wrought by pounding waves. For surfers and sun-bathers alike, there's a popular lunch wagon and beach facilities.

One mile (1.6 km) east of Sandy Beach, Kalanianaole Highway curves up around Makapu'u Point and descends to **Makapu'u Beach,** probably the most famous beach for bodysurfing in the islands; surfboards are not permitted. Its name means bulging eye—after a stone image with eight protruding eyes said to have been in a cave at the base of Makapu'u Point.

Makapu'u's wide square of white sand is flanked by a finger of shiny black lava in the water on the left, and the tall lava cliff of Makapu'u Point on the right. As there is no protecting reef, enormous swells roll in slowly before crashing near shore, and surfers have a long ride without fear of hitting coral. These waters are dangerous for the inexperienced; in winter the waves break at the shoreline and bodysurfers and swimmers can be caught in the pounding break. In summer the waves break offshore and the swimming is good close to the beach. Lifeguards use the flag system here—red for dangerous waters and green for safe.

Makapu'u Point is a craggy palisade rising 420 feet (128 m) above crashing seas. On its summit, facing the perilous Ka'iwi Channel at the easternmost tip of O'ahu, is the Makapu'u Point Light House, land-fall light for vessels bound from the mainland. Its light is visible from the deck of a ship at a distance of 28 miles (45 km), and its reflection has been seen from 45 to 50 miles (72 to 80 km) at sea. The light is turned on a half-hour before sunset and secured a half-hour after sunrise.

A few hundred feet (80-100 m) down the highway is the entrance to **Sea Life Park,** marine world home of the hybrid wholphin (whale and dolphin), great tanks filled with marine life, water exhibitions, and research programs.

■ WINDWARD O'AHU

The windward shore runs from Makapu'u Point up the eastern side of the island to Kahuku Point. You can drive to the windward side following the shoreline all the way around from Makapu'u and through Waimanalo town. Or, you can travel there from central Honolulu by taking the tunnels that pierce the Ko'olau Mountains (Nu'uanu Pali Highway-HI-61, or Likelike Highway-HI-63)—a distance of 10 miles (16 km). The two main windward towns of Kailua and Kane'ohe are large suburbs beside deep bays. Further north, villages dot the shoreline.

The **Ko'olau Mountains** drop almost straight down in volcanic folds onto a collar of lush agricultural lands that meet miles and miles of uncrowded beaches, some with wonderful swimming, others filled with coral. This is one of the most spectacular drives in the islands, past the convolutions of sheer, green-blanketed *pali* looming inland. In the evening light, the mountains grow shadowed from green to purple to deepening black.

Because they are exposed to the northeast tradewinds, windward waters are popular with windsurfers and with sailboat and motor vessel enthusiasts. One of the fine beaches located off Kalanianaole Highway is **Waimanalo Beach Park and Recreation Area**, a three and one-half mile (6 km) stretch of soft white sand accompanied by 38 acres of county park. The beach is at the southeast end of the bay; a distant coral reef about a mile out breaks up the surf. The recreation area is a mile north in a grove of ironwood trees (residents call it Sherwood Forest), and it has facilities, lawns, camping, and sports grounds. Both areas are excellent for year-round swimming. Board- and bodysurfers find the largest waves in the bay off the recreation area. The view from **Waimanalo** (Potable Water) takes in two offshore seabird sanctuaries, Kaohikaipo or Turtle Island, and Manana, usually called Rabbit Island for its crouching profile.

A quarter of a mile (400 m) north of the state recreation area is **Bellows Field Beach Park**. Located on Bellows Air Force Station, the long, broad, finely-packed sands are backed by a dense grove of ironwood trees. It's an excellent family beach; the swimming is safe and coral free; and boogie-board surfers can play in the small waves. Most of the beach is open to visitors on weekends, and camping by permit is allowed. It is two miles (3 km) to the beach from the highway marker.

Kailua Beach in Kailua town is set before ironwood trees and bisected by Kailua Stream. The sands are broad and white, and the seabed slopes gently. Long known to canoe paddlers, Kailua has been discovered by windsurfers and is considered one of the best sites for this sport in the islands. Even if you don't get wet, go on the weekend just for the sight of ballooning sails patterned with flying fish and rainbows, skimming over turquoise water at an awesome speed.

Seldom visited **Ulupo (Night Inspiration) He'iau**, one mile (1.6 km) south of central Kailua, is perhaps the best place on O'ahu to see a sacred temple. (Ironically, it's located behind the YMCA at 1200 Kailua Road.) Legend has it that *menehune*, or elves, built it, and being *menehune,* they did it in a single night. The large open platform, 30 feet (9 m) high and 140 feet (43 km) long, is well preserved.

Up the windward shore and past the rural villages in the district of La'ie lies **Malaekahana State Park,** 23 miles (37 km) north of Kane'ohe town. This beach park is one of O'ahu's best kept secrets. If you're in the mood to while away a day at a tropical beach park about as far from Waikiki as you can go on O'ahu, this is the place. The long and narrow sands are backed by acres of coco palms, ironwood, and *hala* trees. Watching the sun disappearing from the empty, rosy sands at sunset, you might imagine you're in paradise—and you are.

Offshore, opposite the curve of white beach, lies Moku'auia or **Goat Island** (the goats are gone). Small and low-lying, the island is a state bird refuge open to visitors. Swimming, snorkeling, and picnicking are permitted at a small, white beached cove on its inland side. If you wade out at low tide, beware of spiny sea urchins.

This area is seldom crowded; it has good year-round swimming, body, board, and windsurfing; and its extensive facilities attract families. Malaekahana also has a fine camping site (state permit required), or you can rent a tent-camp, or one of the five large and rustic cabins. The rentals are handled at a kiosk near the north entrance from the highway. (For reservations, call 293-1736.)

In the district of La'ie stands a gleaming white Mormon temple and visitor center, and the Hawai'i campus of Brigham Young University. Nearby, the Mormon

Early on a weekday morning the freeway into Honolulu is jammed with commuters from the Kailua area. (opposite) Before the days of highways, trains such as this on Maui, hauled sugarcane and other products to the islands' ports.

church operates the Polynesian Cultural Center, one of the best entertainment tours in the islands—where Polynesians from throughout the Pacific live and perform. Reservations for this all-day tour can be made at your hotel desk.

As it continues north, the road passes old cane fields, new aquafarms, and roadside stands selling cultivated shrimp and homegrown fruit. The windward shore ends at the one resort hotel on this coast, the Turtle Bay Hilton (hotel and condos) on Kahuku Point. Surrounded by flowering bougainvillea and flamboyant trees, a green golf course, bright red hibiscus, and tall cocos, it's a peaceful retreat, far away from the city, where only the sounds of the surf fill the night.

■ CENTRAL O'AHU

Branching off H-1, Highways 750, 99, and H-2 lead through the saddle between the Ko'olau Mountains on the east and the Waianae Mountains on the west, to **Wahiawa.** An old Army town in the middle of the island, it has bars, pawn shops, fast food reataurants, and a lovely old restaurant called Kemo'o Farm. Wahiawa is the site of the U.S. Army's **Schofield Barracks,** traditional home of the Twenty-fifth Division. The central Leileihua plain, now studded with modern bedroom towns, has become the population center of O'ahu.

H-1, H-2, and H-3 are *interstate* highways, an amusing term for highways which adjoin an ocean. "Interstates" came to Hawai'i after statehood was achieved in 1959, when Sen. Hiram Fong argued that the large body of water between Hawai'i and California was not the fault of Hawai'i's residents, and that they deserved to receive a fair share of interstate highway funds. Congress agreed.

If you'd like to visit a plantation town, turn west off HI-750 on Kunia Drive. It makes a one-and-a-quarter-mile (2-km) loop through **Kunia,** an old Del Monte town in the pineapple fields. Here weathered green frame houses raised on low stilts are topped with corrugated tin roofs. Chickens peck in front yards, and bougainvillea bushes erupt in crimson and orange blossoms.

Kolekole Pass is the winding gap (1,724 feet [524 m] high) in the Waianae Mountains that leads to leeward O'ahu. The pass is on Army property and sometimes closed during maneuvers. Enter at Schofield's Foote Gate off HI 750 and check there for information and directions. It's about a 10-mile (16-km) trip through the rocky volcanic pass. The splendid view of white beaches along the Waianae Coast is one few visitors experience.

If you continue north beyond Wahiawa, you'll pass through miles of pineapple fields. At the intersection of HI-99 and HI-80 is the triangular **Pineapple Garden**, where commercial varieties of pineapple grown around the world are planted and described. The Hawaiian pineapple, called "smooth cayenne," is planted in its different growth stages—each plant producing two pineapples. Just north of the garden is the Dole Pineapple Pavilion on HI-99. Stop here for fresh pineapple juice or to buy pineapples packed to carry home.

Further north, fields of tall sugarcane replace pineapple, and the Leileihua saddle begins to widen. Broad views of blue-green ocean lie ahead.

■ NORTH SHORE

Washed by some of the most celebrated and daunting winter surfing waters in the world, O'ahu's north shore is a 20-mile (32-km) stretch of piney ironwoods, coconut, and mango trees, their leafy profusion concealing narrow lanes where beach homes face the sea. The north shore seems a piece of old Hawai'i—many of its buildings weathered and secluded in the tropical green of long established palms and plantings. North shore mountain streams gently flow across beaches to the ocean. There's a South-Seas ambience, and it is easy to realize you are on an island in the most isolated archipelago in the world.

If you've heard of surfing, you've heard of the north shore. In winter months, world-class surfers from every nation where the sport is pursued come to challenge some of the most formidable surf in the Pacific. Even if you know little about the art of surfing, it's an extraordinary experience to watch powerful young men and women riding in the maw of towering 30- to 40-foot (9- to 14-m) waves and gliding down nature's most fearsome walls of heaving water.

For years surfers have come to the dazzling cobalt waters of **Waimea Bay** for the international competition of the Duke Kahanamoku Surfing Classic. Now much of the action centers on nearby **Sunset Beach** and **Haleiwa**, where surfing's Triple Crown is held from early to late December. In summer, Waimea Bay waters are placid, and swimming is good at its wide cream-colored beach. The valley extending up from Waimea Bay is a wilderness where time has restored the land tenderly, and man has trod it lightly.

Pupukea, a marine reserve and snorkeler's haven next to Sunset Beach, has some of O'ahu's best underwater sights. In open water, look for *ulua,* the blue crevally jackfish that swims close to shore. Opposite the beach several narrow lanes bolt upward through green hills that rise steeply from the road to a high plateau. During World War II, Pacific Army forces trained for jungle warfare here, and a large encampment sprawled before the expansive view of distant, blue-water ocean. Visitors now drive here to buy fresh tropical fruits sold at the roadside all summer long by islanders who tend small orchards and ranches.

In ancient times the most important *he'iau* on the north shore was Kahokuwelowelo, across from the present Kawailoa Beach Park. Named for a comet, it was here that the *kahuna-kilokilo* (specialized priests) pondered the stars. Only traces of stonework remain at this oval-shaped scientific temple.

From April until late August, every Sunday is polo day on the north shore. If you drive west over the one-lane Haleiwa Bridge to Mokule'ia (Place of Abundance), you'll find the **polo field** a couple of miles before the western north shore roadhead. Throughout the season the Hawai'i Polo Club plays host to visiting international teams. The Honolulu Polo Club also plays matches with visiting teams year-round on Saturdays in Waimanalo on the windward shore.

Beyond Mokule'ia the road ends, and a rugged two-mile (3-km) track leads out to the end of the island. At the western end of the north shore, along uninhabited coastline, the track leads through tidepools to **Ka'ena Point**. This sliver of sand and lava rock pierces the ocean under a pointed cliff rising to separate the north shore from the leeward side of the island. The cliff, shaped like the prow of a huge ship, creates a bow wave in the sea.

■ LEEWARD O'AHU

The **Waianae Coast** is the arid, leeward side of O'ahu. At its northern tip the island is untouched by roads. Farrington Highway (HI 93) follows the length of the shoreline from central Honolulu north to the end of the paved road. From the roadhead, if seas are calm, you can walk, wade, and inspect tidal pools for some four miles (6 km)—all the way to the sharp tapering point of Ka'ena that separates leeward O'ahu from the north shore.

Even though developers have come into the area, leeward O'ahu is still a place apart. Along the coast there are no souvenir shops or tour buses. Leeward residents, living in rural towns, have resisted both development and visitors. Muggings and car thefts have given the area a bad reputation. One resort hotel, the

Sheraton Makaha, a haven for golfers, lies in Makaha Valley. For some unknown reason, wild peacocks gather each evening at the two adjacent condo towers to preen and screech. Some 3,000 of the birds inhabit the valley, including a number that are all white.

During the summer, along the wide, white strands of the Waianae coast, swimming is good. In winter the seabeds steepen and the breakers become some of the most formidable surfing waves in the islands. Each year at **Makaha Beach** competitions are held. The Buffalo Big Board Surfing Classic in March is the best time for spectators, when old-time surfers use the old-fashioned long boards that can weigh nearly one hundred pounds. (Also see the "SURFING" chapter.)

North Shore surfers, swimmers at Banzai Pipeline; winter surf. This wave probably measures about 8 feet from the back and 15 feet from the front. (following pages) A pod of spinner dolphins.

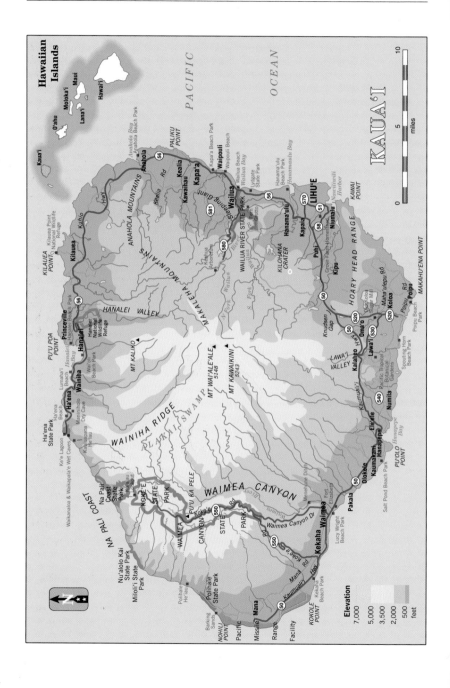

K A U A ' I
G A R D E N   I S L A N D

FROM THE UNPEOPLED HEARTLAND OF KAUA'I, plunging waterfalls, lacy streams, and canyons slash down in every direction, creating habitats for plants and birds that exist nowhere else. Wai'ale'ale, its central misty peak, is the wettest spot in the world, and Kaua'i's seven rivers are luxuriantly lined with tropical growth in more shades of green than you can name. Chartreuse leaves lined with magenta veins adorn plants growing in wild abundance. In contrast, from its largely impenetrable center, a rift cuts toward the southwest, creating a deep and arid chasm that rivals the splendor of the Grand Canyon.

Kaua'i is the oldest, most northerly of the main Hawaiian Islands. Its forests are perfumed with the licorice-scented *mokihana* berry found only on the wild terrain of this island. The spindly *mokihana* tree grows to about 20 feet (6 m) and bears small greenish flowers. Its pastel-green, leathery, and cubeshaped berries are strung to make a lei associated with its king and acclaimed in Kaua'i island chants. Because the intoxicating scent is long-lasting, ancient Hawaiians once dried *mokihana* and placed them among their ceremonial *kapa* garments.

Visitors flying toward Kaua'i catch sight of a green glimmer on the sea, then the central peak of the roughly circular island seems to rise like a coned hat from the water. Below, the island's fields and beaches form a luxuriant flat brim, encircling all but the untamed northwest Na Pali coast. Fringing the brim are 50 miles (80 km) of white sand beaches studded with coco palms falling away toward limpid seas. These soft, white, sandy strands of Kaua'i are the "tropics" of Hollywood movies. Here the director of *South Pacific* found Bali Ha'i, Elvis Presley warbled in *Blue Hawaii*, and Indiana Jones fled for the beach from headhunters in *Raiders of the Lost Ark*.

If you take a helicopter tour of any island, do it here, though be prepared for a strange reaction known as "Gasp Syndrome." Even highly experienced travelers speak in superlatives of Kaua'i. The intrepid English traveler Isabella Bird wrote in 1873 that "Kaua'i, though altogether different from Hawai'i, has an extreme beauty altogether its own, which wins one's love."

Modern Kaua'i was built on a sugar-based economy. In a world market burdened with falling prices, sugar plantation agriculture, born on Kaua'i and a

EARLY KAUA'I

Englishwoman Isabella Bird, an intrepid world traveler, visited Kaua'i in 1873. The following is an excerpt from a letter written to her sister Henrietta back home in Edinburgh.

We took three days for our journey of twenty-three miles from Koloa, the we, consisting of Mrs. ____, the widow of an early missionary teacher, venerable in years and character, a native boy of ten years old, her squire, a second Kaluna, without Kaluna's good qualities, and myself. Mrs. ____ is not a bold horsewoman, and preferred to keep to a foot's pace, which fretted my ambitious animal, whose innocent antics alarmed her in turn. We only rode seven miles the first day, through a park-like region, very like Western Wisconsin, and just like what I expected and failed to find in New Zealand. Grassland much tumbled about, the turf very fine and green, dotted over with clumps and single trees, with picturesque, rocky hills, deeply cleft by water-courses were on our right, and on our left the green slopes blended with the flushed, stony soil near the sea, on which indigo and various compositæ are the chief vegetation. It was hot, but among the hills on our right, cool clouds were coming down in frequent showers, and the white foam of cascades gleamed among the *ohias*, whose dark foliage at a distance has almost the look of pine woods.

Our first halting place was one of the prettiest places I ever saw, a buff framehouse, with a deep verandah festooned with passion flowers, two or three guest houses, also bright with trailers, scattered about under the trees near it, a pretty garden, a background of grey, rocky hills cool with woods and ravines, and over all the vicinity, that air of exquisite trimness which is artificially produced in England, but is natural here.

Kaluna the Second soon showed symptoms of being troublesome. The native servants were away, and he was dull, and for that I pitied him. He asked leave to go back to Koloa for a "sleeping *tapa*," which was refused, and either out of spite or carelessness, instead of fastening the horses into the pasture, he let them go, and the following morning when we were ready for our journey they were lost. Then he borrowed a horse, and late in the afternoon returned with the four animals, all white with foam and dust, and this escapade detained us for another night. Subsequently, after disobeying orders, he lost his horse, which was a borrowed one, deserted his mistress, and absconded!

The slopes over which we travelled were red, hot, and stony, cleft in one place however, by a green, fertile valley, full of rice and *kalo* patches, and native houses, with a broad river, the Hanapépé, flowing quietly down the middle, which we forded near the sea, where it was half-way up my horse's sides. After plodding all day over stony soil in the changeless sunshine, as the shadows lengthened, we turned directly up towards the mountains and began a two hours' ascent. It was delicious. They were so cool, so green, so varied, their grey pinnacles so splintered, their precipices so abrupt, their ravines so dark and deep, and the lower slopes covered with the greenest and finest grass; then dark *ohias* rose singly, then in twos and threes, and finally mixed in dense forest masses, with the pea-green of the *kukui*.

It became yet lovelier as the track wound through deep wooded ravines, or snaked along the narrow tops of spine-like ridges; the air became cooler, damper, and more like elixir, till at a height of 1500 feet we came upon Makaueli, ideally situated upon an unequalled natural plateau, a house of patriarchial size for the islands, with a verandah festooned with roses, fuchsias, the water lemon, and other passion flowers, and with a large guest-house attached. It stands on a natural lawn, with abrupt slopes, sprinkled with orange trees burdened with fruit, *ohias*, and hibiscus. From the back verandah the forest-covered mountains rise, and in front a deep ravine widens to the grassy slopes below and the lonely Pacific,—as I write, a golden sea, on which the island of Niihau, eighteen miles distant, floats like an amethyst.

—Isabella Bird, *Six Months in the Sandwich Islands,* 1890

Poi *makers pounding taro to make the staple food of Hawai'i was a sight typical of the island in the days of Isabella Bird's visit. (Bancroft Library)*

thriving industry for more than 150 years, may soon disappear. This possibility distresses the people of Kaua'i. Sugar has provided a treasured lifestyle, where rural simplicity and stability foster strong family values. Kaua'i tries to maintain that way of life with alternative crops, particularly seed corn. However, tourism is outpacing diversified agriculture. Hotels sprout on the island's eastern shores, from Poipu in the sunny, dry south to Princeville and Hanalei in the north, where dark green beds of taro flourish in the stream-fed valley.

As the economic base of the island shifts to tourism, residents struggle to reconcile Kaua'i's beauty with development. Open horizons are preserved by a county law stating that no hotel on Kaua'i can be taller than a coconut tree. In September of 1992, both the sugar and tourism industries were met with the devastation of Hurricane Iniki. Despite severe damage, Kauaians jumped to make repairs with typical *aloha* spirit.

Wind-rippled, green-gold sugarcane fields ring the southern town of Lihu'e, Kaua'i's county seat. The fields creep up volcanic ridges separated by valleys slanting into the island's center. Valleys and ridges radiate from the forest reserve's center like slices of green fruit. A single highway follows the flat coast around three-quarters of Kaua'i, linking Lihu'e in the southeast with 11 country towns along the coastline. The highway travels up the island's eastern flank to Princeville and the north shore, coming to a dead halt at Ha'ena and the Na Pali cliffs of the northwest. From Lihu'e, the road loops southward to Poipu and around southern shores, to end at the southern base of the Na Pali coast. Another highway climbs from Waimea in the south and ends in mountain parks.

■ HISTORY

The first Polynesians arrived on Kaua'i between A.D. 500 and 700. Probably from the Marquesas, they were subdued by later arrivals who came from Tahiti in A.D. 1000. One theory has it that the Tahitian word *manahune,* or outcast, gave rise to the legends of the *menehune*—Hawai'i's "little people," or elves. Kaua'i, usually considered the home of the *menehune,* is filled with tales of them and their engineering feats in stone. They are credited with building the mysterious irrigation ditches, fish ponds, and temples found on the island.

Menehune worked only at night, always completing a project requiring great strength by dawn—or leaving it eternally undone. They were believed to be jolly, noisy little fellows with big eyes and red faces, who stood about three feet (1 m) *(top)* Konane *board, a traditional form of Hawaiian checkers. (above)* Hokule'a *is an authentic recreation of a double-hulled canoe such as those sailed by the first Tahitian colonists to Hawai'i. In 1976, it made a roundtrip voyage to Tahiti covering 6,000 miles (9,650 km).*

tall. Long ago they supposedly numbered in the thousands, and legend has it that their king, Ola, was worried about *menehune* marrying into the newly arrived Tahitians, an alien race. He ordered his people to go from Kaua'i, decreeing that if a *menehune* was seen on the island, he would be turned to stone. The *menehune* left no hint of their destination, and the builders of the island's gigantic structures even now are a mystery to archaeologists.

Some islanders believe the *menehune* returned to their legendary home on the fabled lost continent of Mu, now beneath the seas of Polynesia, and that Kaua'i is its crown. Others will tell you that not all the *menehune* left—and that some still lurk in remote valleys, hiding so they won't be seen and turned to stone.

When Captain Cook arrived on Kaua'i in 1778, he found people fishing from canoes on the reefs and farming on the coastal plains and in the valleys of the Na Pali coast. In wintertime when pounding surf kept canoes ashore, Na Pali villagers hacked trails across the island's jungled center, using coconut fiber ladders to pass over the steepest ridges.

In 1815, Anton Schaeffer, an ambitious German, showed up on the shores of Kaua'i. Posing as a medical doctor and agent of the Russian-American Trading Company of Alaska, he had in fact been sent to retrieve the cargo of a wrecked Russian ship. An insatiable opportunist, Schaeffer came up with a scheme to take advantage of the young king of Kaua'i, Kaumuali'i, and at the same time claim Kaua'i for the czar of Russia. Schaeffer promised Kaumuali'i that the Russians would fight on his side against the increasingly predatory King Kamehameha of the Big Island, if, in return, he'd allow Schaeffer to build a fort at Waimea.

Hoping to keep Kamehameha out of Kaua'i, Kaumuali'i agreed, and Schaeffer built his fort. After mounting it with 38 cannons, he named it Elizabeth after the czarina and flew the flag of Russia over the bay where American whalers and sandalwood trading vessels laid at anchor.

The alarming news of the menacing fort was brought to O'ahu and then to Kamehameha on the Big Island by American traders. In 1816, an expedition ship of Imperial Russia called at Honolulu, and its commander, Lieutenant Otto von Kotzubue, told everyone who would listen that the "Russian" Schaeffer was an imposter. Von Kotzebue sailed on to Kailua-Kona and repeated this to Kamehameha. Agitated by reports from the Americans that Schaeffer and the young king might be preparing to invade O'ahu, Kamehameha sent a message to Kaumuali'i on Kaua'i that Schaeffer must be ousted, or the Americans would drive him out. By that time Schaeffer's imperious manner had alienated Kaumuali'i, who took

Kamehameha's message seriously. In May of 1817, the young king of Kaua'i stripped Schaeffer of the lands he had given him, and an irate mob drove the imposter from the island.

In his onslaught to unite the islands years earlier, Kamehameha had attempted to invade Kaua'i and was thwarted by ferocious channel storms that took a heavy toll on his war canoes. In the end, Kamehameha utilized his formidable political acumen to entice Kaumuali'i to yield his domain, while allowing him to retain control of Kaua'i as its governor. Although the people of Kaua'i take pride in the fact that they never were defeated in war, it was Kamehameha who realized he could achieve his end without bloodshed—and his diplomatic acuity was equal to the task.

After Kamehameha's death in 1819, he was succeeded by his son Liholiho, who became Kamehameha II. Distrusting Kaumuali'i, the new king tricked him into taking a cruise on a luxury ship Liholiho had acquired in exchange for sandalwood. The kidnapped Kaumuali'i was taken to O'ahu and forced to marry Ka'ahumanu, the great warrior's widow and favorite wife. Through the grand design of royal plotting, Kaua'i was secured. Kaumuali'i died on O'ahu in 1824.

By the mid-nineteenth century, life on Kaua'i was dominated by the sugar industry. It all began in 1833 when three New Englanders with missionary ties, William Ladd, Peter Allan Brinsmade, and William Hooper arrived in Honolulu to establish a trading house. They formed Ladd & Company and leased 980 acres at Koloa on Kaua'i from Kamehameha III at an annual rent of $300.

Local chiefs didn't like what was happening and placed *kapu* on Hooper's effort to plant sugar. Although he was "well nigh starved into a retreat," in 1835 the stubborn Hooper laid out 12 acres. This planting marked the beginning of the sugar industry in the Hawaiian Islands.

A year later Ladd & Company plantation was grinding cane for molasses. The company's third mill, built in 1837 on property later known as Koloa Plantation, set the pattern of plantation-style agriculture in the islands, with channel irrigation, mills, churches, schools and stores. Workers, most of whom were imported, received medical care, housing, a ration of fish and *poi,* and meager wages. Sweet cane became the king of Kaua'i.

Koloa was placed on the National Register of Historic Places in 1962. It is of major significance—for sugar played the dominant role in Hawaiian economics and politics, and probably was the key factor in America's annexation of the Hawaiian Islands.

■ SOUTH KAUA'I

Land of sunshine and infrequent coastal rain, southern Kaua'i is contoured by miles of wide, white beaches. Following the coast from the capital of Lihu'e, on the island's east shore, Highway 50 travels in a southwesterly direction. At the gap in the Hoary Head Range, HI-520 veers straight south through Koloa sugar lands to the sunlit beaches and hotels of Poipu. Between Lihu'e and the beaches, visitors can see an old-fashioned sugar plantation, the old sugar mill that marks the birth of the cane industry in the Hawaiian Islands, a fish pond said to be the work of *menehune*, and tropical gardens. If you just zip through, it's easy to backtrack; Poipu is about 30 minutes from the airport.

Highway 50 continues across the bottom of the island, ending in the dry southwest at Mana. About half-way between Poipu and the end of Highway 50, HI 550 branches up to the mountain parks—Waimea Canyon slashing through an ancient dry rift zone and, higher up, the rain-watered lands of Koke'e State Park.

LIHU'E AND VICINITY

In the mid-nineteenth century, thousands of acres of sugar cane were planted in southern Kaua'i. To serve this agricultural area, two transplanted Americans, Boston businessman Henry Peirce and banker Charles Reed Bishop, founded the town of Lihu'e near a natural slash in the eastern coastline at Nawilwili Bay, where the island begins its southern curve.

Japanese and Filipino immigrant laborers came to work in the fields around Lihu'e, and by 1860, rural villages dotted the area, each dominated by a sugar mill and doused in the scent of molasses. Lihu'e became the center of activity and county seat for Kaua'i and Ni'ihau.

For history buffs, Lihu'e holds a gem. Mid-town, across from the government buildings on Rice Street, is the two-story **Kaua'i Museum**. Small and accessible, its collection of Hawaiian artifacts is considerable and includes featherwork pieces, a hand-carved canoe, stone tools, rare native bowls, and a missionary fourposter *koa*-wood bed with Hawaiian quilts. An exhibit called "The Story of Kaua'i" describes the history, geography, and cultural heritage of the island in skillfully conceived displays, including a contour map and diagram of Waimea village as it was in 1778 when Captain James Cook landed his launch there.

At the south end of Lihu'e, drowsy Nawiliwili Stream flows into a bulge where it meets Nawiliwili Bay Harbor. A stone wall more than 900 feet (274 m) long forms the ancient **Menehune (Alakoko) Fish Pond,** still in use for raising mullet. It pre-dates the arrival of Tahitians, and its origin is unknown. Tradition has it that the wall, now tree-covered, was built in a single night by *menehune.* Further up Hulemalu Road, stop at the overlook for a fine view of the harbor.

On December 30, 1941, a little-known incident occurred at Nawiliwili Harbor. A Japanese submarine surfaced in the bay under a full moon and shelled the shoreline. No one knows why their fire was not returned. Some say the U.S. soldiers stationed at the harbor were manning a new gun and hadn't received their ammo yet; others say the concrete gun base hadn't hardened.

Grove Farm Homestead off Nawiliwili Road is a beacon to those interested in the sugar industry and its relationship to Hawaiian politics from the monarchy into territorial days. Now a museum, this spacious two-story home is set on a broad lawn edged in gardens. Once the headquarters of an 80-acre complex that

Luau outside a grass house; c. 1890. (Bancroft Library)

flourished from the 1860s into the 1930s, it is Hawai'i's finest example of a plantation period home. Inside are salons once used for entertaining or quilting, two libraries, a music room, upstairs bedrooms, morning room, formal dining room, and extensive kitchens.

Quilting was a tradition at the Homestead. The book, *The Wilcox Quilts In Hawaii*, is a record of generations of family quilting, with pictures of antique quilts and stories about the quilts and their makers and collectors. Also in the book is a recipe for concocting *ko'ele pala'u*—a sweet potato wine everyone guzzled for a week in celebration of a completed *pu'iki*, or quilt.

When George Norton Wilcox founded the plantation, oxen hauled the cane from field to mill, and the molasses to Nawiliwili Harbor. Later, steam-powered sugar trains did the same work, running on narrow gauge rails. As late as 1957, four locomotives plied Grove Farm fields.

OLD KOLOA SUGAR MILL

About five miles (8 km) south of Lihu'e, the main road forks at Knudsen Gap in the Hoary Head Range. If you turn *makai* onto HI 520, you'll find arching branches of eucalyptus trees forming an unbroken mile (1.6 km) of leafy tunnel on the way to the old sugar town of **Koloa**. At the junction of Maluhia and Koloa Roads stands a weathered chimney, relic from the last mill of Ladd & Company, the first successful sugar plantation in Hawaii. Built in 1841, the massive square stone foundations of the plantation's third mill lie in ruins at the edge of a cane field bordering Waihohonu Stream. Although few mills continue to grind sugar, the land still sprouts cane.

Close to the ruins is a sculpture honoring ethnic groups who worked on the plantation—Hawaiian, Japanese, Chinese, Korean, Filipino, Portuguese, and Puerto Rican. There was one more figure in the grouping—a Caucasian on horseback representing the foreman. He has disappeared. A number of plaques are placed in the area, with facts about the history of sugar on Kaua'i.

Off HI 50, near Lawai, Hailima Road leads to two famed gardens that may be seen on a combined walking tour. The well-planned displays of the **National Botanical Gardens** cover 186 acres devoted to science, nurseries, and education.

Lawai Kai, popularly called the Allerton Gardens, and famed for its artful landscaping, follows Lawai Valley. Its manicured trail passes a purple cascade of bougainvillea, a Japanese teahouse, gazebos, and an Italian garden. Anthurium,

HAWAIIAN QUILTS

When the missionary ladies of New England introduced quilting to the Sandwich Islands over 170 years ago, a new avenue was opened for Hawaiian creativity.

Hawaiian designs always represent a single emotion—wisdom or love, or a quilt may tell a story. Perhaps the imagery was disclosed in a reverie and celebrates the birth of a child, or it may be a visualization of fish in a bright coral reef, a sun-dappled valley, or even a faithless lover. Hawaiians take their inspiration from the flowers, trees, and fruits of the islands, and from the mysteries of dreams. Contemporary designs tend to flow in bolder, larger patterns with more colors than earlier quilts.

The traditional Hawaiian quilt is made from a single piece, with two contrasting colors. Patterns are cut from fabric folded into eighths, in the manner of snowflake patches taught by the missionaries, and the stitching is done in the echo or contour style, which suggests an undulating wave as it radiates out to the borders. The rows of Hawaiian stitches are six-eights of an inch apart; mainland American quilting rows are wider—from one to two inches apart.

In the heady days of monarchy, quilts celebrated objects—such as King Kalakaua's crystal—and recorded great events in Hawaiian history. Beds were adorned with quilts of the Royal Hawaiian flag and coat of arms, which were named *Ku'u Hae Aloha* (My Beloved Flag). During the 1890s, an anguished time for Hawaiians with the monarchy overthrown and the beloved Queen Lili'uokalani imprisoned, flag quilts were made in secret and kept disguised. Hawaiians made them as a form of personal allegiance. The small museum at the Coco Palms Hotel on Kaua'i exhibits a quilt in a striking flower design —turn it over and there is the quilted flag.

The warmth of *aloha* comes through the quilter's hands, and a Hawaiian quilt is a treasured gift, one passed through generations carrying its *aloha*, the gift of sharing.

Quilt maker demonstrating his art at the Bishop Museum.

ficus, tall shower trees of pink or bright yellow, plumeria, and colored gingers gather round waterfalls; night-blooming cereus and cactus turn toward the sun.

Begun by Queen Emma in the 1860s, the gardens were enlarged by sugar baron Alexander McBryde, and perfected by the hand of Robert Allerton, an American businessman who bought the estate in 1938. Allerton and his son John Gregg added new specimens and European statuary. Surprises lurk in the gardens. Down each curving path, a totally different landscape is revealed—from a bamboo jungle to a manicured lawn where a mermaid dances in a fountain.

Both gardens were placed in trust in 1986 and are managed by the National Botanical Gardens. It's wise to make reservations well in advance; only some 15 people at a time are taken through the research gardens and down Lawai Kai. (Call 332-7361.)

POIPU BEACHES

Past Koloa town, where old plantation buildings have been transformed into craft galleries, boutiques, and cafes, the Poipu Road continues three miles (4.8 km) to **Poipu** (Crashing Waves), on the southernmost tip of the island. Here along the southern shore, separated from the wet mountains by lowlands, the climate is dry, though it can cloud over in the afternoon.

As sugar wanes, tourism waxes. Poipu, once a sleepy beach where the Kimball family (of Waikiki's Halekulani Hotel) kept a 50-room leafy hideaway named Wai'ohai, has emerged as the center of tourism on the island. When the Hyatt Regency Kaua'i announced it would build at Poipu, those who care about preserving Kaua'i's beauty were understandably nervous. They heaved a sigh of relief when the hotel opened in 1990. Designed by Honolulu architects who utilized *koa* wood and lava rock gardens, its cool and restful ambiance feels Hawaiian and is reminiscent of Wai'ohai.

At Poipu, visitors and residents play on three beaches. Between two rocky points, 500-yard (456-m) long Poipu, a strip of soft white sand, lies before a small bay flashing with the colored sails of windsurfers. Because the waves are predictably steady and for most of the year not too formidable, intermediate and beginning body- and board-surfers migrate here for smooth blue-water rides. The small adjacent beach, **Wai'ohai**, is the realm of snorkelers. Underwater, golden butterflyfish dart in the reef. The Achilles tang fish (with a big orange spot near the tail glowing like neon on its black body) and shimmering-gold white-banded surgeonfish peck at the coral for tiny bits of food. Sheltered on each side with facilities and a lifeguard tower, the adjoining **Poipu Beach Park** is one of the safest swimming beaches on the island. Because it's a fine place to take children, residents call it "Mama's Beach." At the west end, the shoreline forms a *tombolo*—a sand bar that connects an island with the mainland or with another island. This *tombolo* joins the park shore with an offshore islet, creating a point of velvety beach called Nukumo'i.

West of the hotels and beaches is Poipu's **Spouting Horn Beach Park.** One of Hawaii's many blowholes, Spouting Horn lava tube builds geysers of ocean spray reaching up 50 feet (15 m). Breaking surf rushes into a narrow chimney of lava, forcing a column of whitewater spray and compressed air to leap like a briny fountain from its hole in a noisy blast. If you go in the afternoon, the spray is colored in rainbows of the setting sun.

Legend says the howl caused by shooting water and air comes from a sorrowful and enraged *mo'o,* or lizard. The *mo'o* swam from Ni'ihau to Kaua'i sobbing over the loss of two sisters. Unable to see through his tears, he overshot his landing and was carried into the blowhole, to be trapped forever. We hear him moan when the horn spouts. Spouting Horn is popular with visitors; tour buses stop here, and shell jewelry sellers set up shop in the parking lot.

WAIMEA

Continuing west along the coast, HI 50 passes through small rural towns where wet taro beds flourish and avocado trees shade farmsteads. Chickens scrabble and dogs laze in sun. Here, where the south coastline curves inward, lies Waimea. The name, meaning "red water," refers to waters flowing down over the red earth of the Koke'e Plateau, rising behind the coast.

The ambience of dusty, sleepy **Waimea town** does little justice to its history. At a small, palm-fringed park in the middle of downtown stands a lava monument to Captain Cook, who made his first landing in Hawai'i here in 1778. In bronze bas-relief the two ships of Cook's expedition are depicted entering Waimea Bay, as Hawaiians, in profile, turn toward them. Waimea wakes up once a year on the last weekend in February for a Captain Cook carnival with games, rides, and gallons of beer.

At the mouth of the Waimea River, the stone walls of Fort Elizabeth (named for the czarina of Russia) stand in mute testimony to the attempt by the imposter

Anton Schaeffer to take Kaua'i for the Russian crown—which had not authorized any such action.

The fort's ten-foot (3-m) stone walls now blossom with fragile yellow *'ilima* flowers. A short footpath leads from the highway parking lot to the site, where you can pick up a self-guided trail map from a box. Markers on the platform tell what used to be there. The fort was acquired by the state in 1969, and ten years later was designated a National Historic Landmark.

Menehune Ditch Road turns *mauka* from the mouth of the Waimea River, up into the valley about a mile to the Swinging Bridge, a footbridge that gives access to the east bank. Near the west side lies **Menehune Ditch** (Kiki a Ola), a narrow irrigation ditch sliding into a tunnel cut into the base of a bluff. An ancient row of rectangular stones, cut to fit tightly, edges the ditch and is still in use to divert water into taro patches. How this ditch, wall, and tunnel were devised in an engineering style not practiced by Hawaiians confounds archaeologists. Surely the elves of Kaua'i, the industrious, nocturnal *menehune* were here.

■ WAIMEA CANYON AND KOKE'E STATE PARK

Twenty minutes up into the mountains behind Waimea town an astonishing panorama opens—the Grand Canyon of the Pacific, a spectacular sight even on an island rife with scenic views.

On the brink of a great gorge 3,400 feet (1,034 m) deep, colors stream toward you. As though a giant were pouring rainbows in an everchanging kaleidoscope, clouds billow by and are reflected in orange, red, and purple, the dry hues of the desert. Changing patterns crawl over canyon walls. Tropical greens and yellows sprinkle the chasm floor below, where a sun-lit thread of water seems too insignificant to have carved such a spectacle. And we are reminded that there are times when the placid Waimea River, gorged by waterfalls pouring down from the mountains, transforms into a raging flood carrying off rocks and trees and endlessly resculpting the contours of the canyon.

From the lookout, etched by wind and water, fluted lava strata expose geologic time. Cutting into the heartland of Kaua'i, measuring one mile (1.5 km) across and ten miles (16 km) long, Waimea Canyon is one of nature's tributes to cloud and shadow, sunlight and water.

Waimea gorge is often called the Grand Canyon of Hawai'i. (Reg Morrison)

From town, Waimea Canyon Drive sweeps up in a winding well-angled road that merges with another from Kekaha. Both are numbered HI 550.

KOKE'E STATE PARK

Continuing up the Waimea-Koke'e ridge, the road (now called Koke'e) ends in the mountain refuge of Koke'e State Park on 4,345 acres of rainforest. Here, just 40 miles (64 km) from warm Lihu'e, the air is brisk and sometimes cold. On a tree-fringed open meadow, birds and jungle fowl chatter. If you are lucky, you might see the bright red *i'iwi* bird here, with its hooked salmon-colored bill.

There is a small natural history museum, a basic restaurant, and state-operated rustic cabins and camping facilities. From here at the Koke'e park center at 3,600 feet (1,094 m), 45 miles (72 km) of strenuous hiking trails lead westward into the Alaka'i wetlands. These 10 square miles of rainy, chilly swamp-forest extend toward mist-covered Mount Wai'ale'ale. In the depths of the swamp may live the last Kaua'i *'o'o* bird.

Of Alaka'i Swamp, Eric Knudsen, scion of a Kaua'i family, wrote in 1940:

> Alakai means to lead—and if ever you need a guide it is there. The land undulates like the waves of the sea, little lines of stunted lehua trees run hither and thither, long open glades lie between and all are dotted with water holes of all shapes and sizes. Some are supposed to be deep enough to drown a person, and if you fall in and try to climb out the turf breaks like rotten ice and you cannot pull yourself out. All is wet, the turf you walk on is soggy . . . To step on a seemingly solid piece of earth and sink to your knees instead is a bit disconcerting . . . When the fog swirls in and all turns grey it is impossible to tell the points of the compass and every hillock and swale looks exactly alike and it is impossible to see the person ahead and when rain comes as it so often does it is very cold. Many a man has lost his way . . .

■ MOUNT WAI'ALE'ALE

Hidden in rain clouds, the central mountain of Wai'ale'ale (Overflowing Water) seldom shows its crown. Rigorous and remote, its soggy hiking trails wind through the Alaka'i wetlands. On the slopes of this boggy, sunless land, trees grow no higher than your kneecap.

Up an oozing trail high on a squashy ridgeline stands a rain gauge. Rainfall measurements vary from 426 to 624 inches (1,065 to 1,585 cm)—more than 50 feet (16 m) per year, making this the wettest spot on earth (although Cherrapunji in India's eastern Meghalaya state makes the same claim).

KALALAU LOOKOUT

Past Koke'e meadow, the road climbs to Kalalau Lookout. From here at its head, the lush green valley plunges to the distant north shore seas of the rugged Na Pali Coast. Towering 4,000-foot (1216-m) cliffs cradle the valley as it slips onto a perfect beach. Birds flutter beneath you. Clouds form and disperse. It is this isolated Eden, nearly inaccessible and bursting with wild fruit, that Jack London chose for his tragic story of the fugitive "Koolau the Leper," who hid here to avoid being shipped off to the Moloka'i leper colony.

The best way to see the canyon, Koke'e, and the lookout is to start at the top. Go straight to the lookout in the morning, before clouds build up in Kalalau. Then picnic at Koke'e (or buy a snack) and come down to the canyon overlook. Toward the end of the day, descend from the canyon down the switchbacks and stop often for stunning panoramas of the canyon in ever-changing light, each stratum a different color—from black to tan to red, and finally, to white.

■ WEST KAUA'I

Western Kaua'i curves in a shore of continuous wide, white sands bathed in hot sun. Facing open sea and with no protecting reef, the shore is thrashed by incoming rollers in wintertime, when swimming becomes perilous.

Where the southshore highway ends at Mana, a secondary road leads northward through towering cane fields to the almost desert sands of Polihale. One of the longest, widest beaches in the islands, the **Mana (Arid) Shore** (say "ma-NA") runs for 15 miles (24 km)—from Kekaha in the south to its abrupt end in the southwest at the massive bulk of the Na Pali cliffs.

Pacific Missile Range Facility (called PMR) stretches around Mana's Nohili point, and reaches across **Barking Sands** beach. This civilian-operated U.S. naval facility is crammed with electronics—under the sea, ashore, and up at Koke'e. Its radar can pinpoint the range, depth, and bearing of vessels within 1,000 square

After Iniki

In September of 1992, Hurricane Iniki slammed into the island of Kaua'i, its 160 mile per hour winds destroying homes and hotels, flattening sugarcane fields, and ripping up macadamia orchards. What fascinated those who visited the island soon afterwards was the aloha *spirit of generosity and helpfulness which seemed to animate so many of Kaua'i's people. This story appeared in the* San Francisco Chronicle *a few days after the storm.*

Lihu'e, Hawai'i

Under a shelter made of broken branches and palm fronds, Herman Kane served freshly barbecued chicken and fish, and a basket of oysters. From the darkness beneath his table, he brought forth a jug of orange juice mixed with homemade rice liquor.

"Eat," he said, the light from a warming fire catching his smile and the sweat on his barrel chest. "Eat until you're tired."

Many have done just that since Kane built his lean-to under the coconut trees in Kalapaki Beach the day after Hurricane Iniki shattered Kaua'i.

Think of living in a place where you can't get ice, or phone your friends in the next town. This is daily life in Kaua'i six days after the hurricane.

Kane has no ice and no gas, but he has a roof he made himself. And what he has under it will make you forget about the things you thought you needed. The 20 people gathering there daily think so.

Kane will stay open until people stop coming to him because the rest of the island is again offering what he has. The way the relief effort is shaping up, that could be a long time.

When meat runs out, he'll serve fish. He is piling coconuts behind the cabana. When he can get his band together, he plays ukelele and entertains under the stars with traditional Hawaiian music.

"We leave this place open 24 hours a day," said Kane, 54.

His family and friends honor him as Uncle Herman, because he is an elder of a native Kaua'i family and because he has a reputation for having a big heart. He helps people through tough times. For him, the hurricane is no different, only bigger.

Each day that goes buy since the disaster, the word about Kane's place gets deeper into the blacked-out island and more friends come.

On a recent night, the group included his friend Donna Garrioch-Kamehiaku, an expatriate Californian born in Hillsborough. There was Larry Vigne, 50, a retired Pacific Bell manager from Santa Cruz who realized his longtime dream of opening a deli in Kaua'i only to see it washed away by Iniki.

Tony Rita, 40, was there with his van. A member of Kane's extended family, he is a native whose main love is paddling traditional dugout canoes in competitions between the islands.

Helping out was Tony Perez, 45, a native of Oakland who has lived on Kaua'i since 1975 and hopes to find steady work in the aftermath of the hurricane.

They and one or two of their children gathered around the shelter in the park on Nawiliwili Bay, with an Army transport brigade camped next door. Across the bay were the darkened hulk of a huge hotel and a row of homes on a ridge, with spaces where some had been knocked out like teeth by the last hurricane in 1982. There were no lights, just the moon on the surf.

In the camp, a chicken and Rita's pit bull played around an uprooted banyan tree where white pigeons lived before the storm.

"Uncle Herman is a *kupuna*—a highly respected man," said Vigne, who came to the island with his family last June. Every time Vigne has visitors, Kane weaves them traditional *ti*-leaf leis.

"That's the wise man over there," Perez said, nodding toward Kane. "Everybody asks him for everything, gets his OK."

The spirit of Kane's camp seemed to rub off on the soldiers of the 25th Transportation Co. from Honolulu. They had not yet received their first assignment, so they feasted with Uncle Herman.

"Yesterday, I taught them how to open coconuts, and they're eating them instead of MREs (rations)," said a sergeant with the company. "They're loving the juice."

—Rick DelVecchio, *San Francisco Chronicle,* September 17, 1992

Herman Kane kept his makeshift shelter open 24 hours a day after Hurricane Iniki hit Kaua'i.

miles (3,860 sq km) of ocean. From its high-frequency radio station operated by the U.S. Department of Commerce, time signals are received by trans-Pacific ships and aircraft.

PMR maintains a close relationship with the community, and access is easy. Fishermen and surfers, swimmers and beach fans need only arrive at the security gate with a driver's license and automobile registration. If you'd like a guided tour, call in advance to make sure the facility is not closed for an infrequent military exercise (335-4111).

At Major's Bay, within the boundaries of PMR, sand dunes 60 feet (18 m) tall back the beach at Barking Sands. You might be able to make the sands bark—or woof or sing or hoot. Stirring up the sands by rapidly sliding down a dune is said to produce a dog-like yelp, or a hoot like an owl's. Old chants speak of "sounding sands," *keone kani*. Even if the sands won't bark for you, you'll find the beach majestic. It is 300 feet (91 m) wide in summer months.

At the end of the Mana shore more than two miles (3.2 km) of beach merge into **Polihale State Park.** Where HI 50 ends near the PMR, follow signs five miles (8 km) west to the beach through sugar fields on well-maintained cane haul (dirt) roads.

Polihale Beach is hot and dry with brilliant white sand—a sunbather's dream of heaven, sprawling over 140 acres. This is a wilderness place and there is no lifeguard; basic facilities are available. When you're ready to swim, try Queen's Pond. It's protected by a small reef, about mid-way along the beach, and is popular for swimming and all kinds of surfing. Follow the main park road south to an access road leading up to the dunes above the pond. Watch for deep sand.

If you like tent camping beneath a star-spangled sky with the only sounds those of the falling surf, Polihale is the place to be. State permit required.

■ NORTHWEST KAUA'I/NA PALI COAST

Remote, nearly inaccessible, soaring volcanic cliffs and emerald valleys form the coastline of the Na Pali Coast State Park. Stretching from Polihale beach at the south end to Ha'ena beach at the north, the Na Pali coast spills into the sea—sheer cliffs slashed by beach-fronted valleys, one after the other, each isolated from the next by a cascade of mountainous lava, each valley lush and fertile with a stream, each razor-sharp barrier blanketed in green. Seen from a helicopter or boat, the raw power of nature, building cathedral-like spires and domes of sharp or rounded lava, fills you with awe.

In summer months a boat can deposit you with a picnic lunch on a valley beach for the entire day. (Please leave no trace of your visit.) Although there is no access by land, next to Kalalau—the valley seen from the lookout above Koke'e—lies Honopu, where you'll feel as if you've been dropped on a heavenly planet. Behind wide searing sands, sheer cliffs rise in a solid semicircle. At one side waves have carved a lava archway on the beach. Through it drops a waterfall trickling off into the sea. A perfect place. (Hollywood chose the Valley of Honopu to film for the home of *King Kong*.) Beyond the arch lies a double beach, where the water is whitecapped, brilliant royal blue, and deep.

From the Ha'ena side on the island's north shore, an 11-mile (18-km) trail snakes into Kalalau and down to its beach. If you go, carry water and plan on a full day trek to go there and back. In ancient times Hawaiians lived in the isolated valleys, leaving a record in temples, burial grounds, and legend. Kalalau was a major community and important in the cultivation of taro. As the new sugar towns developed, many Hawaiians were lured away from Kalalau, and by 1919 the last inhabitants had left. The following year cowboys and cattle were brought in by barge, and grazing continued in Kalalau until the early 1970s, when the state acquired the valley.

Attracted by its remote beauty and mysterious structures (said to be the work of *menehune*), many hippies moved into Kalalau in the late 1960s, and the ecology was seriously disturbed. In 1980, the state stepped in to erect facilities and regulate camping, which now is only at the shoreline and by permit. The intruders are gone, and the tropical growth renewed. Today, the valley beckons to trekkers in search of the perfect wilderness.

Though placid in the summer months, during the winter season the seas off Na Pali crash ashore in thunderous waves that pound the beaches of each valley, and push off the cliffs in powerful back-waves that collide in riptorn currents, dispersing the sandy beaches, only to bring them back in the spring.

■ EAST KAUA'I

From Lihu'e, beaches and rural towns follow the contour of the island up its east flank. HI 56 runs through cane lands, past hotels that dot beaches of the Wailua area to the north shore.

Just north of Lihu'e, a single-lane paved road leaves the highway and curves up through four miles (6.4 km) of sugar field to **Wailua Falls** on the 12-mile (19-km) long **Wailua River**, Hawaii's only navigable waterway. Dropping 80 feet (24 m), the falls usually are seen as two. When waters draining from the island's central core are heavy, Wailua (Two Waters) merges into a solid line of wide falling water. Fish, tossed in the air by its force, often take flying plunges into the cold pool below.

On a bluff above the river lies the *he'iau* named for the snow goddess Poliahu, a sister of Pele. Ruling chiefs prayed at this large temple that closely resembles a Tahitian *marae* (temple). Once a site where human sacrifice was offered, the area now overlooks a scene of pastoral calm, as cattle graze the river banks.

Directly south of Poliahu a dirt road leads to the **Bell Stone**, once a means of transmitting news. When struck, the stone sent a ringing peal out over wide distances to announce the birth of a royal child. Some scholars believe the stone might have served as an alarm should an attacking force enter the river. There are two stones; no one is quite sure which was the Bell Stone. Many have tried to ring the stones; you can, too.

At the marina near the river mouth at Wailua Bay, visitors board launches that wind up the Wailua River, past dense tropical greenery to see the **Fern Grotto**. From the ceiling of the lava cavern, tropical ferns hang in canopy-like green stalactites. In the natural amphitheater, expect a serenade—or a wedding; it's a favored place to say "I do." If you'd rather skip the touristy trip, the river is open to kayaking and water skiing. The grotto itself is accessible only by boat.

At the mouth of the river, waves breaking on a sand bar at Wailua beach attract body and board surfers. The 100-foot (30-m) wide beach is long and unshaded—good for sun-

Petroglyphs such as this on Lana'i are found on most of Hawai'i's islands.

bathing. It's wise to remember that caressing tradewinds make you feel deceptively cool, and you easily can forget the burning power of the sun. After a heavy rain engorges the river, the sand bar at its mouth is eroded away by pouring water, revealing boulders carved with petroglyphs.

Past Wailua Beach, HI-56 moves north, up the east coast, through rural towns and past beaches. Just past Waipouli Complex (shops) look west to the mountain formation named the **Sleeping Giant**. According to legend a huge and friendly creature slept on the ridge after a great feast. *Menehune* tried to waken him by tossing stones, so he swallowed them and turned into rock. The giant's feet are in Kapa'a, his head in Wailua.

Through fields of sugarcane, just north of the 15-mile marker another formation emerges. **Hole in the Mountain** pierces the ridge at the right of the tallest spire. After Hurricane Iwa in 1982 the hole was packed with debris that now is washing clear. The legend of this hole is nearly the same as the Tahitian tale of the island of Mo'orea, where a hole was made when a giant hurled his spear through the mountain to release water.

The Na Pali Coast is one of the Hawaiian Islands' most dramatic sights.

■ NORTH SHORE

Swathed in tropical growth, Kaua'i's north shore seems nearer to paradise than any other place in the islands. The landscape has the effect of inspiring the mind to conjure up visions of *menehune*, and gods appear to rest on misted peaks blanketed in forest green. Rain brings rainbows, and on moon-filled nights you might see a moonbow—moonbeams coloring a misted arc.

Following the island contour, HI 56 turns west along the north shore, through Hanalei and on to the end of the road at Ha'ena. Luscious beaches dapple the shoreline and no tourist development intrudes on this dreamy scene. In 1873, the traveler Isabella Bird wrote of Hanalei, "Indeed, for mere loveliness, I think that part of Kaua'i exceeds anything that I have seen."

The most northerly neck of land in the eight main islands is **Kilauea Point,** jutting out to sea below the highway. Topped with a picturesque lighthouse, its sea-battered cliff shields a tiny cove. Down at the end of the short, pot-holed Kilauea Road, you'll hear a clamoring din. Here the overlook opens onto a view of fluttering massed sea birds.

Visitors quickly become bird watchers at the **Kilauea Point National Wildlife Refuge.** Red-footed boobies cling to cliffs; frigate birds with their forked tails wide to the wind, zoom over pounding surf to steal dinner from other birds with their long hooked beaks; Laysan albatross fly in from the low atolls of the northwest; and wedge-tailed shearwaters spend the summer nesting in burrows that pock the cliff.

In the cove sea turtles swim and porpoises play while Hawaiian monk seals sun on rocks below the point. During their annual winter visit to Hawaii, whales cavort offshore on their way to Lahaina Roads, then back again when spring comes.

At the visitor center housed in a former Coast Guard station, you can borrow binoculars or use their telescope for a closer look.

HANALEI PLATEAU AND BAY

In the 1850s, the Hanalei Plateau was a sugar plantation owned by an Ayrshire Scotsman, Robert Wyllie (1798-1865), who bestowed the name Princeville on the area in honor of Prince Albert Kauikeao'uli, son of Kamehameha IV and Queen Emma. This prince, last child born to Hawaiian monarchs, died at the age of four. Wyllie later became the King's foreign minister. Other plantation owners introduced ranching here, and you still may see cattle grazing on the plateau.

Princeville, the largest development on Kaua'i, was built on the plateau and may be more of everything than the north shore should sustain. Its mega-resort complex sprawls over 11,000 acres above Hanalei Bay. There are 10 condo complexes, a shopping center and restaurants, two golf courses, endless upscale homes, tennis courts, and a small airport. The Sheraton Princeville hotel, built down a hillside, was gloomy and dark until mid-1991, its lobby cut off from the soaring scenery and its decor more New Guinea Expedition than graceful Hawaiian. Recently the gloom has been relieved by skylights, and the South Pacific decor replaced by marble and European antiques. Picture windows now open onto a broad view of the bay.

A red-footed booby chick. (Greg Vaughn)

Past Princeville the road bends and broadens into an overlook. Below, the **Valley of Hanalei** (Wreathed Bay) stretches out in a sweeping patchwork shaded with the dark green of taro farms and the flashing silver of the water caught in glinting sunlight. Edging the farms, the Hanalei River wanders down to the wide bay, its banks carpeted green. At the back of the valley blue-green mountains rise into shadow and dissolve in cloud-shrouded peaks. Waterfalls ribbon down cliffs. Pastoral and serene, there are no mega-resorts here.

Much of the upper valley is the 917-acre **Hanalei National Wildlife Refuge** under the aegis of the U.S. Department of the Interior. The private farms are within the Refuge, created to preserve the fields and the rare birds nesting in the taro leaves. Brown-bodied, with a red bill and brow, rare Hawaiian gallinules *('alae 'ula)* live here and never leave. Ancient Hawaiians believed the red markings were made by the gods after a bird snapped off one of their firebrands.

Nearly all of the *poi* consumed in Hawai'i comes from the taro patches of Hanalei. One of the oldest cultivated foods in the world, taro is crammed with vitamins, minerals, and fiber. All parts of the plant are eaten. In their double-hulled canoes, Hawaii's first settlers brought taro wrapped in *ti* leaves to plant as their staple crop in the new land. Today the bulbous purple roots are shipped to *poi* factories in Honolulu. Known to visitors as a lu'au staple, *poi* digests easily, is nonallergenic and a traditional food for babies.

A wooden, single-lane span over the river, **Hanalei Bridge** is the entrance to Hanalei Valley. From time to time there have been moves to raze the quaint span built in 1912 and replace it with something more modern. That might encourage development, however, so the bridge, repaired and repainted, stays. No tour buses or heavy equipment can pass.

Except for the utility poles and paving on the road leading through Hanalei Valley toward the bay, the scene before you remains almost as it was generations ago. No buildings rise until you reach slow-paced **Hanalei Village.** At the **Hanalei Museum,** have a look at the photos dating from around the turn of the century. The scenes are very like those you see today. The museum was once home to the family of a successful Chinese immigrant laborers, and its old wooden floors slant a bit under display cabinets full of old bottles and examples of taro and rice cultivation. Works of the Hanalei Artisans Guild are displayed downstairs.

Because the town is still quiet, and a long way from the whirl of Lahaina's art colony, artists are drawn increasingly to the awesome workings of nature at Hanalei Valley. The laid-back art scene of Hanalei Village attracts painters and artisans who work in every medium you can think of—glass, ceramics, jewelry, clothing, basketry, mosaic, and photography.

The **church and mission at Wai'oli** (Joyful Water) are named for the musical sound of a nearby waterfall. Here, teacher-missionaries Abner and Lucy Wilcox worked to convert Hawaiians. Their offspring produced a dynasty of part-Hawaiian civic leaders on Kaua'i. Their green-painted New England style church established in 1835 once had a congregation of 1,000 Hawaiians. The Wilcox's two-story frame house, built in 1837 in typical New England style, is now a museum containing period furnishings including a melodeon, a spinning wheel, and lanterns.

If you seek a large and perfect crescent beach, you need look no further than Hanalei Bay, where the beaches are considered by some residents to be the best on the island. Trees frame white sands, a silvery river wades into turquoise ocean, and there are two miles (3 km) of curving beach. Along this shore three county beach parks offer facilities and tent camping by permit.

At the eastern end where the Hanalei River joins the sea, Hanalei Beach Park faces a gentle sloping bottom good for summer swimming. Known as **Black Pot**—after a cooking pot once kept there to prepare fish feasts—the beach is next to **Hanalei Pier.** Traditionally a gathering place, the pier has accommodated all kinds of surfing, canoe, and kayak paddling since the 1940s. Because a sand bar at the river mouth comes and goes, only shallow draft hulls can cross at any time. Other boats must wait for high tide. Yachts anchor offshore in the summer.

Hanalei Pavilion Beach Park, where the surf breaks on the sand bar, is a good place for summertime beginning surfers; winter brings pounding waves. **Wai'oli Beach Park** at about the middle of the bay's shore is the site of north shore surfing competitions. The beach is known also as Pinetrees for its backdrop of ironwood trees (they're actually acacias).

LUMAHA'I BEACH AND BEYOND
A mile beyond Hanalei, around Makahoa Point, lies Lumaha'i beach, where Mitzi Gaynor tried to wash that man right out of her hair in *South Pacific.* Wide and smooth, nearly a mile (1.6 km) long and backed by cocos, the beach curves around a slight bay. Though it's an ideal setting for paintings and photos, this isn't the place to swim. Exposed to open ocean, Lumaha'i is bashed by waves year round. This is no beach to turn your back on; accidents can happen and rogue waves have been known to take sunbathers. The green sands near the lava outcroppings are made of water-worn olivine. Walk and photograph Lumaha'i and move on.

West of Lumaha'i, **Ha'ena Beach** tags the end of the road at the northern edge of the Na Pali cliffs, just as Mana and Polihale tag the ends of the roads at their southwestern edge.

About five miles (8 km) past beaches favored by fishermen, Ha'ena is one of the most popular spots on Kaua'i. Beaches of two adjacent Ha'ena parks face open ocean, a bay, and at its west end, the reef-protected **Ke'e Lagoon,** where visitors and residents come from all over Kaua'i to swim, snorkel, and take underwater photographs of rainbow-colored reef fish. (Don't swim in the fast-running channel.)

Largely wilderness, the 230 acres of **Ha'ena (Red Hot) State Park** contain ruins of Hawaiian communities dating from A.D.1000. On the point above Ke'e, a state-owned house marks a trail leading to Ke Ahu o Laka, a terrace for hula performance, and Kauluapaoa He'iau—a temple dedicated to Laka, goddess of hula.

Across from the beach park is broad, deep **Maniniholo Dry Cave,** where dripping water sinks into a sandy floor. Legend has it that the goddess Pele dug the cave, as well as two others, called "wet caves." Public facilities are nearby.

If you've circled Kaua'i, enjoyed its beaches and rare tropical beauty, you've found the island is "a promise kept." And like Isabella Bird, you may find it hard to leave Kaua'i.

Elizabeth Chandler, one of the last pure-blooded Hawaiians in the islands, threads plumeria blooms into a lei at her home in Kaua'i.

NI'IHAU
Forbidden Island

In sun or shadow, the island of Ni'ihau rears a brooding face 17 miles (27 km) across the Kaulakahi Channel from Kaua'i. More than a century ago, New Zealander Elizabeth Sinclair bought Ni'ihau from King Kamehameha V for $10,000. Today, the island is off-limits to all but those who live there. There are no guns on Ni'ihau, no modern electricity, no telephones, paved roads, crime, or traffic. Residents ride horses, communication is by shortwave radio, and transportation to neighboring Kaua'i is made in a World War II landing boat or a seven-passenger helicopter. Visitors may take helicopter tours (which originate in Kaua'i) of Ni'ihau, and land briefly at bleak points well to the north and and south of the main village.

The island men are employed by Mrs. Sinclair's descendants at Robinson's Ni'ihau Ranch; they herd its 30,000 sheep and produce honey and kiawe charcoal. Except for an occasional visit by an official from the Department of Education, Ni'ihau's 226 residents, all of whom are native Hawaiian, live undisturbed in the main village of Pu'uwai. Hawaiian is spoken almost exclusively, although English is taught at the single elementary school. After eighth grade, students move to schools on Kaua'i, or, funded by Robinson scholarships, to the Kamehameha School on O'ahu.

Ni'ihau found itself briefly involved in World War II when a Japanese pilot who had attacked Pearl Harbor crashed his plane in a Ni'ihau field on December 7, 1941. The island's residents took him prisoner, but because he had no way to leave the island, he was not confined. After forcing a Japanese-American ranch employee, Yoshio Harada, to help him lay hands on a machine gun from the downed plane, the flyer terrorized the islanders for five days. In a splendid display of courage and strength, the islander Hawila Kaleohano disarmed the man and confiscated his papers. The pilot drew a hidden pistol and attacked another islander, Benehakaka Kanahele. Kanahele, with five bullets in his body, grabbed the pilot and smashed his head into a stone wall. Newsmen later dubbed the incident the Battle of Ni'ihau —America's first victory in World War II. Kaleohano and Kanahele were decorated for heroism under fire and Kanahele received the Congressional Medal of Honor. Harada committed *hara-kiri.*

Ni'ihau is famed for its lei—six-yard (5-m) multi-strands of tiny, smooth, ivory-white shells called *pupu.* The shells are found only on Ni'ihau and were favored by Hawaiian royalty.

FLORA AND FAUNA

There was then, as there is now, no place known on earth that even began to compete with these islands in their capacity to encourage natural life to develop freely and radically up to its own best potential. More than nine out of ten things that grew here, grew no where else on earth.

—James Michener, *Hawaii*

HAWAI'I'S FLORA ONCE CONSISTED OF SOME 1,800 SPECIES, 96 percent unique to the islands. Over the past 200 years, more Hawaiian plant and animal species have fallen into extinction than on the entire land mass of North America.

The few that have survived the competition of imported plants, animals, microbes, and development exist in remote Hawaiian valleys and mountains. One example are the tree lobelias, which are a source of nectar to birds whose beaks are adapted to the curve of their flowers. Some of Hawai'i's endangered species are well-known, such as the silversword growing on Maui's Haleakala. Most are virtually unknown—such as the *kaneoha* mint, found only in the Wai'anae mountains of O'ahu.

When the first Polynesians beached their canoes in Hawai'i around A.D. 700, they burned lowland forests to clear the land for cultivation of crops native to Tahiti. Soon they were growing the taro, breadfruit, sweet potatoes, coconuts, and bananas they had brought with them as seedlings from Tahiti. They nurtured groves of *wauke*, the paper mulberry, for its bark—which was peeled and beaten into *kapa* cloth. *'Olona* and *hau* provided fibers for canoe lashings and fishnets; coco husks provided sennit (braided cords); and plant materials were harvested for building homes, for medicines, dyes, and canoes.

Centuries later, a new wave of foreigners began importing another wave of plants adding up to some 2,000 non-native species. The new plants ran rampant over the landscape, in the process destroying an enormous percentage of the indigenous species. Introduced guavas and Java plum, lantana, bamboos, and gingers escaped into the wild and pushed aside native flora. Today, close to 1,000 Hawaiian plant species have become so rare they are considered nearly extinct.

If the European incursion began the destruction of much of Hawai'i's natural world, it was also the beginning of the scientific study of its flora and fauna.

The Bird of Paradise (top) is one of the many flower species introduced from other parts of the world; (above) Protea thrive on the leeward slopes of Haleakala on Maui between 2,000 and 4,000 feet.

Aboard Captain James Cook's ships *Resolution* and *Discovery*, naturalists collected samples and made notes of species never before seen by Europeans. By the 1990s, an enormous body of biological information about Hawaiian species lay in museums, books and tracts, manuscripts, journals, and files. That body of knowledge, wrapped in the findings of a report released in 1991, contributed to the documentation of an extinction rate that has been called phenomenal. (See "Hawai'i's Extinction Crisis," prepared by the U.S. Fish & Wildlife Service, the State Department of Land and Natural Resources, and the Nature Conservancy of Hawai'i.)

The astounding assemblage of native plants and birds marks the Hawaiian archipelago as a place apart, and an example of the works and vulnerability of nature. If the report has an impact, long-term protection should halt the accelerating, deadly descent into extinction of Hawai'i's unique living laboratory.

■ FLORA

Following is a selective list of Hawaiian plants.

'Ahinahina, Silversword
Argyroxiphium sandwicense
Maui's indigeneous plant is the Hawaiian silversword, famed the world round for its single spike thrusting straight up from the volcanic slopes of Haleakala. A rosette of leaves covered in silvery-white hair hugs its base. The sword-like flowering stalk bears up to 500 nodding light yellow flower heads, and grows to a height of about 7 feet (2 m).

There was a time when silverswords were so profuse that it became a popular sport to uproot and roll them down the mountain, or they were cut and shipped as decorative pieces to China. Further depedation was caused by feral goats and introduced insects. Once the silversword was reduced to fewer than 100 plants in the crater. The National Park Service has followed conservation procedures since 1927. It is illegal to cut down a silversword.

'Ena'ena, Hawaiian Cudweed
Gnaphalium sandwicensium, var. Molokaiense
Found only in western Moloka'i, *'ena'ena* grows on the hot coastal sand dunes behind the beach. These hairy little plants grow about a foot (30 cm) high and bear

tight clusters of muted yellow flowers. The Moloka'i variety differs from other cudweeds in its thick covering of delicate hair that tints the leaves a silvery blue color. *'Ena'ena* means "hot" in Hawaiian and may refer to the arid environment in which it grows.

Kauna'oa, Dodder
Cuscuta sandwichiana
In ancient songs the island of Lana'i was noted for its *kauna'oa,* a strange, ground-running plant that thrives on leeward beaches and whose smooth bare tendrils are the peachy color of baby-skin. A parasite rooted in the sand above the highwater mark, *kauna'oa* attaches itself to the stems of host plants, its thread-like stems resting on the sand. The tendrils, gathered in handfuls, are twisted or braided to make a thick lei. Small pieces of greenery add contrasting color. The lei requires no tie; after a few hours the tendrils bind themselves together.

Loulu Palm
Prichardia kaalae
Discovered in the forests at the foot of Mount Ka'ala, O'ahu's tallest mountain, the *loulu* is indigenous to that island. A graceful, medium-tall palm, its fringed fronds branch out in a symmetrical pattern around its trunk. Still rare in nature, these palms now are propagated for decorative planting. The first cultivated O'ahu *loulu* grows to the right of the main terrace garden in Honolulu's Foster Botanical Garden.

Mokihana
Pelea anisata
The perfume of the *mokihana* berry scents forests only on the island of Kaua'i. A spindly native tree that grows to about 20 feet (6 m), it bears small greenish flowers and pastel green berries, or seed capsules. Leathery, cube-shaped, and anise-scented, the berries are strung to make a lei that is associated with Kaua'i island chants. Hawaiians once placed dried *mokihana* amongst their ceremonial *kapa* garments.

'Ohi'alehua
Metrosideros collina

The *lehua* blossom of the *'ohi'a* tree may be the most sacred flower of the islands, for it belongs to the fire goddess Pele, who now makes her home on the Big Island. Its flaming red pompoms are worn in *hula* dedicated to the goddess. *Lehua* are gathered only on the way down a mountain, never going up, because Pele surely would cause a heavy mist to descend.

An abundant Hawaiian tree and one of the first growths on new lava, *'ohi'a* is found in all sizes and shapes—from small bonsai-like gnarled forms in arid lands to slender giants 80 feet (24 m) tall in fertile forests. *'Ohi'alehua* creates micro-habitats for herbs and mosses, and Hawaiians once steeped its young reddish leaves *(liko lehua)* for a tonic. Canoe hulls and temple idols were carved from its trunk, and when missionaries learned of the dark sturdy *'ohi'a* wood, they sent great teams of men up into the mountains to cut and haul down logs for new churches.

Legends and chants recount tales of Pele and this tree. One recounts that 'Ohi'a and Lehua were lovers. Pele, attracted to the handsome 'Ohi'a was rebuffed. Enraged, she slew both lovers. Regretting her outburst, Pele eternally joined the lovers by making the young man's body into a tree capped with the delicate, feminine *lehua* flower.

Another legend tells that Pele believed her younger sister Hi'iaka, guardian of the *'ohi'alehua* forests, betrayed her by seducing Pele's lover, Lohi'au. In her fury, Pele erupted, spewing fire and lava to engulf Hi'iaka's trees. Only then did Hi'iaka act, taking revenge by embracing the young chief. To this day Pele's eruptions pour down lava that consumes *'ohi'alehua* trees.

Pua aloalo, Hibiscus
Hibiscus tiliaceus

Pua aloalo, the hibiscus, sports large, showy, cup-shaped flowers with five petals surrounding a yellow stamen. While it is a favored flower to tuck behind the ear (snip off the powdery stamen first), the hibiscus shrivels quickly, making it unfit for a lei. In the early days of tourism it was said a flower behind the left ear meant a lady was committed—the left side belonging with the heart. Behind the right ear—well, maybe. Hibiscus has been Hawai'i's official flower since its designation by the Territorial Legislature in 1923.

LEIS

Flower leis are worn like necklaces and may be wide and flat, thick and round, a single circlet, many strands tied together, or U-shaped. Their message is love, and they are bought for occasions great and small, or for no reason at all.

Traditionally, lei makers relied on inventive usage of greenery and natural fibers, seeds, pods, nuts, and the tip or base parts of a flower to create leis. When missionary women introduced roses to the islands along with carnations, marigolds, violets, and pansies, the new materials were adapted rapidly by creative Hawaiian lei makers.

Learning about leis is learning more about Hawai'i's stories and traditions. For instance, hula dancers believe they gain inspiration from Laka, goddess of the hula, and long ago they placed leis of the shiny, scented, green *maile* leaves on her altars.

Jasmine flowers or *pikake* (peacock) are traditionally used in courtship and marriage. (They were given the name "peacock" because Princess Kia'ulani had jasmine bushes and peacocks in her garden.) The *pua kika* or cigar lei, also associated with marriage, is presented to bridegrooms and is made from hundreds of tubular, red-orange, and white cigar flowers strung in a slender round of geometric patterns.

Traditional *haku-lei* styles, which take enormous skill to create, recently have returned to popularity. *Haku* means to set or mount flowers on a backing of banana or other natural fiber, positioning them face-up in greenery, much as jewels are placed into a setting.

The most cherished and elegant of Hawaiian leis is made of the *'ilima* flower. Although it ranges in color from yellow to deep gold to rusty orange, bright orange is preferred. This slender, velvety lei requires 2,000 tiny and easily bruised flowers, which must be picked unopened before dawn, then strung before they blossom in late morning. This fragile lei is associated with, though not restricted to, royalty, and tradition has it that *'ilima* strands many feet long were presented early each morning to Hawaiian monarchs.

Each island has its treasured lei, as described below.

Hawai'i	Red *'ohi'alehua,* delicate and feathery; sacred to Pele, goddess of volcanoes.
Kaua'i	*Mokihana,* a fruit; tiny berries that grow only on Kaua'i, are anise scented and long-lasting.

Lana'i	Light orange *kauna'oa,* thread-like bare strands gathered in handfuls and twisted into a thick rope; a parasite, it binds itself together.
Maui	Pink *lokelani,* the sweet-scented rosebud of heaven.
Moloka'i	Silver-green *kukui* (candlenut) tree leaves.
Ni'ihau	White *pupu* shells; smooth small shells that are found along the rocky shoreline of this private island.
O'ahu	Orange *i'ima,* velvety and delicate.

Five thousand types of hibiscus are bred today in a range of reddish colors or brilliant yellow, sometimes double-petalled. The blossom of a lowland tree known as *hau*, the hibiscus at one time was crushed and mixed with sap for medicine. The sturdy light wood of the *hau* was used for outriggers on canoes.

■ BIRDS

Blown off course or clutching onto driftwood, a few land birds—15 original species from 11 bird families—long ago found their way across the seas to the isolated islands of Hawai'i. Encountering no predators and no competition, they evolved into some 70 different kinds of birds unique to the Hawaiian chain. More than half are extinct; the others are rare and endangered.

Some of nature's weirdest mutant changes and diversification of a species from a single ancestor are found here. Hawai'i is known to the world's ornithologists for an entire family found only in the Hawaiian islands—the honeycreepers. They illustrate the process of evolution to a greater degree than any other bird family in the world. From a single ancestral species, 22 species developed on various islands. Some honeycreepers were endemic to a single island—the extinct *aki'apola'au* and *mamo* to Hawai'i, and the *ani'ani'au* to Kaua'i.

Since the first pigeons were released in 1796, more than 156 species of non-indigenous birds have been introduced in the islands. The most familiar species are the common mynah, white-eye and red-crested cardinals, common sparrow, and barred dove.

'A'o, Shearwater
Puffinus auricularis
The *'a'o* once nested on all the islands, and today lives only on Kaua'i. Black with a white front and one foot (25 cm) in body length, the *'a'o* has a wingspan of 35 inches (89 cm). Also known as the Townsend's or Newell's Shearwater, the *'a'o* nests in mountain burrows. Traveling in large flocks, its young fly away to sea one evening and do not return for two years. Often on the first flight they are confused by city lights, crash into street lamps, and flounder on the ground. To protect them from cats and cars, Kaua'i residents collect the stricken fledglings, patch them up, and send them off. It is estimated that some 10,000 shearwaters have been saved to fly again.

'Alala, Hawaiian Crow
Corvus tropicus
Once common on the Big Island, the *'alala* is one of the world's rarest birds, and is now down to a wild population of only a few dozen. About 18 inches (46 cm) long with a dull black body and brown-tipped wings, it was trapped by early Hawaiians who used its feathers for *kahili,* the royal standards and symbols of royalty. *'Alala* roamed the island, eating red *'ie'ie* and *'ohelo* berries—sacred to Pele.

The bird's adaptability was its downfall: At home on ranches in the 1800s, *'alala* were shot as pests feeding on dead stock. A federal and state breeding program on Maui works to re-establish the *'alala.*

'Apapane, Honeycreeper
Himatione sanguinea.
Because the red-feathered *'apapane* feeds on the red flowers of the *'ohi'alehua,* it is difficult to spot, blending naturally with the flower. Most common of the surviving honeycreepers, it lives in forest treetops and is found on all the main islands.

'Elepaio, Flycatcher
Chasiempis sandwichensis.
Less than 6 inches (15 cm) in length, the endangered brown and white *'elepaio* lives in the forests of Kaua'i, O'ahu, and Hawai'i. An Old World flycatcher, its name comes from its song—e-le-pa-i-o. The bird was the goddess of canoe makers. In early times, Hawaiian canoe makers looking for a good tree trunk learned to avoid those the 'elepaio were pecking. It meant the trunk was infested with insects and unsuitable for a canoe.

'I'iwi
Vestiaria coccinea
Found on all the islands at the turn of the century, the brilliant orange-red *'i'iwi* now lives on Hawai'i, Maui, and Kaua'i. Its long tail and wings are black. *'I'iwi* feathers were used extensively in featherwork capes and helmets. The beak is curved to feed on flowers of the endemic lobelias.

'Io, Hawaiian Hawk
Buteo solitarius.
The broad-winged *'io* lives in the forests of Hawai'i. Utilizing its sharp talons, it preys on rats and spiders. Adults grow to 18 inches (46 cm) and build nests more than a foot (30 cm) deep. The female is large and has dark and light brown color phases. Esteemed by some as an *'aumakua* or ancestor spirit, the endangered bird's lofty circling flight became a symbol of royalty; its name is honored in the name of 'Iolani Palace.

Nene, Hawaiian Goose
Branta sandwichensis
Hawai'i's official state bird, the *nene* is a Hawaiian success story. Roaming free today on the slopes of Haleakala on Maui, on Mauna Loa and Kilauea on the Big Island, in bird parks, on a private estate on Hawai'i, and at the Honolulu Zoo, the *nene* has been saved from extinction by human intervention. A big, bright, multi-colored goose that grows to weigh five pounds and measure 28 inches (70 cm) in length, the *nene* originally thrived on rugged lava flows, away from ponds or running water. Nesting at elevations between 4,000 and 8,000 feet (1,216 to 2,432 m) on Mauna Loa, its food and water sources were native Hawaiian grasses and *'ohelo* berries. Far from water for generations, the webbing on the *nene's* feet decreased.

At the time of Captain Cook's arrival in 1778, it is believed the *nene* population was close to 25,000 birds on Hawai'i (and possibly Maui). The near-demise of the *nene* began with sandalwood logging in nesting areas. As the native habitat was hacked away, the *nene* fell victim to attacks by intro-duced mongooses, wild pigs, dogs, and

Hawai'i's native nene *goose. (Greg Vaughn)*

cats. By the early 1950s, only 30 birds remained. Alarmed, the state declared the *nene* protected and the Division of Fish and Game began a breeding program at Pohakuloa on Hawai'i. By the 1960s, more than 800 *nene* were hatched.

Today, hundreds of *nene* released on Hawai'i and Maui romp in the rough lava. Still, problems continue to confront the *nene*. Although the goose will hatch in pens, it must overcome the causes of its near-extinction—changes in habitat and animal attacks when it tries to breed in the wild. *Nene* means "to sit together and talk." Watch them. The *nene* seem quite sociable.

'Feathers of the i'iwi were used in the making of capes and helmets. (Greg Vaughn)

'O'o
Moho nobilis

Once known as the king of Hawaiian plumage birds, the *'o'o*, a honey eater, was first collected during Captain Cook's expedition of 1779. More than a foot long (30 cm), its yellow feather tufts under each wing were highly valued for feather capes and helmets. It is believed that yellow feathers from some 80,000 *'o'o* went into the feather cloak of Kamehameha the Great.

Once common, it virtually disappeared around the turn of the century. Possibly, the endangered Kaua'i *'o'o* still exists, living in the Alakai wetlands, but it has not been sighted there recently and may be extinct.

Pueo
Asio flammeus sandwichensis

One of the few owls to hunt in daylight, the short-eared *pueo* soars above the fields, hovering before making a straight dive on its prey—usually a small rat or mouse which it swallows whole. The *pueo* grows to some 18 inches (46 cm) in length, has yellow eyes and white-streaked brown feathers, and lives on all the islands, from sea level to mountain top. Many consider it an ancestor spirit, and it is worshipped in some Hawaiian homes.

Palila
Psittirostra bailleui.

On the cold high slopes of Mauna Kea on Hawai'i, the *palila* survives in an ecological niche with the *na'io* and *mamane* trees. Grasping a pod with its foot, it pecks out the seeds. *Palila* eat the flowers of the *mamane* and feed their young on caterpillars snatched off the leaves. The *palila* is six inches (15 cm) long, has a large head and short dark bill, and is yellow, the color of the *mamane* flower. It nests in both trees. Once found throughout Hawai'i, destruction of its habitat, disease, and competition from introduced birds have reduced its population. *Palila* now live above the 7,000 foot (2,128 m) level amid protected stands of trees. Feral sheep that once fed on leaves and seedlings have been removed.

■ MAMMALS

When the great Polynesian ocean migrations found Hawai'i's shores 1,500 years ago, ancient whale and dolphin species may have roamed island waters. Only seals and tiny bats frolicked on the land. The sea-going canoes carried pigs and dogs—and the Polynesian rat.

Hawaiian Monk Seal
Monachus schauinslandi

Found no other place on earth, the monk seal was separated from relatives in the Caribbean and Atlantic when the Isthmus of Panama appeared some 200,000 years ago. Perhaps the seal was the first mammal ashore on Hawai'i. Hunting the monk seal, explorers and seamen nearly annihilated the species by 1900, yet scientists had no clue it existed. Not until 1905 was the seal "discovered." Now protected, more than 1,000 monk seals populate the Hawaiian Islands National Wildlife Refuge at the northern end of the island chain—around French Frigate Shoals and Kure Atoll. Joining humans in its love of sandy beaches and nearby shallows, the sweet-faced creature has reappeared on Kaua'i.

Hoary Bat
Lasiurus cinereus
Somehow, thousands of years ago, the little reddish-colored hoary bat flew to the islands under its own steam. Probably descended from the hairy brown bats of the Americas, its original relatives were migratory. Hawai'i's bat hasn't quite lost that instinct—while hoary bats store a summer layer of fat before a long flight, Hawai'i's bats lay on the fat and fly nowhere. Breeding mainly on the islands of Hawai'i and Kaua'i, they have been spotted on O'ahu and Maui.

Pig
Sus scrofa
In need of meat for his crew, Captain Cook found in 1779 that the largest pigs he could barter for weighed 50 to 60 pounds (23 to 27 kg). Probably the early pigs lived much as they do today, and their population was limited. The native pig of Cook's time interbred with pigs (from imported breeds) that escaped into the wild, and together they evolved into a fearsome beast akin to an enormous European wild boar. Today, they rummage in the lush forests, digging muddy wallows that disturb the native flora, and spreading introduced plants. A boar's head still is a respected hunting trophy. With luck, on Kilauea volcano you might see an open-jawed toothy boar's head brought in the night and offered to Pele.

Dog
Canis familiaris
Dogs, to the early Polynesian voyagers, were everything—except man's best friend. Apparently small and unresponsive dumbbells, dogs were used for barter and in religious rites, the flesh eaten and the bones carved. Cultivated in pens on a vegetarian diet, dogs were a food staple; hundreds might be served at a feast. In 1889, Robert Louis Stevenson was the guest of honor at a lu'au given by King Kalakaua. Of that day, Arthur Johnstone writes, "It is here that the novelist is said to have tasted his first dish of Hawaiian baked dog, which he did with the best grace at his command, and, after the first bite, with more or less gusto." One of three rabies-free areas in the world (the other two are Australia and Great Britain), Hawai'i maintains a stiff state quarantine.

Polynesian Rat
Rattus exulans

Rats infested Polynesia, and the Maori of New Zealand ate them. Scientists suppose the Polynesian rat arrived in Hawai'i by stowing away in voyaging canoes. Once in Hawai'i, it evolved into a distinctly Hawaiian rat. The Hawaiians didn't eat them, but they played with rats, placing them in a contest arena where the rats were done in with spears. (Hawai'i seems to be the only part of Polynesia to play this game.) To counteract the rat's havoc in the cane fields, sugar planters developed tough strains of sugar. Today the Polynesian rat is an intractable pest that eats rare birds and is an anathema to wildlife conservationists.

Other Feral Mammals

Mammals brought to the islands since the arrival of Captain Cook in 1778 include horses, donkeys, cats, dogs, cattle, goats, and rabbits. Some members of every species escaped into the wild and developed feral populations. Wild mammals introduced for sports hunting include axis and mule deer, pronghorn antelope, mouflon sheep, and even some wallabies on O'ahu. All now endanger the islands' environment, as does the Indian mongoose which was introduced for rat control.

Hawaiian monk seal, an endangered species now protected in the Hawaiian Islands National Wildlife Refuge. (Greg Vaughn)

French Frigate Shoals are part of the Northwest Hawaiian Islands and are home to the monk seal.
(Greg Vaughn)

REEF FISH

Reef fish are those the snorkeler will most likely see. There are many varieties in Hawai'i. Listed below are a few you're apt to notice.

Parrotfish

Growing to two feet (61 cm) in length, adult males are brightly colored, and the females, red, grey, and brown. Parrotfish are named for their beaks, which they use to bite off coral for its algae, crushing the coral with teeth at the back of the throat. The rubble passes through the digestive tract and is ejected; in this way they recycle coral into sand. Parrots graze the reefs and are not bothered by peering snorkelers.

red-lipped parrotfish

The blue-mottled parrotfish *(uhu)* adult male has yellow scales with light blue edges, and pink and blue dorsal fins and tails. The red-lipped adult male parrotfish *(uhu)* has a chartreuse green head, back, and dorsal fin, and a light blue underside.

uhu

Goatfish

Attaining a length of about 16 inches (41 cm), goatfish are gaudy, plentiful, and have double whiskers under the mouth. Once used in ceremonial rites of launching new canoes or entering a *hula halau* (hula school), today they are valued for food and can be found at good fish markets.

saddleback wrasse

Whitespot goatfish *(kumu)* are orange-colored with a white tail and a black horizontal stripe through the eye. They are seen hugging reefs scattered throughout groups of damselfish and carnivorous wrasses. A delicious fish, they often are caught by spear. The red or yellowstripe goatfish *(weke)* has a bright pink body with horizontal yellow stripe, and a blue back. *Weke* swim in schools in large circles near reefs, and are good eating. White goatfish *(weke'a'a)* are pure white. Don't eat this model during the summer months when it is said to produce a temporary delirium or "nightmare."

Hawaiian scorpionfish

Scorpionfish

Scorpionfish have many names—among them turkeyfish, dragonfish, tigerfish, and lionfish. They perch everywhere in the reefs, often hanging upside down, and they snatch small fish that venture close to examine spiny bits hanging from scorpionfish faces. Some 10 inches (25 cm) long with spots and stripes and long spindly fins, their camouflage makes them difficult to see. This weird-looking fish carries venom in the anal, dorsal, and ventral fin spines. A puncture wound is painful though not fatal. (Indo-Pacific stonefish with fatal venom are not found in Hawaiian waters.)

moorish idol

Hawaiian scorpionfish *(nohu pinao),* a mass of black, brown, and white stripes and spots is a popular aquarium fish that should not be handled.

Butterfly Fish

Usually up to about six inches (15 cm) in length, brightly colored, and dainty, the body of the butterfly fish is short and narrow.

bluestripe butterflyfish

Many of these fish pair off while still small and stay together for life, always swimming one behind the other, darting in and out of reefs.

The long-nose butterfly *(lau wiliwili nukunuku 'oi'oi)* has a bright gold body topped with 12 dorsal spines, a long nose on a black head, and a black tail with black circle beneath. The bluestripe butterfly *(lauhau)* has horizontal blue stripes on a gold body, and is one of the few butterflies in Hawai'i that has no vertical black bar through the eye.

threadfin butterflyfish

Triggerfish

Triggerfish are odd-looking coral denizens with eyes in the middle of their bodies. They are slow swimmers and stay close to home.

The painted triggerfish *(humuhumu nukunuku apua'a)* was made famous by the song, "My Little Grass Shack;" and Hawai'i's small fish with the big name still "goes swimming by." Although it now holds the rank of official state fish, early Hawaiians weren't overly impressed by the *humuhumu nukunuku apua'a,* considering it an insignificant inshore fish for food. Often, it was used like a twig to cook more tasty morsels from the reef. *Humuhumu,* meaning "to fit pieces together," may refer to the nest it builds, and *nukunuku apua'a* means "nose like a pig." With black painted stripes, brown wedge to the rear,

manta ray

mottled moray

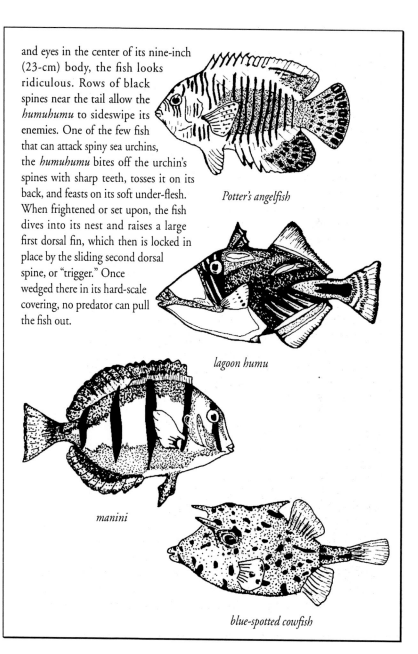

and eyes in the center of its nine-inch (23-cm) body, the fish looks ridiculous. Rows of black spines near the tail allow the *humuhumu* to sideswipe its enemies. One of the few fish that can attack spiny sea urchins, the *humuhumu* bites off the urchin's spines with sharp teeth, tosses it on its back, and feasts on its soft under-flesh. When frightened or set upon, the fish dives into its nest and raises a large first dorsal fin, which then is locked in place by the sliding second dorsal spine, or "trigger." Once wedged there in its hard-scale covering, no predator can pull the fish out.

Potter's angelfish

lagoon humu

manini

blue-spotted cowfish

S U R F I N G

WHEN YOU SEE OCEAN RISING IN A WALL OF SHIMMERING BLUE and curling over hollow space with its edge tipped in foam, you can feel the excitement. Riding a wave, sliding across its face on the front of a board, is one of the great exhilarations known to man.

The secret of surfing isn't about conquering the ocean. Surfing is flowing *with* the ocean. It takes discipline and training, excellent physical condition, grace, and bravery.

Hawaiians have loved the sport for more than a thousand years. In petroglyphs you can see today on the Big Island, there are board-riding stick figures , carved by the early Tahitian colonists. Originally known as *he'enalu,* or sliding on a wave, surfing was a sport everyone enjoyed, from *tutu* (grandmother) to *keiki* (child).

In Kona a *he'iau* dedicated to surfing once stood at Kahalu'u Bay, its terraced rock facing the sea and possibly used as bleachers. The *he'iau kahuna,* or priest, picked vines, handing some to the surfers, and they all beat the water and chanted prayers to the god of the ocean for large waves. In those early times, surfing waters favored by the *ali'i* or royalty were *kapu* to commoners and the penalty was death. Occasionally a commoner with fine surfing skills could earn the privilege of riding royal surf.

Wintertime, beginning in November, was the favorite time to surf, when stormy winds roiled the ocean and huge waves came pounding ashore on island beaches. Competitions were held and the people wagered pigs, dogs, canoes, and fishing nets on the surfers. The winners and losers were celebrated in *mele,* or chants.

The acknowledged "father of modern surfing" was the Olympic swimmer Duke Pa'oa Kahanamoku (1890-1968). In the early 1900s, on a long 114-pound *koa* wood board, he perfected new maneuvers on the waves at Waikiki—riding backward, performing headstands, and surfing at an angle to slide left or right along the face of a wave. Sometimes he surfed with a dog sitting on the front of his board. Duke was the first Hawaiian to take women along to ride tandem on the board; in ancient times tandem surfing was *kapu.*

Duke introduced the sport to Australia in 1915, and after winning Olympic golds in swimming in the 1920s, he introduced surfing to the United States, performing in waters off California, New York, and New Jersey.

The heyday of the old-time Hawaiian beach boys, all consummate surfers, began in the thirties and still exists to some extent. Movie stars, writers, and wealthy tourists came by ship and ensconced themselves at the Moana, Royal Hawaiian, and Halekulani hotels in Waikiki. They made friends with the beach boys who spent their days tending to the visitors, taking the rich and famous out in outrigger canoes and teaching them to ride surfboards. The Hawaiian surfers played music and sang on the beach, drank with the moneyed, enjoyed the rubbed-off glamor, and earned enormous tips.

As surfing became a lifestyle in the 1960s, in Hawai'i and on the mainland, surfers began cultivating a tattooed, long-haired, bad-boy image. While non-surfers wondered what their passion was about, the "surf bums," as they were called then, simply went on pursuing the next wave. As time passed surfing gained recognition as a sport of intense athleticism. Professional surfers now are as well re-garded in their watery arena as most-valuable-players are on a dry-land football field.

Their passion is the challenge of joining with the wave and flowing with its high-powered energy. The greater the wave the greater the challenge and thrill. In monstrous surf, waves tower 10 to 15 times higher than the surfer.

(above) Surfing Waikiki, c. 1950 (Oakland Museum). (following page) Surfing has developed into an international sport fetching prize purses of thousands of dollars.

Today, winter is still the best time to surf, and at international competitions on O'ahu's north shore beaches, winter waves may tower up to 30 feet (9 m). Although pigs and fishing nets aren't wagered now, there is big prize money from corporate sponsorships. At competitions the internationally accepted Hawaiian wave scale is used. The measurement, from trough to peak, is taken in buoy readings and represents the size of the waves moving in open ocean, not the size of the face when the waves approach the shore and become vertical. If you hear that waves are "10 to 12 (feet)" (3 to 4 m), it means they will build to a 20-foot (6-m) drop on the face. Surfers come from all over—California, Texas, Australia, South America, South Africa, and Singapore—to compete on these enormous waves.

Since the hollow board was invented, surfboards have undergone many changes. Designs are far different from the days of Duke's heavy redwood or *koa* boards, and board-making spawned an industry. "Shapers" make light-weight boards, eight to 12 feet (2.5 to 4 m) long, filled with polyurethane foam and a "stringer" or thin strip of wood sandwiched in the center. Skegs (fins) are fitted to the bottom, and the boards are laminated with fiberglass cloth and resin. Finally, the surface is sanded to a slick finish. Today's popular surfboards are called "Longboards," "Guns," "Twin Fins," and "Tri-Fins." Under 18 inches (46 cm) wide, they are narrower, longer, thicker in the middle, and carry more tail than earlier designs.

One man who became a surfing legend was Hawaiian Eddie Aikau, who spoke little and surfed from morning to night. In 1977, he was listed 24th in a field of master surfers at the Duke Kahanamoku Classic competitions. With scores rated by length of ride, maneuvers, performance style, and judgment of wave selection, Eddie won that day at O'ahu's Sunset Beach.

Surfboard chic.

JACK LONDON LEARNS TO SURF

When Jack London sailed into Honolulu in May of 1907 aboard his barely seaworthy ketch, the Snark, *he was already a celebrated writer. He and his wife Charmian settled into a Waikiki cottage at the Seaside Hotel and were at once introduced into the life of Honolulu. Together they met the dethroned Queen Lili'uokalani; Prince Jonah Kuhio Kalanianaole, Hawai'i's delegate (non-voting) to Congress; A. S. Cleghorn, father of the late Princess Ka'iulani; and Sanford B. Dole, politician and pineapple baron. It was after this trip that London wrote* The Cruise of the Snark, *in which, among other things, he describes learning to surf.*

I deserted the cool shade, put on a swimming suit, and got hold of a surfboard. It was too small a board. But I didn't know, and nobody told me. I joined some little Kanaka [Hawaiian] boys in shallow water, where the breakers were well spent and small—a regular kindergarten school....When a likely-looking breaker came along, they flopped upon their stomachs on their boards, kicked like mad with their feet, and rode the breaker in to the beach. I tried to emulate them. I watched them, tried to do everything that they did, and failed utterly. The breaker swept past, and I was not on it. I tried again and again. I kicked twice as madly as they did, and failed. Half a dozen would be around. We would all leap on our boards in front of a good breaker. Away our feet would churn like the sternwheels of river steamboats, and way the little rascals would scoot while I remained in disgrace behind.

I tried for a solid hour, and not one wave could I persuade to boost me shoreward. And then arrived a friend...

"Get off that board," he said. "Chuck it away at once. Look at the way you're trying to ride it. If ever the nose of that board hits bottom, you'll be disemboweled. Here, take my board. It's a man's size."

. . . He showed me how to properly mount his board. Then he waited for a good breaker, gave me a shove at the right moment, and started me in. Ah, delicious moment when I felt that breaker grip and fling me! On I dashed, a hundred and fifty feet, and subsided with the breaker on the sand. From that moment I was lost.

. . . So it was, next morning, when Ford came along, that I plunged into the wonderful water for a swim of indeterminate length. Astride of our surfboards, or rather, flat down upon them on our stomachs, we paddled out through the kindergarten where the little Kanaka boys were at play. Soon we were out in deep water where the big smokers came roaring in. The mere struggle with them, facing them and paddling seaward over them and through them, was sport enough in itself. One had to have his wits about him, for it was a battle in which mighty blows were struck, on one side, and in which cunning was used on the other side —a struggle between insensate force and intelligence. I soon learned a bit. When a breaker curled over my head, for a swift instant I could see the light of day through its emerald body; then down would go my head, and I would clutch the board with all my strength. Then would come the blow, and to the onlooker on shore I would be blot-

Jack and Charmian London, Waikiki, 1915. (Bancroft Library)

ted out. In reality the board and I have passed through the crest and emerged in the respite of the other side. . . .

The whole method of surf-riding and surf-fighting, I have learned, is one of nonresistance.

—Jack London, *The Cruise of the Snark,* 1908

The Londons returned to Hawai'i a second time in 1915, settling into a cottage on Beach Walk in Waikiki, and later into a cottage near the Halekulani Hotel. London wrote several stories during this time, including Shin Bones, *its theme centering on Hawaiian burial ritual;* The Kanaka Surf, *a surfing tale of a love triangle; and* The Water Baby, *the story of a Hawaiian boy who hoodwinks sharks.*

A few months later he sailed aboard the *Hokule'a,* a re-creation of a double-hulled Polynesian voyaging canoe. It was on its second 3,000-mile (4,800-km) trip from Hawai'i to Tahiti, and being navigated in the ancient way, when, near midnight on March 16, 1978, five hours out of Honolulu, the craft was hit by a rogue swell in the Moloka'i Channel and capsized.

As a storm formed, the crew clung to the craft, hoping to be spotted by commuter aircraft. By morning currents were pulling the vessel out to sea. Against heavy odds, Eddie chose to go for help on his surfboard, though the channel was seething with 20-foot (6-m) whitecaps that would hit a surfboard broadside from all angles. Wearing a life vest and rain slicker and carrying a knife and light, he set off for Lana'i, about 12 miles (19 km) distant. Later in the night the other crew members were rescued. Eddie was never seen again.

The big-wave riders of O'ahu's north shore feel that Eddie's spirit hovers at Waimea Bay. On January 21, 1990, the Eddie Aikau Contest was surfed at Waimea, and the day is remembered for perfect 18- to 25-foot (5- to 8-m) waves. Surfers and spectators still talk about that day of positive energy, when the sound of a Hawaiian drumbeat carried over the beach and the wind came out of the valley (a rare occurance), and surfers rode spectacular waves in memory of Eddie Aikau.

■ WHERE TO CATCH WAVES

■ O'AHU

O'ahu is considered *the* surfing island. Here, year-round surfing is the hottest in the Hawaiian islands, and the international competitions are held annually in the big winter surf of O'ahu.

South Shore Beaches

Surfers find spots to launch their boards all along the south shore of O'ahu. Following are some Waikiki hot spots, listed from south to north:

The surfing breaks of Waikiki are out beyond the swimming areas, and while traffic with outriggers, catamarans, and long-distance swimmers can be frustrating, the waves are reliable year-round. Facing the beaches of Waikiki from Diamond Head to the Hawaiian Village Hotel, the long-ride breaks are: Diamond Head, Tongg's, Old Man's, Publics, Castle, Cunha's, Blowhole, Queens, Canoes, First

Break, Cornucopia (Moana Hotel), and Popular. Behind First Break, a long way out to sea, is Zero Break.

In the sixties surfers discovered Point Panic, at the foot of Ahui Street between Waikiki and downtown. North of the small breaks beyond the reef outside of Ala Moana Beach Park is Kewalo Basin, where commercial fishing and cruise boats tie up. At the north end of Kewalo lies rocky Point Panic. There is no sand beach. Here the surf zooms in to a sea wall at the University of Hawai'i's Pacific Biomedical Research Center and board surfers must know how and when to cut off rides, a situation that gives rise to this spot's apt name.

Leeward Beaches

Makaha. At 84-369 Farrington Highway. Makaha is the most famous surfing beach on the northwest coast. Surfers rode the big winter waves at Makaha well before they attempted the north shore breaks. The first surfers came here with their old-style heavy wooden boards in the 1930s, and in 1952 the first Makaha international surfing championships were held. Contests are held each year when the north swells run and the waves tower up into walls of moving energy. In winter the pounding surf erodes the wide summer beach into a narrower strand with a steep seabed dropoff. The name Makaha, meaning "savage," refers to robbers who once congregated here. Makaha is a place with two personalities—the one, turned inward, friendly, and Hawaiian. The outward face is somewhat hostile and the casual surfer elicits a frigid greeting from locals, who consider the Makaha surf one of their last few possessions.

Yokohama Bay. North of Makaha at the end of the Farrington Highway paved road. Located between two rocky points, this is the last beach on the northwest coast. The popular surfing spot is at the bay's center. Here the waves meet a dangerous rocky shelf and exposed reef. Steep and rapid over a seabed with exposed rocks near the beach in winter, the waves pound on shore in heavy foam.

North Shore Beaches

From November through mid-May, the big winter surf on the north shore draws experienced board-surfers from around the world. First surfed in the 1940s by Waikiki surfers on heavy redwood boards, the north shore became popular with surfers using modern boards in the early fifties.

Sunset Beach is a two-mile (3-km) stretch of wide sands where many sections have acquired specific names to indicate surfing sites. Today Sunset refers only to one surfing spot. Public rights-of-way lead to all beaches. Hot spots are east of Hale'iwa town. Moving east up the shoreline, they are:

Laniakea Beach. Between Papa'iloa and Pohaku Loa Way. This beach is named for a freshwater spring and the actual surfing site is off a rocky point to the left. In high winter waters, the fast current in the wide channel on the town side can sweep unwary surfers seaward and rescues are many.

Chun's Reef Beach. On the eastern side of Pohaku Loa Way. Named for a family of surfers, the wave break is on the right side of a mound in the shoreline Pu'u Nenue. One of the most popular north shore surfing sites, the reef is close to shore and meets the beach. In uncommon fashion, a wind called Hukamakani (Wind Whistles) blows here from the mountains instead of the sea.

Waimea Bay Beach. At 61-031 Kamehameha Highway, Waimea. Internationally famous Waimea Bay, with the tallest rideable surf in the world, is the ultimate goal of all big surf riders. The name Waimea refers to the runoff of red soil from Waimea Valley after a heavy rain. Enormous waves, perilous and exciting in the wide deep bay, challenge surfers and spectators alike. When the high surf runs and international competitions are held, huge crowds gather on the beach and on the highway above the bay. When the wave breaks up, it pounds ashore in a crashing roar. Only the most experienced surfers should think about attempting this surf, and then think again before dipping a board into these furious winter waters. In summer Waimea is a flat calm pool with wonderful waters for swimmers.

Banzai Pipeline. At the right side of Banzai Beach, between Ke Waena and Ke Nui Roads, Pupukea. Banzai is the Japanese word for "Ten Thousand Years," an equivalent to Hurrah! Here the winter swell travels through offshore deep water and builds rapidly as it approaches the seabed shelf. The waves are steep, tossing the crests forward to form tubes, or "pipelines." The waves crash onto a shallow reef and many accidents have occurred. The famous surf site is between Banzai beach and 'Ehukai Beach at 59-337 Ke Nui Road, Pupukea. The beach park is the best place to watch surfers in the Banzai Pipeline. *'Ehukai* (Red-tinged water) describes the after-spray of a breaking wave: when sunshine lights the spray, it appears reddish.

Rocky Point. Right of 'Ehukai. Named in 1960 by Australian surfers, this area is favored for quick sessions, when a surfer wants to catch a few waves. **Sunset Beach,** shoreline off the 59-100 section of Kamehameha Highway. Powerful and perilous, the waves here climb to 20 feet (6 m) and break on a dangerous shallow reef. This surf is the site of several annual competitions.

■ M A U I

There are many surfing beaches outside reefs with adequate year-round surf along the western shores of Maui. On the north shore, at the top of the head-shaped knob of west Maui, furious waves make surfing dangerous. Exposed to open ocean and never safe, the boulder-strewn beaches are pounded constantly by heavy surf. Yet some board riders go out in the winter surf that seethes through Honokohau Bay. The road here is a series of switchbacks through gulches and valleys behind the sea cliffs. The best surfing spots probably should be hard to reach. **La Perouse Bay** on the south coast is the hottest spot on Maui. It is past Makena and beyond the end of the paved road. Here the swells and wind are reliable for most of the year, and there always will be a few surfers.

■ H A W A I ' I : B I G I S L A N D

The surfing sites on Hawai'i are best for intermediate and advanced surfers; there are few wave breaks for beginners. The hottest spots are on the western Kona Coast.

Kahalu'u Beach Park. North of Keauhou Bay, off Ali'i Drive, South Kona. This is the beach where Hawaiians once beat the water with vines and prayed for big surf. At the seaward side of the reef outside Kahalu'u Bay, experienced surfers can count on superior waves during periods of high surf. These waves create a rip current that moves north along the rocky shore before dispersing in deeper waters. Surfers caught in this seaward rip must flow with it, then, beyond the surf line, paddle south around it and ride in.

Ke'ei Beach, Palemano Point. South of Kealakekua Bay, South Kona. The seabed is shallow and rocky. Offshore, a 300-yard (274-m) reef fronts the beach, creating the biggest waves and some of the longest rides in the stretch between Napo'opo'o and Honaunau. Here, in 1866 on a one-hour canoe trip, Mark Twain paused to watch whole families of Hawaiians surfing together.

White Sands Beach Park, north of Kahalu'u off Ali'i Drive, South Kona. When high winter surf builds up off Kona, this little pocket of white sand beach is one of the hottest spots in the Hawaiian Islands for experienced bodysurfers. The break is located outside the point opposite the rest rooms building. Here you can ride waves up to ten feet (3 m) without a board.

Spectators crowd the shore for the annual winter Magic Sands Bodysurfing Championship, the only bodysurfing contest held on the Big Island. During winter, White Sands Beach often disappears, washed away by the watery assault. This can happen overnight, giving rise to the beach's other names of Disappearing Beach, Vanishing Sands, and Magic Sands. The beach is rebuilt each year when the big rollers cease.

A kneeboarder submerged in the rolling waters off the Kona Coast.

■ BIG WAVE BOARD SURFING COMPETITIONS

The dates of surfing competitions depend on the size of waves during a scheduled period of time. When the wave measurements indicate big waves, the exact days of the one-to-three-day competitions are determined. The telephone numbers listed give up-to-the-minute information.

October 31—November 15
XCel Pro International. North Shore, O'ahu. 637-6239
Hawaiian Pro Surfing Classic. North Shore, O'ahu. 638-7266

Late November—Mid-December
Triple Crown of Surfing. North Shore, O'ahu. 377-5850. The Triple Crown includes the Hawaiian Pro Men's and Women's event at Ali'i Beach Park, Hale'iwa; the Annual Marui Pipeline Masters at Banzai Pipeline; and the World Cup of Surfing at Sunset Beach.

Early December—Late-February
Quiksilver/Eddie Aikau Memorial Big Wave Classic. Waimea Bay, North Shore, O'ahu. 732-4563. This event is not part of the Triple Crown, although it takes place during the famous triple competition: the Triple Crown takes a day-off on the day the Quiksilver is held. This one-day competition honoring Eddie Aikau is held only when waves reach 20 feet (6 km) or more, and surfers compete by invitation only.

December—February
Makaha Point Challenge. Makaha Beach, Leeward O'ahu. 732-4563
Annual Buffalo's Big Board Surfing Classic. Two-day event where old-timers surf with the old-style huge and heavy wooden surfboards. Rides are fast. Makaha Beach, Leeward O'ahu. 696-0120

TALKING SURF

Surfers like to get together and regale listeners with tales of the wild waves they've surfed. They use English in a style all their own. Here are a few terms to help you decipher their stories.

Aerial	To leave and re-enter a wave.
Backwash	The back-flow of a wave after breaking on the beach.
Bailing out	Jumping off a surfboard to avoid harm.
Close out	A wave breaking all at once along its length; unridable.
Cloud breaks	Big waves that break on an outside reef.
Curl	The curve of the wave's breaking water.
Covered or tucked away	To be inside a wave's curl where the water curves above a surfer's head.
Down the line	A long ride.
Drop in	To take off on a wave another surfer is riding; bad form.
Elephant gun	A giant surfboard used to ride giant waves.
Face	The part of a wave for riding at the wave's inner curve.
Fin or skeg	The rudder beneath the back end of a surfboard.
Free fall	When the surfer drops straight down the curl of the wave, and for a moment surfer and board hang in air.
Hang ten	All ten toes grab the board over the front (or nose) of the surfboard.
Island pull out	Leaving a wave by pushing the front of the surfboard beneath the water's surface.
Inside	The water between the wave break and the beach.
Kick out	Leaving a wave by moving your weight to the back (tail) of the board.
Leash	The cord on the rider's ankle attached to the rear of the surfboard.
Locked in	Standing on the surfboard, inside its curl; the ideal place to be on a wave.

Monolith or monster	An enormous wave.
Over the falls	To be pulled over the crest of a wave and down into roiling whitewash water.
Pearl	Pushing the front of the surfboard beneath the surface, causing the rider to deep-dive before a wave; derived from pearl diving, which implies a mistake, not a deliberate exit.
Quiver	A set of surfboards for differing wave states.
Rails	The edges of the surfboard.
Ripe	An ideal wave.
Roller coaster	The movement of a surfer up and down the wave face.
Shore break	Small waves that break onshore.
Sliding	Slanting to left or right down a wave.
Smokin' a pipe	Tearing down the face of a wave in the tube.
Snake or shoulder hopper	Another surfer who cuts in on a rider's right of way.
Spinner or 360	A turn full-circle.
Soup	Dangerous whitewash breaking water.
Stall	Slowing a surfboard until the wave closes in.
Stoked	Excited, especially after a supreme ride on a supreme wave.
Trough	Bottom slope between two waves.
Tube or pipe	The tunnel-shaped inside curve of a wave.
Tubed or glasshouse	Riding in the wave's smooth hollow area.
Waiting room or line up	The area of ocean swells beyond the breakers where surfers wait to catch waves.
Wall	An enormous wave that cannot be ridden.
Walking the dog	Walking forward and back on a surfboard to change speed.
Walking the nose	Walking on the front (nose) of the surfboard.
Wipe out	Falling off the surfboard during a ride.
Zigzag	Changing rails, shifting weight, while speeding down a wave face.

PRACTICAL INFORMATION

Compass American Guides makes every effort to ensure the accuracy of its information; however, as conditions and prices change frequently, we recommend that readers also contact the Hawai'i Visitors Bureau for the most up-to-date information. On O'ahu, call (808) 923-1811, or write 2270 Kalakaua Ave., Suite 801, (Waikiki Business Plaza) Honolulu, HI 96815. Each island has its own Chamber of Commerce and Visitor's Bureau; a listing of these and other helpful sources of information can be found under "Tourist Information" in this chapter.

■ AREA CODE

The area code for all islands is **808**.

■ GETTING THERE

Honolulu International Airport is the focal point of Pacific travel. Honolulu, the nation's eleventh largest city, is serviced with multiple daily flights by the major domestic carriers and many charters. Neighboring islands are serviced with direct daily flights, and via Honolulu, from U.S. mainland cities.

A dozen foreign airlines service Hawai'i, connecting Honolulu with the mainland, Asia, Australia, and New Zealand. Direct charter flights from Europe are increasing. Service to islands in the South Pacific runs out of Honolulu on U.S.-owned carriers with frequent flights to Samoa, Tahiti, Rarotonga, Guam, and Micronesia.

Luxury cruise ships voyaging in the Pacific regularly stop at Hawaiian ports: Hilo and Kona on the Big Island of Hawai'i; Kahului, Maui; Honolulu, O'ahu; and Nawiliwili, Kaua'i.

■ GETTING AROUND IN THE ISLANDS

BY AIR

Locals treat island hops like taking a bus ride, and you can, too. The five major airports of the Hawaiian Islands are Honolulu, O'ahu; Kahului, Maui; Kona and Hilo airports on the Big Island; and Lihu'e, Kaua'i. Two Honolulu-based companies equipped with wide-bodied jet aircraft, Aloha Airlines and Hawaiian Airlines, service the five major airports with some 200 daily flights each, from 6 A.M. to about 9 P.M. (Late night flights are not made between islands.)

Small piston aircraft also service the islands with multiple daily commuter flights out of Honolulu. They service major airports as well as small ones, the latter including Kamuela on the Big Island; Kapalua and Hana, Maui; Kalaupapa, Moloka'i; Lana'i City, Lana'i; and Princeville, Kaua'i. Aloha IslandAir, a subsidiary of Aloha Airlines, is the largest commuter airline. Small-plane flights are wonderful for close up aerial views.

AUTO RENTALS

The best way to see the islands and travel at your own pace is to rent a car. The state requires a valid driver's license from any signature country to the United Nations Conference on Road and Motor Transport, which very nearly covers the world. Rental agencies require either an English language license or an international driver's license. By state law, seat belts must be used. Safety seats (which can be rented) are required for children under three.

The major domestic car rental agencies are on all islands. Advance reservations are recommended; most have an 800 telephone number. Prices vary and you may want to shop around. Mileage usually is free. There's a drop-off charge for cars returned to a location different from your pick-up point. If you pick up a car in Hilo and drop it off in Kona, there will be a charge.

BUSES

The City and County of Honolulu, which is the entire island of O'ahu, has excellent public transportation on THEBUS. The fare to any destination is the same, and you can ride all the way around the island for one fare. If your stay is extended, you can buy a one-month bus pass at any branch of the *Bank of Hawai'i* (passes are sold at the beginning of each month).

The Big Island of Hawai'i offers an infrequent public bus service between Hilo and Kailua-Kona, and to Volcanoes National Park.

Maui has no public transportation. A free shuttle runs between Ka'anapali and Lahaina, and a private bus operates along the Kihei shore. Kaua'i also has no

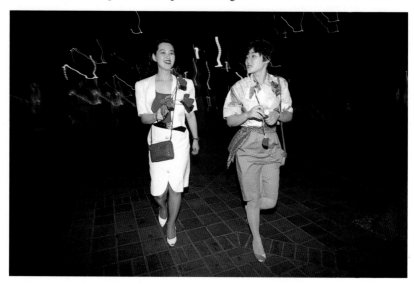

Young Japanese women on holiday in Waikiki.

public transportation. A private shuttle operates between Lihu'e and Po'ipu. Nor does Moloka'i have a bus—though you can ride a mule to Kalaupapa.

CRUISES, FERRIES, AND BOAT TRIPS

Regular inter-island passenger ferries never have been operated on a large scale in the Hawaiian Islands. The open-ocean seas are too rough. However, there are a couple of opportunities to go from one island to another by boat: Between Lahaina, Maui, and Manele, Lana'i, a small 24-passenger boat runs twice-daily round-trips. One way is one-hour. *Expeditions;* Lahaina, Maui; 661-3756. Between Lahaina, Maui, and Kaunakakai, Moloka'i, the **Maui Princess** operates twice daily. One way is one and a quarter hours. *Sea Link of Hawai'i;* Maui: 661-8397; Moloka'i: 553-5736; O'ahu: 533-6899; Mainland: (800) 833-5800.

American-Hawai'i Cruises, 550 Kearny St., San Francisco, CA 94108, (800) 227-3666, sail exclusively in Hawaiian waters on seven-day island voyages. Two cruise ships with accommodations for nearly 800 passengers each, sail out of Honolulu in opposite directions every Saturday night.

As water activities are an integral part of the island experience, the following is a limited list of the various cruises, charters, and diving excursions available:

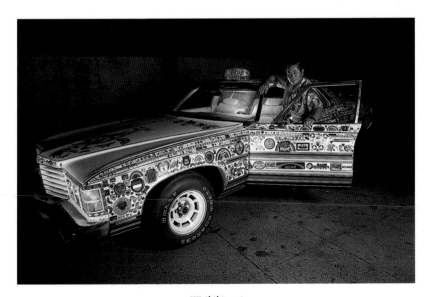

Waikiki taxi.

■ H A W A I ' I (B I G   I S L A N D)
Atlantis Submarine; Kailua-Kona, 329-6626. Captain Cook VII; Kailua-Kona, 329-6411. Captain Zodiac; Kailua-Kona, 329-3199. Hawai'i Sailing Academy; Kailua-Kona, 329-6411. The Party Boat; Kailua-Kona, 329-2177. Whalewatch Cruises; in season, by Hawaiian Cruises, 329-6411.

■ K A U A ' I
Blue Odyssey; 826-9033. Bluewater Sailing; 822-0525. Captain Andy's Sailing Adventures; 822-7833. Kayak Kaua'i; Hanalei, 826-9844. Na Pali Cruise Line; 826-9696. Na Pali Zodiac; Hanalei, 826-9371. Paradise Adventure Cruises; Hanalei, 826-9999. Smith's Motor Boat Service; 822-4111.

■ M A U I
Captain Nemo's Emporium; Lahaina, 661-4743. Captain Zodiac; Lahaina, 667-5351. Club Lana'i; Lahaina, 871-1144. Frogman; Ma'alaea, 667-7622. Lin Wa; glass-bottom "Chinese junk," Lahaina, 661-3392. Ocean Activities Center; Ma'alaea, 879-4485. Pacific Whale Foundation; Kihei, 879-8811. Sea Sails; Ka'anapali, Sheraton Hotel, 667-2759. Trilogy Excursions; Lahaina, 661-4743.

■ O ' A H U
Aikane Catamarans; 552-1533. Atlantis Submarines; 522-1710. Glass Bottom Boats Hawai'i; 537-1958. Jada Yacht Charters; 955-0722. Paradise Snorkeling Adventures; 923-7766. Royal Hawaiian Cruises; 672-4141. Steve's Diving Adventures; 947-8900. Windjammer Cruises; 521-0036.

MOPEDS AND BICYCLES
Moped agencies abound in Waikiki. Rental offices are found on most of the side streets; most are small companies. The only major company renting mopeds is **Budget** and their fees are high. It's best to shop around.

Bicycles are popular. Most cycle shops rent all-speed bikes and some specialize in biking tours. Bike races are sometimes held and information is available from any bike shop in Honolulu, Kona, or Lahaina. Coasting down Haleakala volcano on Maui is a popular bike tour. Companies in Lahaina take bus tour groups up to the summit for the 38-mile ride coasting down from 10,000 feet (3,048 m) to sea level. **Cruiser Bob** is the original company; (800) 654-7717. On the Big Island,

Kona cycle shops rent two-wheelers and offer escorted tours, including cycle-camping tours.

TAXIS
All islands offer taxi services. Fares are based on mileage and there's no charge for additional passengers.

■ CLIMATE

All of the eight main Hawaiian islands are in the tropics. Northeasterly trade winds prevail most of the year, and the climate is generally comfortable. Visitors should beware of taking too much sun; the cooling trades tend to lead you to forget its burning powers. From summer to winter, average temperatures vary slightly. Coastal areas average between 85° F (30° C) and 65° F (20° C). The average year-round temperature of ocean swimming areas is 74° F (25° C) and in summer the waters are around 80° F (27° C).

The heavy rains come between December and March. These winter rains may last all day for several days, or occur only at night. Rainfall varies more by location than with the season. It's an old story in Hawai'i that you can cross to the other side of the street to avoid a shower. In the verdant valleys, daily showers fall in the afternoon.

On every island the windward shores receive more rain than leeward coasts. Volcanic peaks seize the trade winds and block rainclouds from pouring down on the leeward sides. The abundant rain falls on the peaks and on the windward sides. In Hilo, on the windward side of the Big Island, the average annual rainfall is 130 inches (330 cm), making it the rainiest city in the U.S. Conversely, in Kona, on the leeward shore of the same island, you can sunbathe nearly all year long and watch rain clouds drench the slopes just two miles away. Because the volcanic peaks capture the rain, the leeward sides also are the sunniest and driest, with placid ocean waters and an average annual rainfall of 10 to 25 inches (25 to 63 cm).

The trade winds move infrequently from the northeast to the south, when *kona weather* (south wind) comes up. Then, without the cooling trades, you're in for a day or two of sticky weather, or a sudden Kona storm.

On the Big Island in winter, the summits of Mauna Kea and Mauna Loa are white-capped with snow, and atop Haleakala on Maui, the mercury also drops below freezing. Mauna Kea, the tallest mountain, is the coldest spot in the islands. A record low of 11° F (-10° C) has been recorded at the summit observatories; and the highest record there, 66° F (21° C).

A location near the summit of Mount Wai'ale'ale, at an elevation of 5,075 feet (1,547 m), on the island of Kaua'i, holds the world's record for the highest annual average rainfall with an amazing 450 inches (1,143 cm) every year. Only 15 miles (24 km) to the southwest, just leeward of the peaks, lies an arid zone with only 20 inches (51 cm) of rain fall on average, per annum.

■ ACCOMMODATIONS

Hawai'i offers a wide range of lodging facilities across a spectrum of prices and amenities. The travel experience you plan will determine the type of accommodation. When choosing a destination, plans should include a decision whether to stay at simple lodgings while making day trips on an island, a luxury resort where you stay close to its activities, or a combination of the two. Every island except Hawai'i is sufficiently compact and you can return from any day trip to home-plate.

Halekulani Hotel and Pool, Waikiki.

(opposite) The total eclipse in 1990 filled hotels on all the islands.

The Big Island is another matter. Distances are great. Here you can base part of your time in Kona or Kohala in the west, and part in Hilo in the east, then make day trips. Better still, if you are adventurous and want to see Hawai'i thoroughly, drive your rental car all the way around, staying in small inns of country towns. Before statehood, jet planes, and resort complexes, family-operated lodging houses catered to traveling salesmen who brought their wares into rural towns. While only a few remain, they are strategically located, the tariffs are low, the rooms basic and clean, and the old-time island atmosphere is relaxed and friendly. These lodgings are not for everyone—there may or may not be a TV in the room and probably there is only one telephone. Neither are there *mai tais,* room service, or movie moguls as fellow guests, although you might meet a tractor or feed salesman. Some inns have cavernous restaurant-bars where you can hear the lilting inflections of local pidgin.

A selective list of accommodations follows. Most are listed under town names; in those cases town names are not included in addresses. Reservations always are recommended. Rental cars often can be included in packages. There is an **808 area code** for all the Hawaiian Islands. Prices, based on double occupancy per night, are indicated as follows:

B = Budget, up to $60; M = Moderate, $60–120; L = Luxury, over $120.

■ HAWAI'I (BIG ISLAND)
There are 68 Bed & Breakfast establishments on the island. Representing 38 B & Bs, *My Island* publishes a pamphlet; Box 100, Volcano, HI 96785; 967-7110. Daily, weekly, and monthly rates; B–M

CAPTAIN COOK
Manago Hotel. Family-managed, right on Hwy. 11, with plenty of old-island atmosphere and an international following. Original frame building and 3-story modern wing with ocean views of Kealakekua Bay; the Japanese Room has beautiful decor with an *ofuro* (Japanese bath); airy local restaurant. Near Pu'uhonua O Honaunau National Historical Park, Box 145, HI 96704; 323-2642; B

HILO
Dolphin Bay Hotel. Residential area four blocks above downtown; color TV, fans, kitchens, sunken baths. 333 Ili'ahi St., HI 96720; 935-1466; B

Hilo Hawaiian Hotel. Modern highrise overlooking Coconut Island. 71 Banyan Dr., HI 96720; 935-9361; (800) 367-5004; M

Naniloa Hotel. Largest Hilo hotel; modern highrise. 93 Banyan Dr., HI 96720; 969-3333; (800) 367-5360; M

Waiakea Villas. Set amid gardens and ponds; some rooms with kitchens; weekly rates available; shops and restaurants. 400 Hualani St., HI 96720; 961-2841; B

HONOKA'A

Hotel Honoka'a Club. Family-managed, old-style island lodging popular with the *paniolo.* Ten basic rooms with mountain views; cavernous restaurant and bar. Book well in advance. Box 185, HI 96727; 775-0678; B

HOLUALOA

Holualoa Inn. Large modern wood building, B & B; 4 rooms. Pool, billiards, TV in lounge. Box 222, HI 96725; 324-1121; M

KAILUA-KONA

There are more condos than hotels from Kailua to Keauhou, many managed by rental agencies which publish a brochure or partial listing. A good agency is *Kona Vacation Resorts,* 77-6435 Kuakini Hwy., HI 96740; 329-6488; (800) 367-5168; B–L

Hotel King Kamehameha. Large hotel on the only beach in town; historic Kamehameha the Great site; excellent exhibit of artifacts. 75-5660 Palani Rd., HI 96740; 329-2911; M–L

Kanaloa at Kona. Owned by Colony Hotels & Resorts; 118 deluxe 1, 2, and 3 bedroom suites. 78-261 Manukai St., HI 96740; 322-2272; L

Kona Hilton. Large hotel in sweeping design; tasteful. Fine pool. 75-5776 Kuakini Hwy., HI 96740; 329-3181; M–L

Kona Seaside Hotel. Modern 6-story wing and an older wing. 75-5646 Palani Rd., HI 96740; 329-2455; B

Kona Village. On beautiful beach at foot of old lava flow. Elegant bungalows, gardens. Water activities; famous buffets. Exclusive and expensive. Box 1299, HI 96745; 325-5555; (800) 367-5290. Inter-island: (800) 432-5450; L

KAMUELA (WAIMEA)

Kamuela Inn. Located in the cool uplands, its best feature is the third-floor penthouse for up to 6 people; full kitchen, fireplace, cable TV; private lanai (patio), no telephone. Box 1994, HI 96743; 885-4243; M

Parker Ranch Lodge. Mainland style motel-type lodgings; 20 rooms with kitchenettes, AC, KS-beds, telephones, and large TVs. In town, next door to Paniolo Country Restaurant. Box 458, HI 96743; 885-4100; M

KOHALA COAST

This is the area of glamorous resort complexes and golf courses that rise out of lava fields. They offer complete amenities and services; tours, shops, and restaurants.

Mauna Kea Hotel. The doyen of this elegant, art-filled locale, on Kauna'oa Bay. The hotel has maintained its original atrium-design; built by Laurance Rockefeller. Box 218, HI 96743; 882-7222; (800) 882-6060. American Plan; L

Mauna Lani Resort. Includes **Mauna Lani Bay Hotel and Bungalows,** Box 4000, HI 96743; 885-6622, (800) 992-7987; and the **Ritz-Carlton,** 1 N. Kaniku, HI 96743; 885-2000; L

Waikoloa Resort. Includes the **Hyatt Regency,** resembling a theme park; swim with dolphins; HC02 Box 5500, HI 96743; 885-1234; and the **Royal Waikoloan Hotel;** HC02 Box 5300, HI 96743; 885-6789; L

NA'ALEHU

Shirakawa Motel. Southernmost lodging in the U.S.; rural; 13 motel-type lodgings set amid hibiscus. Near Mark Twain's Monkeypod tree. Box 467, HI 96722; 929-7462; B

PUNALU'U

Sea Mountain. At Punalu'u; well furnished units with standard amenities; adjoins golf course. There are 76 units although some are time-share; restaurant. Box 70, Pahala, HI 96777; 928-8301; (800) 367-8047; M

VOLCANO

Chalet Kilauea. B & B in a former manor home; 3 rooms and treehouse; fireplace; library; French spoken. Box 998, HI 96785; 967-7786; M; 967-7216; B

Volcano House. Unlike mainland national parks, there are no large hotel facilities within park boundaries in the islands. The one exception is this hotel across from the park headquarters; sited on the rim of Kilauea caldera. Ordinary rooms with views that are not what they could be; large restaurant often filled with group tours at lunchtime; fireplace lounge. Box 53, Hawai'i Volcanoes National Park, HI 96713; 967-7321; M

W A I P I ' O

Tom Araki's. This no-name, 5-room hotel is the ultimate in basic in nearly inaccessible Waipi'o, the Valley of the Kings. Surrounded by ginger and fruit trees, located beside lotus and taro farm. Plenty of charm and no electricity. Kerosene lamps, Coleman stoves in basement kitchen; shower and commode at end of hall. No hot running water. Bring your own food, bedroll and towel. Mail: 25 Malama Pl., Hilo, HI 96720; 775-0368 Waipi'o; 935-7466 Hilo; B

Hamakua Hideaway. Modern bungalow above Waipi'o with fine view. Kitchen, fireplace, sunken tub. Often rented by the month. Box 5104, Honoka'a, HI 96727; 775-7425; M

■ K A U A ' I

Due to storm damage from Hurricane Iniki, some hotels and resorts may be closed. Good sources for condos are *Aston Hotels & Resorts,* 2255 Kuhio Ave., Honolulu, HI 96815; (800) 321-2558; and *Colony Hotels & Resorts,* 11340 Blondo St., Omaha, NB 68164; (800) 777-1700.

H A N A L E I

Hanalei Bay Resort. Set in 22 acres of north shore hillside; fine views; walk down to beach. Standard amenities; 2 pools. HI 96714; M–L

K A P A ' A

Lae Nani. Owned by Colony Hotels & Resorts; tropical, beachfront resort with 84 suites, featuring full kitchens. 410 Papaloa Rd., Kapa'a, Kaua'i, 96746; 822-4938; L

L I H U ' E

Tip Top Motel. Motel-type lodging in town; no pool. Join locals in the restaurant, famous for its cookies. 3173 Akahi St., HI 96766; 245-2333; B

Westin Kaua'i Hotel. On beautiful Kalapaki Bay beach, Nawiliwili. Greco-Roman design glitzy resort with marble beasts, antiques, and howling birds.

The highrise that led to Kaua'i's height limitation of buildings to no taller than a coconut tree. Boat and Clydesdale horse carriage rides through gardens. Kalapaki Beach, HI 96766; 245-5050; (800) 228-3000; L

PO'IPU

The Po'ipu Beach Resort Association is a good information source; brochure; Box 730, Koloa, HI 96756; 742-7444. Condos: *R & R Rentals,* RR1, Box 70, Koloa, HI 96756; 742-7555; (800) 367-8022; M–L

Garden Isle Cottages. Above Koloa Landing; 7 cottages and 2 houses, 1 with lap pool. Paintings by owner. Studios with refrigerator; 1 & 2 BR with kitchens. 2666 Pu'uholo Rd., HI 96756; 742-6717 daily until noon; M

Hyatt Regency Kaua'i. Resort and spa opened end of 1990. Comfortable atmosphere. Dining in open-sided huts over lagoon. Paddling in lagoon. Fresh & saltwater pools. Golf, tennis, riding. 1591 Po'ipu Rd., HI 96756; 742-1234; (800) 233-1234; L

Sheraton Kaua'i Beach Resort. Facing the ocean; and **Sheraton Kaua'i Garden Hotel** facing inland. *Koi* (carp) ponds; 2 pools; ocean gear and activities. Modified American Plan available. 2440 Ho'onani Rd., HI 96756; 742-1661; (800) 325-3535; L

Stouffer Waiohai Beach Resort. Extensive ocean activities; scuba instruction. Fine amenities; 2 pools, wading pool, health club. 2249 Po'ipu Rd., HI 96756; 742-9511; (800) 468-3571; L

PRINCEVILLE

Here there are 10 condo complexes. A good source is *Blue Water Vacation Rentals,* Princeville Shopping Ctr., Box 366, HI 96722; 826-9229; (800) 628-5533; M–L

Sheraton Princeville. Recently renovated. European antiques and marble decor redeemed by scenic views of Hanalei Bay. Full amenities; a golfer's paradise. Box 3069, or 5520 Kahaku Rd., HI 96722; 826-9644, (800) 325-3535; L

WAILUA

Coco Palms Resort. Located in a coconut grove; known internationally for its old-Hawai'i charm and traditions. Elvis filmed *Blue Hawaii* here. Wedding chapel and small museum. Box 631, Lihu'e, HI 96766; 822-4921; M–L

■ LANA'I

There are exactly 3 lodging selections on the island. Two are new, owned by Dole Food Co. and operated by Rockresorts, who run a shuttle between them.

The Lodge at Ko'ele. The state's only new mountain hotel. Designed like a Victorian country manor; fine woods in central great hall; luxurious rooms and butler-serviced suites; putting course; golf course amid pines, opened in 1992. Tours, horseback riding, pool & spa. Box 774, Ko'ele HI 96763; 565-7300; (800) 321-4666; L

Manele Bay Hotel. A seaside villa with modern, airy rooms overlooking Hulopo'e Bay, the island's best beach. More Rockresort elegance. Address and phone numbers same as Ko'ele; L

Hotel Lana'i. Cozy mountain lodge built by Dole in early twenties. 10 basic rooms, some with *lanai* (patio); TV in lounge. Box A119, 565-7211; B

■ MAUI

The west coast is awash in condos, especially at Kihei and Napili. A reliable source is *Aston Hotels & Resorts*. Packages offered throughout Maui; children up to 18 usually free. 2255 Kuhio Ave., Honolulu, HI 96815; (800) 321-2558; M–L

HANA

Hotel Hana Maui. At Hana Ranch on the secluded east end. Originally an exclusive resort for millionaires, it still is posh and expensive. Beautifully appointed bungalows; standard amenities. Many outdoor activities (the hotel also arranges east end activities for non-guests). Hana Ranch, HI 96713; 248-8211; L

KA'ANAPALI

Embassy Suites Resort Ka'anapali. 413 spacious suites with wet bars, stereo, standard amenities. Landscaped oceanfront. 104 Ka'anapali Shores Pl., Lahaina, HI 96761; 661-2000; (800) 464-6284; L

Hyatt Regency Maui. Premier hotel on the strip for those who like Greco-Roman design. 720 rooms with standard amenities, shops, restaurants, and health club. Pool has curving waterslide, grotto, and bar with seating in the water. 200 Nohea Kai Dr., Lahaina, HI 96761; 661-1234; (800) 233-1234. L

Ka'anapali Beach Hotel. 431 rooms with standard amenities, shops, and restaurants. 2525 Ka'anapali Pkwy., Lahaina, HI 96761; 661-0011; M–L

Royal Lahaina Resort. The only Ka'anapali hotel that's not boxed in by other hotels. 521 rooms and bungalows with kitchens on broad grounds and beach; standard amenities; 3 pools, 11 tennis courts (6 lighted). 2780 Kekaa Dr., Lahaina, HI 96761; 661-3611; L

K A H U L U I

Maui Seaside Hotel. Town hotel with standard amenities, pool. Car packages available. 100 Ka'ahumanu Ave., HI 96732; 877-3311; B–M

K A P A L U A

Kapalua Bay Hotel & Villas. Elegant luxury resort complex; 194 rooms and condos, 2 pools, 3 restaurants; 3 beaches; shops; golf. 1 Bay Dr., HI 96761; 669-5656; (800) 367-8000; L

L A H A I N A

Maui Islander. 372 rooms and condos in gardens about 3 blocks inland from Front St.; standard amenities, pool. 660 Waine'e St., HI 96761; 667-9766; M

Maui Plantation Inn. Victorian style B & B in town; 9 rooms decorated with antiques and stained glass. Breakfast in Gerard's French restaurant downstairs. 174 Lahainaluna Rd., HI 96761; 667-9225; M

Napili Shores. Owned by Colony Hotels & Resorts; tropical beachfront resort with 152 units, featuring lanais and full kitchens. 5315 Honoapi'ilani Hwy., HI 96761; 669-8061; L

Pioneer Inn. 48 rooms facing harbor; original building has surrounding veranda on second floor; noisy though plenty of local color; outdoor covered restaurant and bar with live music. 658 Wharf St., HI 96761; 661-3636; B–M

U P C O U N T R Y

Kula Lodge. Attached bungalows; some with fireplaces. Restaurant; paintings of Curtis Wilson Cost in gallery downstairs. RR1, Box 475, Kula, HI 96790; 878-1535; M

W A I L E A - M A K E N A

Offering 2,739 rooms, suites, villas, and condos on 1500 acres along 5 beaches; there are 6 properties in the Wailea complex: **Destination Resorts; Four Seasons**

Resort; Grand Hyatt Resort & Spa; Inter-Continental Resort; Kea Lani Hotel; Maui and Stouffer Wailea Beach Resort. The *Wailea Destination Association* is the source for this area; brochure. 3750 Wailea Alanui, HI 96753; 879-4258; (800) 782-5642. Good packages for families, seniors; M–L

Maui Prince. At Makena near end of the paved road. Japanese style; heavy walls surrounding tropical courtyard; 300 rooms with standard amenities; ocean views. 5400 Makena Alanui, HI 96753; 874-1111; L

■ MOLOKA'I

KAUNAKAKAI

Hotel Moloka'i. Polynesian style on south shore; 55 rooms with fans, refrigerators; no TV. Pool, restaurant. Box 546, HI 96748; 553-5347; B–M

Pau Hana Inn. In town; basic rooms in longhouse; poolside rooms; 1 beachfront suite. Wonderful old-island flavor in restaurant-bar; live music on weekends. Box 546, HI 96748; 553-5342. O'ahu: 536-7545; B–M

WEST END

Kaluako'i Hotel & Golf Club. Owned by Colony Hotels & Resorts of Hawai'i; Polynesian-style resort; 300 rooms and condos with standard amenities, pool, tennis, bicycles, golf course. Uncrowded area; transportation from airport. P.O. Box 1977, Kepuhi Beach, HI 96770; 552-2555; (800) 777-1700; L

■ O'AHU

There are more visitor accommodations on this island than any other in Hawai'i, concentrated mainly around the beach at Waikiki. (See "Waikiki" below.)

DIAMOND HEAD

Diamond Head. Owned by Colony Resorts & Hotels; deluxe 14-story, European-style, ocean front hotel. 2947 Kalakau Ave., HI 96895; 922-1928; L

KAHALA

Kahala Hilton. Luxury resort hotel in residential area. Dolphins in lagoon. Golfer's haven; site of annual Hawaiian Open Tournament. 5000 Kahala Ave., Honolulu, HI 96816; 734-2211; (800) 445-8667; L

LEEWARD O'AHU

Sheraton Makaha Resort & Country Club. In Makaha Valley; the only hotel on the leeward coast. Sheraton high standards with 2 golf courses. Wai'anae, HI 96792; 695-9511; (800) 325-3535; M–L

WAIKIKI

Sixty-nine thousand hotel and condo units available. According to a state source, Honolulu takes first rank in occupancy percentages—some 86 percent (the national average is about 65 percent), and reservations are recommended. Packages are numerous, for rooms, family suites or condos; standard amenities, pools, restaurants; with and without kitchenettes. Children under 17 usually free. Wide range of budget lodgings; B–L. Headquarters for sources are in Waikiki (Honolulu, HI 96815). Some are: *Aston Hotels & Resorts,* 2255 Kuhio Ave.; (800) 321-2558. *Outrigger Hotels* (22 hotels in Waikiki), 2375 Kuhio Ave.; (800) 733-7777. *Sheraton Hotels* (5 hotels); (800) 325-3535. *Hilton Hotels* (large Waikiki complex at Hilton Hawaiian Village); (800) 445-8667.

Three elegant hotels are on the beach: **Sheraton's Royal Hawaiian,** the doyen "Pink Lady of Waikiki," dignified, with a dining terrace right at the beach, and beach-side ballroom; and the **Moana-Surfrider,** the first Waikiki hotel, carefully restored in 1991. Open, airy and light; terrace dining. Breezeway on 6th floor of the Moana. Both have the feeling of gracious Hawai'i; contact Sheraton: (800) 325-3535. The **Halekulani Hotel** is the premier hotel in the Hawaiian Islands, airy and posh with state-of-the-art computerized services. 2199 Kalia Rd., Honolulu, HI 96815; 923-2311; (800) 367-2343; M–L

Boutique hotels pack elegance into spacious rooms and luxurious corporate suites with mirrors, glass and wood, marble and metal; top amenities, decorative art, and fine restaurants.

Waikiki Joy Hotel. (Boutique); 320 Lewers St., HI 96815; 923-2300; (800) 733-5569; M–L

Park Plaza Hotel. (Boutique); 1956 Ala Moana Blvd., HI 96815; 941-7275; (800) 367-6070; M–L

Waikiki Royal Suites. (Boutique); only all-suite hotel in Waikiki; 225 Beach Walk, HI 96815; 926-5641; (800) 535-0085; L

WINDWARD O'AHU

Turtle Bay Hilton & Country Club. The only complete resort on the windward coast. Normal Hilton; golf, tennis and riding. Kahuku, Oʻahu, HI 96731; 293-8811; (800) 445-8667; M–L

■ SPAS

■ HAWAIʻI

Anara Spa. Separate saunas for men and women, steam room, cold baths, lounge areas with Jacuzzi. Massage. Full beauty salon services, nutrition and meditation training. A facility with 25,000 square feet. Hyatt Regency Waikoloa, Waikoloa Beach Dr., Kohala Coast, HI 96743; 885-1234

Ritz-Carlton. Separate saunas for men and women, steam and workout rooms. Massage and loofah scrubs. Full beauty salon services. A stress program featuring the *Moor Back Treatment*. Mauna Lani Hotel Spa, N. Kaniku Dr., Kohala Coast, HI 96743; 885-2000

Paradise Spa. A smaller spa beside the swimming pool. The workout room does not offer classes. Jacuzzi, cold baths, wet and dry saunas. Three types of massage offered: Swedish, shiatsu and *lomilomi* (Hawaiian). Naniloa Hotel, 93 Banyan Dr., Hilo, HI 96720; 969-3333; (800) 367-5360

■ KAUAʻI

Anara Spa. Low-impact aerobic classes, 25-meter lap pool, workout rooms. Separate facilities for men and women: sauna, steam and Jacuzzi. Full beauty salon services. Diet and fitness programs. Massage and Hawaiian *ti* leaf wraps. Snack bar. Hyatt Regency Kauaʻi (Poʻipu), 1571 Poʻipu Road, Koloa, HI 96756; 742-1234; (800) 233-1234

Prince Rejuvenation Spa. An addition to the new Prince Golf Course clubhouse. Aerobics, fitness and lifestyle programs. Massage and hydrotherapy. Hiking, kayaking, horse riding and bicycling. A 15,000 square ft. (4,572 m) facility operated by the Paris-based *Institut de Beaute*. Sheraton Princeville Hotel, P.O. Box 3069, Princeville, HI 96722, 826-9644; (800) 325-3535

■ MAUI

Hotel Hana-Maui Wellness Center. Programs for physical and spiritual wellbeing. Water exercises in a 25-meter lap pool. Workout room, planned hiking. Massage. P. O. Box 8, Hana, HI 96713, 248-8211

Spa Grande. Workout rooms, racquetball and squash courts. Jacuzzi, pool, sauna and steam rooms. Fitness and nutrition programs. Full beauty salon services. Massage: 42 treatment rooms for various types of therapies and baths, including *Maui Mud.* Restaurant, 2 juice bars, cosmetic shop. A multi-level facility with 50,000 square feet. Grand Hyatt Wailea, Maui, 3850 Wailea Alanui Dr., Wailea, HI 96753; 875-1234

■ O'AHU

The Plantation Spa. In a rural section of windward O'ahu, this destination spa is located on 7 acres of lawn and forest at the foot of the Ko'olau Mountains. Quiet cottages for 18 guests. Vegetarian menu; no coffee or sodas. Pool exercises, yoga and kayaking. Supervised dieting, Swedish massage, evening programs. 51-550 Kamehameha Highway, Ka'a'awa, HI 96730; 237-8685

■ EATING HAWAIIAN STYLE

Elegant, romantic dining is widely available on all islands, and in Waikiki you can eat in almost any language. Or, choose from other categories throughout the islands—family-type ethnic restaurants, diners, fast food emporia, glitzy discos and "yuppie" nouvelle cuisine establishments. In the tradition of fine restaurant dining, impressive views and fine service enhance cuisine made with fresh home-grown and imported ingredients.

Yet the most interesting eating is "local food," a catch-all description for a blend of ethnic tastes. Dishes such as Hawaiian style chopped steak, *saimin* (Japanese; broth with noodles, scallions, and fishcake) or *chicken adobo* (Filipino style), are favored by the general populace, and by suit-and-tie attorneys or legislators, business executives, and beach buffs.

The "Hawaiian plate lunch" is the way to explore this unique culinary experience. Begun in World War II when fleets of lunch wagons offered meals to wartime workers who toiled around the clock, plate lunches are modelled on the Japanese *bento* (cold box lunch) with one big difference—hot, home cooked meals.

The epitome of the Hawaiian plate lunch is beef stew and rice. Or, try a microcosm of Hawai'i's people in a "mixed plate," for example: sweet and sour spareribs (Chinese), chicken *katsu* (Japanese), *Kalua* pig (Hawaiian), and a side order of *kim chee* (Korean). Choose any combination you'd like from an enormous selection that includes pork or chicken *teriyaki, kalbi* (Korean) shortribs, oyster-sauce chicken (Chinese) chili and rice, mahimahi fish with 2 wedges of lemon and tartar sauce, *manapua* (Chinese steamed bun with sweet pork filling), jumbo shrimp, American roast turkey, stuffed cabbage, or a tuna sandwich. Whatever you select for your plate lunch, it will come heaped on a paper plate together with two constants: "two scoops rice" and a scoop of macaroni salad.

Dispensed from painted wagons at busy locations, an entire family conducts the operation. Preparing the food at home (kitchens are inspected and licensed by the health department) at 4 in the morning, by 9 A.M. they're ready for business. In a set-up that takes only 20 minutes, a generator is hooked up, an awning extended and relishes placed on the counter. Dozens of entrees shelved in every nook and cranny of the wagon are stacked above sodas and "shave ice."

The late 1970s brought high-powered competition to the wagons when mainland fast food franchises erupted all over the cities and towns of the islands. While the new arrivals eventually levelled off, the Hawaiian plate lunch goes on, endemic to these islands. Local franchisers have adapted in curious ways: At the Zippy's on north Vineyard Street in Honolulu—where the decor is trendy, and instead of a wagon's cardboard display sign there's colored neon—valet parking is offered to the busy Hawaiian Plate Lunch trade.

■ RESTAURANTS

In the Hawaiian Islands, American, Polynesian, Oriental, and European foods reflect the ethnic population mix. Local food is a traditional gift; don't be surprised if your seatmate on an inter-island flight is carrying taro chips from the Big Island, Tip Top cookies from Kaua'i, potato chips from Maui, honey from Moloka'i, or a cake from Dee Lite Bakery on O'ahu. On mainland flights they may be hauling a shopping bag crammed with bags of *poi* and crack seed, chocolate macadamia nut coffee, and a box of *mochi* crunch.

Restaurant diners and game fishing enthusiasts usually encounter the Hawaiian names for local fish. The most popular menu entree (the main course) is mahimahi, or dolphin fish (dorado), not to be confused with dolphin mammals. Others are:

Ahi	Yellowfin tuna	*Kawakawa*	Bonito (little tuna)
Aku	Skipjack tuna	*Mano*	Shark
Akule	Mackerel	*Onaga*	Red snapper
'Ama'ama	Gray mullet	*Ono*	Wahoo
A'u	Pacific marlin	*Opakapaka*	Pink snapper
	(swordfish)	*Uhu*	Parrotfish
Awa	Milkfish	*Uku*	Gray snapper
Kahala	Amberjack,	*Ulua* or *Papio*	Jack fish
	yellowtail		

The following restaurants, bistros, delis and coffee shops are a selective list for each island. The dress code almost always is casual. A very few luxury restaurants require jacket and tie. There is an **808 area code** for all the islands. Reservations are recommended at moderate and fine dining establishments. Prices for one, excluding liquor and tip, are indicated as follows:

B = Budget, up to $12; M = Moderate, $13–24; L = Luxury, $25 and above.

■ HAWAI'I (BIG ISLAND)
CAPTAIN COOK
Manago Restaurant. Local, family style favorite serving simple Japanese and American food; delicious fresh fish. Manago Hotel; 323-2642; B

HILO
Harrington's. Seafood and Italian-American menu in "yuppie" atmosphere serving dinner only. 125 Kalaniana'ole; 961-4966; M

Ken's Pancake House. American coffee shop; good Belgian waffles. 1730 Kamehameha Ave.; 935-8711; B

Restaurant Fuji. Japanese food served at poolside or indoors. Hilo Hotel, 142 Kino'ole St.; 961-3733; B–M

Roussels. French creole cuisine served in a decor of polished hardwood, columns, arches and high ceilings. Famous for blackened fresh mahimahi and poor-boy seafood French bread sandwiches. 60 Keawe St.; 935-5111; M

HONOKA'A
Tex Drive Inn and Restaurant. Famous for *malasadas* (Portugese donuts without holes). Take-out and sit-down, local style food. Hwy. 19; 775-0598; B

KAILUA-KONA

Fisherman's Landing. Garden fantasy with three outside dining rooms and four inside. Local style stir-fry, Poke Hawaiian raw fish; fresh fish. Good views and value. On Aliʻi Dr. at Kona Inn Shopping Village; 326-2555; B–M

Huggo's. Long-time favorite for grilled American food; beside the shore in town. Aliʻi Dr.; 329-1493; M–L

Jameson's by the Sea. Wonderful fresh seafood served in tasteful light and open decor; continental menu. Oceanfront. Aliʻi Dr. at Magic Sands Beach; 329-3195; M

Kona Galley. Fishing decor is the backdrop for a seafood menu. In town on Aliʻi Dr.; 329-4077; M

Kona Ranch House. American food and atmosphere; coffee shop/steak house. Great breakfasts. Palani Rd.; 329-7061; B

La Bourgogne. With blue velvet booths, dark wood and flowery decor; French food is served from an à la carte menu. Dinner only. Nalani St. in Kuakini Plaza South; 329-6711; M–L

Phillip Paolo's. Italian decor and Italian food. Kona Waterfront Row, No. 2; 329-4436; M

Reuben's Mexican Restaurant. Wide selection of Mexican dishes. In town at Kona Plaza. W. Aliʻi Dr.; 392-7031; B

KAMUELA (WAIMEA)

Edelweiss. Owner-chef, Hans-Peter Hager, draws diners island-wide. International menu popular with meat-eaters. Swiss chalet-like decor with *koa* wood and high ceilings. Kawaihae Rd.; 885-6800; M

Merriman's. Draws diners island-wide for fresh fish and Pacific cuisine; fresh local produce; game in season. Opelo Plaza, Hwy. 19; 885-6822; M

Paniolo Country Inn. American coffee shop with *paniolo* decor. Hwy. 19; 885-4377; B

KOHALA COAST

Batik Restaurant. Elegant dining with Indonesian decor and continental menu; dinner only. Jacket and tie required. Mauna Kea Beach Hotel; 882-7222; L

Canoehouse. Oceanfront with fine views of the coast; seafood and Pacific cuisine. Mauna Lani Bay Hotel; 885-6622; L

Donatoni's. In flashy Hyatt Regency decor, the most expensive pasta on the island; dinner only. Hyatt Regency Waikoloa; 885-1234; L

Gallery Restaurant. Casual fine dining in glass-walled small room with fine views. Fresh seafood, American sauces, Hawaiian plate, and wide selection of fruit desserts. Mauna Lani Resort Racquet Club; 885-7777; M

Garden. Airy, elegant dining, even at breakfast; international and health-aware menu. Jacket and tie required. Mauna Kea Beach Hotel; 882-7222; M–L

Grill Restaurant & Lounge. Dinner-dancing; American menu; dinner only. Mauna Lani Resort's Ritz Carlton; 885-2000; M–L

Terrace. Open-sided, overlooking the beach (converts to Japanese restaurant at night). The mother of lunch buffets in the islands; American food. Mauna Kea Beach Hotel; 882-7222; M

Tiare Room. Elegant dining with ocean views; continental menu; dinner only. Royal Waikoloan Hotel; 885-6789; L

PUNALU'U

Punalu'u Black Sands Restaurant. Overlooks black sand beach. Continental menu; the only fine dining within miles. Sea Mountain at Punalu'u; 928-8528; L

VOLCANO

Kilauea Lodge & Restaurant. A nice alternative to the only other real restaurant in this area. American and continental menu; dinner only. Volcano Village; 967-7366; M

Volcano House. On the rim of Kilauea caldera. Some tables with fine views. Standard American menu. Hawaii Volcanoes National Park; 967-7321; M

■ KAUA'I

Some restaurants may be under repair due to Hurricane Iniki.

HA'ENA

Charo's. Wide glass windows offer fine north shore views. Local ingredients for fresh fish sauces; continental and Spanish menu reflects the owner, entertainer Charo. Good *pupu* (canapes). Colony Resort, Kuhio Hwy.; 826-6422; M

HANALE'I

Foong Wong. Standard Chinese food. In Ching Young Village; 826-6996; B

Hanalei Dolphin. Fresh fish served in rural atmosphere beside the river; dinner only. Kuhio Hwy.; 826-6113; M

KILAUEA
Casa di Amici. Fine Italian dining in country town on the north shore. Fresh local ingredients. 2484 Keneke Rd.; 828-1388. M

LIHU'E
Club Jetty. On jetty extending over water at Nawiliwili. Family restaurant in early evening; the lounge is traditional hangout for local night life; disco. Cantonese food is incidental to atmosphere here; dinner only. 245-4970; B
Cook's at the Beach. Poolside with ocean view; serves American and Mexican food; known for its Cajun french fries. In the Westin Kaua'i mega-resort at Kalapaki Beach; 245-5050; B–M
Gaylord's. Al fresco dining in courtyard of restored plantation manager's home. American menu; game in season served amid tropical greenery. At Kilohana Sq. in Puhi area, 3-2087 Kaumuali'i Hwy.; 245-9593; M
Kiibo Restaurant. Japanese country decor. Simple, local Japanese food; try the green-tea ice cream. 2991 Umi St.; 245-2650; B
Masters. Elegant French restaurant in the Westin Kaua'i mega-resort at Kalapaki Beach; 245-5058; L
Sharky's Fish Market. Seafood house with fine oceanfront views. At Kaua'i Lagoons, 3100 Kapule Hwy.; 246-4470; M
Tip Top Cafe & Bakery. Coffee shop where macadamia nut cookies were invented; known for traditional oxtail soup. Local hangout. 3173 Akahi St.; 245-2333; B

PO'IPU - KOLOA
Breakers. Standard Sheraton American menu at the Sheraton Kaua'i; dinner only. Po'ipu Beach; 741-1661; M
Brennecke's Beach Broiler. Upstairs with wide windows and excellent ocean view. Good food at the beach; seafood appetizers and steak burgers. Across road from Po'ipu Beach Park, 2100 Ho'one Rd.; 742-7588; B
Plantation Gardens. Old plantation atmosphere with photos; veranda lounge; ocean view. Seafood and American menu served in garden. At Kiahuna Plantation, 2253 Po'ipu Rd.; 742-1695, M–L
Tamarind. One of two top restaurants on the island. Formal decor and service. Continental menu with fresh local ingredients, fresh fish; tasteful decor. Dinner only. Stouffer Waiohai Beach Resort, 2249 Po'ipu Rd.; 742-9511; L

Tide Pools. Casual elegance in decor; American menu with fresh ingredients. Dinner only. At the Hyatt Regency Kaua'i, Koloa; 742-1234; M

Waiohai Terrace. One of two top restaurants on the island. Open-air, beachside with ocean view, informal. Continental menu; delicious Sunday brunch. Stouffer Waiohai Beach Resort, 2249 Po'ipu Rd.; 742-9511; M

PRINCEVILLE

Bali Hai Restaurant. Casual atmosphere with live entertainment; fine view of Hanalei Bay. Continental menu. At Hanalei Bay Resort, 5380 Hono'iki Rd.; 826-7333; M

Beamreach. Seafood and steak house; standard, limited American menu. Dinner only. Pali Ke Kua, 5300 Ka Haku Rd.; 826-9131; M

Cafe Hanalei. American coffee shop. Sheraton Princeville Hotel; 826-9644; B–M

La Cascata. Latin American food and decor; dinner only. Sheraton Princeville Hotel; 826-9644; M–L

WAILUA

Lagoon Dining Room. Open-sided, airy Polynesian decor; American menu with fresh local ingredients. Coco Palms Resort Hotel; 822-4921; M–L

Smith's Tropical Paradise. Polynesian decor; American fare; fresh fish. Operated by same family that runs boats up Wailua river to the grotto. Dinner only. Wailua Marina State Park; 822-4654; M–L

Wailua Marina Restaurant. Simple, family style with local American-Oriental menu. Nice river view. Tour buses stop here. Wailua State Park, 5971 Kuhio Hwy.; 822-4311; B

■ MAUI

HANA

Hana Ranch Restaurant. One of two restaurants in Hana. Local plate lunches and take-out counter. Good ocean view from outdoor tables. Across road from post office; 248-8255; M

Hotel Hana Maui Dining Room. Fine dining; garden views. Fresh fish and local ingredients; game in season; continental and Pacific cuisine. Hotel Hana Maui; 248-8211; American Plan for hotel guests. Others prix fixe at dinner; L

KA'ANAPALI

Chico's Cantina. Standard Mexican menu. Whaler's Village; 667-2777; B

Lahaina Provision Company. Features yogurt, salad, and chocolate-dessert bars; American menu. Hyatt Regency Maui, 200 Nohea Kai Dr.; 661-1234; M

Lokelani. Understated pleasant local decor serving seafood specialties. Homemade bread; fresh local ingredients. Maui Marriott Resort, 100 Nohea Kai Dr.; 667-1200; M

Nikko Japanese Steakhouse. Japanese decor with teppanyaki service—tableside grills and chefs who wield knives like fire dancers. Maui Marriott Resort, 100 Nohea Kai Dr.; 667-1200; L

Royal Ocean Terrace. Beautiful garden setting minus the flashy Ka'anapali mega-resort atmosphere. Continental and American menu. Royal Lahaina Resort; 661-3611; M

Sound of the Falls. Seafront, with watery surroundings of waterfalls; flashy decor. Piano music. French and continental menu. Westin Maui Hotel, 2365 Ka'anapali Pkwy.; 667-2525; L

Spats II. Posh decor; dress code (elegant casual). Mediterranean and Northern Italian menu; well-known for veal. Dinner only. Disco dancing. Hyatt Regency Maui, Atrium Tower. 200 Nohea Kai Dr.; 661-1234; M–L

Swan Court. Shore-side setting with large windows overlooking swimming swans and flamingos. Hyatt-style continental menu. Hyatt Regency Maui, 200 Nohea Kai Dr.; 661-1234; M–L

KAHULUI-WAILUKU-PA'IA

Chart House. Always reliable steak and seafood menu; salad bar. Favored by local business crowd. At Kahului Harbor, 500 N. Pu'unene Ave.; 877-2466; M

Chum's Restaurant. American coffee shop and diner with decor of the 50s; local plate lunches. 1900 Main St., Wailuku; 244-1000; B

Hazel's Cafe. True local restaurant with plain tables and Japanese prints on the walls. Fresh fish, curry, beef stew & rice. 2080 Vineyard, Wailuku; 244-7278; B

Ming Yuen Chinese Restaurant. Large dining room with extensive Canton and North China menu. 162 Alamaha St., Kahului; 871-7787; B–M

Picnics Maui. The menu is your map showing everywhere on the island good for a picnic. Pick up a box lunch from extensive selection; no advance reservation required. 30 Baldwin Ave., Pa'ia; 579-8021; B; L for the executive model.

Siam Thai Cuisine. Not much on Thai decor; delicious standard Thai menu; fresh ingredients. 123 N. Market, Wailuku; 244-3817; B–M

KAPALUA

Kapalua Bay Club. Understated elegance with wonderful views of Moloka'i and Lana'i and sunsets. Film stars and dignitaries often seen dining here. International menu. Kapalua Bay Hotel, 1 Bay Dr.; 669-5656; M–L

Kapalua Grill & Bar. If you don't golf, you'll feel an outsider; good views of the course. Seafood; international menu. Kapalua Bay Golf Course, 200 Kapalua Dr.; 669-5653; M

Pineapple Hill. In a former plantation home set on a hill amid pines and ironwoods; fireplace in lounge. Beautiful ocean views with large windows. American-continental menu. Dinner only. 1000 Kapalua Dr.; 669-6129; M–L

KIHEI

Kihei Prime Rib and Seafood House. Steak and seafood served in standard steakhouse atmosphere; tables close together; salad bar. Touristy. At Kai Nani Village, 2511 S. Kihei Rd.; 879-1954; M

LAHAINA

Alex's Hole in the Wall. Upstairs dining in old-time Hawaiian decor. Italian-Continental menu. 834 Front St.; 661-3197; B–M

Avalon Restaurant. Courtyard dining. Chef Mark Ellman serves health-conscious Pacific cuisine; fresh local ingredients. 844 Front St.; 667-5559; L

David Paul's Lahaina Grill. Old Lahaina atmosphere in restored Lahaina Hotel. Owner-chef creates Pacific cuisine. 127 Lahainaluna Rd.; 667-5117; L

Gerard's. Owner-chef, Gerard Reversade, creates Nouvelle and classic French cuisine; fresh local ingredients; game in season. Served in quaintly intimate surroundings at the Plantation Inn Hotel. Dinner only. 174 Lahainaluna Rd.; 661-8939; M–L

La Bretagne. On the main road in a converted home; country decor. Classic French cuisine. Dinner only. 562-C Front St.; 661- 8966; L

Lahaina Broiler. Right on the main drag; standard breakfasts, steak and seafood menu at reasonable prices. 889 Front St.; 661-3111; B

Longhi's. A Lahaina institution. Oceanfront dining on busy, noisy main drag. American-Italian menu. 888 Front St.; 667-2288; M

Old Lahaina Cafe. On the main drag; reliable coffee shop fare, local style. 505 Front St.; 661-3303; B

O L O W A L U

Chez Paul. Bistro in country village on the road to Lahaina. A wide following dines here in casual, stylish ambiance. French and Continental menu. Dinner only. Olowalu Village, Hwy. 30; 661-3843; L (Prix fixe)

U P C O U N T R Y

Casanova Italian Deli. *Paniolo* atmosphere and clientele. Deli menu; homemade pasta; espresso; pastries. Live music and dancing. 1188 Makawao Ave., Makawao; 572-0220; B–M

Kula Lodge Restaurant. Broad mountain views and wood-panel chalet decor; light and airy with standard American menu. Kula Lodge, Haleakala Hwy., Kula; 878-1535; M

W A I L E A - M A K E N A

Hakone. Elegant Japanese woodwork decor in Japanese hotel. The visual sense is everything in Japanese dining and the presentation here is superb. Dinner only. Maui Prince Hotel, 5400 Makena Alanui, Makena; 874-1111; L

La Perouse. Hunting and oriental decor; elegant and excellent Continental dining; fresh local ingredients; known for its seafood and the wine cellar. Dinner only. Maui Inter-Continental Resort, 3700 Wailea Alanui, Wailea; 879-1922; L

Pacific Grill. Flashy dining with ocean views in a Four Seasons hotel. Fresh fish and seafood; fresh local ingredients; Pacific Rim international cuisine. Four Seasons Resort Wailea, 3900 Wailea Alanui, Wailea; 874-8000; M

Prince Court. Airy, with ocean views. Creative Sunday brunch; American cuisine with nouvelle emphasis; fresh fish, seafood; local ingredients. Maui Prince Hotel, 5400 Makena Alanui, Makena; 874-1111; L

Raffles. Asian decor with good ocean views. Continental menu. Dinner only. Stouffer Wailea Beach Resort, 3550 Wailea Alanui, Wailea; 879-4900; L

Seasons. Continental decor in romantic atmosphere with ocean views; Continental menu and California-style seafood preparation. Dancing. Dinner only. Four Seasons Resort Wailea, 3900 Wailea Alanui, Wailea; 874-8000; L

■ MOLOKAʻI
KAUNAKAKAI

Holo Holo Kai. Indoor and outdoor hotel restaurant beside the shore. Standard American menu with Hawaiian touches. Hotel Molokaʻi, Kamehameha V Hwy.; 553-5347; M

Mid Nite Inn. With ceiling fans, formica tables and vinyl floors, it's old island style; a resident and tourist hangout; coffee ready at 5 A.M. American and local menu; famed for beef stew, oxtail soup and fried *akule.* Ala Malama & Komoi streets; 553-5302; B

Pau Hana Inn Dining Room. Hawaiian decor and atmosphere on the shore. Standard American menu with local touches. Good fun local entertainment. Pau Hana Inn, Seaside Pl.; 553-5342; M

KUALAPUʻU

Kualapuʻu Cook House. In converted small plantation residence, it's the only eatery within miles. American diner and Hawaiian plate lunch menu. Entertainment on Fri. nights. Owned by local artist, Nannette Yamashita; stoneware used is by Dan Bennett. Kualapuʻu Village at center of island; 567-6185; B

WEST END

Jojo's Cafe. Old-island style with antique bar. American and local menu; fresh local ingredients. Maunaloa Village (1 mile west of Kaluakoi Resort); 552-2803; B

Ohia Lodge. Polynesian decor with good ocean views; for fine dining at the west end, this is it; the only restaurant available. American menu; fresh seafood; friendly service. Live entertainment in lounge. Kaluakoi Hotel and Golf Club, Kepuhi Beach; 552-2555; M

■ OʻAHU
HONOLULU

American

Coasters. Pleasant open air dining at end of pier at Maritime Museum. Good, fresh seafood menu. Pier 7, Honolulu Harbor; 524-2233; M

Columbia Inn. A Honolulu tradition. Coffee shop atmosphere and bar; hangout of journalists from the News Bldg. next door. Standard American menu, Japanese dishes; service until late hour. 645 Kapiʻolani Blvd.; 531-3747; B

Fisherman's Wharf. Crammed with decor of the sea. Long-time favorite for fresh fish and seafood at fishing and cruise boat harbor. Nice bar. Good service. Ala Moana Blvd. at Kewalo Basin; 538-3808; M

Flamingo Chuckwagon. Western decor, somewhat dark. All-you-can-eat prime rib; reliable family buffet. 1015 Kapi'olani Blvd.; 538-1161; B

Hackfield's. Calm hideaway in busy shopping center. American food with nouvelle touches; wonderful Cobb salad. Liberty House, street level, Ala Moana Shopping Ctr.; 945-5243; M

Hala Terrace. Favorite of residents for elegant and casual breakfast and lunch in light, airy atmosphere beside the shore. Traditional menu; Hawaiian fruits. Tourist favorite at night for Danny Kaleikini show. Kahala Hilton Hotel, 5000 Kahala Ave.; 734-2211; M–L

John Dominis. One of Honolulu's premier restaurants. Decor of the sea; waterside at Point Panic with wonderful views of surfers. Fresh fish and seafood menu. Highly rated and a bit overpriced. Dinner only. 43 Ahui St.; 523-0955; L

King's Bakery & Coffee Shop. Favorite of residents, day and late night. Coffee shop menu; breakfast any time. 1936 S. King St.; 941-5211; B

Orson's. Modern decor, light with big windows to view harbor. Fish and seafood menu; nice bar. Ward Warehouse, 1050 Ala Moana Blvd.; 521-5681; M

Rose City Diner. Fifties atmosphere with juke box listings at booths; standard diner. Restaurant Row, 500 Ala Moana Blvd.; 524-7673; B

Ruth's Chris Steak House. Calm surroundings for the tenderest, tastiest steak in town. Restaurant Row, 500 Ala Moana Blvd.; 599-3860; M–L

Ryan's Parkplace. "Yuppie" meeting place; somewhat noisy. Standard menu. Ward Ctr., 1200 Ala Moana Blvd.; 523-9132, B

Stuart Anderson's Cattle Co. Cowboy decor and fine steaks. Music. Family restaurant; crowded. Ward Warehouse, 1050 Ala Moana Blvd.; 523-9692; M

Tripton's American Cafe. Casual decor and one of the best values in town. Good food and service. Dinner only. On the fringe of Waikiki, upstairs at Diamond Head Ctr., 449 Kapahulu Ave.; 737-3819; M

Chinese

Doong Kong Lau. Typical Chinese dining room with red paint. *Hakka* menu (preparation style of boat residents in China). Seafood, not too spicy. Chinese Cultural Plaza, 100 N. Beretania St.; 531-8833; B

Hee Hing. Chinese dining on the fringe of Waikiki. Extensive menu. Diamond Head Ctr., 449 Kapahulu Ave.; 735-5544; B

King's Garden. Typical Chinese dining room, long a tradition with residents for Cantonese menu. Ask server to speak slowly. Order a steamed mullet in advance for family treat. 3477 Wai'alae Ave.; 732-0724; M

Maple Garden. Ornate entry into typical dining room serving good Mandarin food in residential neighborhood. 909 Isenberg St.; 941-6641; B

Yong Sing. Businessmen and legislators flock to this downtown location; not-too-noisy atmosphere. Cantonese menu. 1055 Alakea St.; 531-1366; M

Continental and International

Alfred's. Swiss-French dining in European atmosphere. Game in season. Near Waikiki, it draws residents and visitors; nice hideaway. Century Ctr., 1750 Kalakaua Ave.; 955-5353; L

Alpine Village. Simple Swiss decor in small room; booths. Excellent continental food near the University. 2700 S. King St.; 949-8889; M

Black Orchid. Elegance in art-deco marble and beveled glass. Standard Continental menu; pricey. Popular bar with live music and dancing. Restaurant Row, 500 Ala Moana Blvd.; 521-3111; L

Crepe Fever. Sandwiches, salads, and health foods. Crepes stuffed with everything from veggies to seafood. Ward Ctr., 1200 Ala Moana Blvd.; 521-9021; B

Greek Island Taverna. Simple decor with good Greek food and wine; hefty portions. Fun place with live Greek music; belly dancer on Wed. and Sat. nights. You might join in Greek line dancing on small dance floor. 2570 S. Beretania St.; 943-0052; B

Hajibaba's. Moroccan decor; standard tables or cushion seats, though a bit close together. Fun place with good Moroccan food; eat-with-your-hands style popular. Belly dancer. In Kahala Mall at 4614 Kilauea Ave.; 735-5522, M

India House. A hole in the wall near the University. Dilapidated entry and Indian decor inside. Excellent North Indian non-vegetarian and vegetarian curries; *samosas, tandoori;* ask for *saag* (the world's tastiest spinach). 2632 S. King; 955-7552; M

Jo-Ni's. Simple restaurant on the fringe of Waikiki, serving Filipino food; chicken *adobo* and Filipino style spring rolls. 1017A. Kapahulu Ave.; 735-8575; B

Maile Room. Long considered the premier restaurant in Hawai'i. Luxurious, conservative decor and fine continental fare. Service personnel in tuxedo or kimono. Full band plays in lounge; good Latin dancing, jitterbug, no rock. Dinner only. Jacket required. Kahala Hilton Hotel, 5000 Kahala Ave.; 734-2211; L (prix fixe or à la carte)

Nicholas Nickolas The Restaurant. The place in town to be seen. Elegant decor atop hotel adjacent to shopping center; views of Waikiki. Fine continental menu. Busy bar. Live music and rock dancing. Dinner only. Ala Moana Hotel, 1410 Atkinson Dr.; 955-4466; L

O'Toole's Irish Pub & Restaurant. Downtowners gravitate to Irish atmosphere and occasional entertainment. Lively bar. Hearty continental food, lunch only. Snacks at night. 902 Nu'uanu Ave.; 536-6360; B–M

The Willows. Traditional favorite of long-time visitors and residents. Continental and Hawaiian menu; Thursday *poi* lunch with Hawaiian entertainment. Building is collection of airy grass-like huts over carp ponds. Quiet and pleasant in residential neighborhood. 901 Hausten St.; 946-4808; M

Hawaiian

Ono Hawaiian Foods. A tiny room on the fringe of Waikiki serving only Hawaiian food. Order dishes individually or in combination plate. 726 Kapahulu Ave.; 737-2275; B

People's Cafe. Simple atmosphere, a longtime tradition of businessmen craving a Hawaiian fix. Order dishes individually or in combination plate. Near downtown. 1310 Pali Hwy.; 536-5789; B

Italian

Andrew's Restaurant. European atmosphere. Popular with residents. Standard menu. Entertainment. Ward Ctr., 1200 Ala Moana Blvd.; 523-8677; M

Auntie Pasto's. Youthful hangout where diners wait outside for seating. Neighborhood place with hefty portions. 1099 S. Beretania St.; 523-8855; B

Che Pasta. Simple elegance in old neighborhood. Fine seafood pastas. 3571 Wai'alae Ave.; 735-1777; M

Castagnola's. In valley marketplace above the University. Good food; crowded, slightly noisy. Manoa Marketplace, 2752 Woodlawn Dr.; 988-2969; M

Il Fresco. Open and airy with bottle of olive oil on every table. Creative pastas with local ingredients. Ward Ctr., 1200 Ala Moana Blvd.; 523-5191; M

Old Spaghetti Factory. Simple surroundings and hearty pastas. Ward Warehouse, 1050 Ala Moana Blvd.; 531-1513; B

Japanese and Korean

Korean Bar-B-Q House. No decor, just substantial Korean barbecued ribs; kim chee. Behind Diamond Head at 3106 Monsarrat Ave.; 737-9598; B

Mrs. Sei's Family Restaurant. Simple booths and counter serving hearty portions of Japanese dishes and American menu. Near the University. 2734 S. King St.; 941-5180; B

Suehiro. Big dining room with booths; banquet rooms upstairs. Wide selection of local Japanese favorites. 1824 S. King St.; 949-4584; M

Mexican

Azteca Mexican Restaurant. Good food in residential area; hefty portions. Try the flan. 3569 Wai'alae Ave.; 735-2492; B

Compadres Mexican Bar & Grill. Light and bright with Mexican decor touches. Wide selection menu; huge portions; famed for the brimming pitchers of margaritas. Upstairs at Ward Ctr., 1200 Ala Moana Blvd.; 523-1307; M

Quintero's Mexican Restaurant. Shiny bright hole in the wall with good food; unusual menu. Closes up when owner feels like it. 2334 S. King St.; 944-3882; B

Thai and Vietnamese

A Little Bit of Saigon. On the edge of downtown's Chinatown. Good Vietnamese food served in small room. 1160 Maunakea St.; 528-3663; B

Chiang Mai. Tiny dark room, there's often a line waiting outside. Superb Thai food. 2239 S. King St.; 941-1151; B–M

Siam Orchid. Near shopping center; light and bright with understated Thai decor. Excellent Thai menu. Ask for Thai tea and take care not to stain clothing. 1514 Kona St.; 955-6161; B–M

WAIKIKI

American

Bobby McGee's Conglomeration. Waiters wear costumes. Noisy and fun; friendly. Standard so-so menu and touristy disco. Dinner only. Colony Surf East Hotel, 2885 Kalakaua; 923-5751; B–M

California Pizza Kitchen. Bright surroundings for pizza with California flair. Good service. 1910 Ala Moana Blvd.; 955-5161; B

Cappuccinos. Elegance and beauty in decor. Chef Ernesto Mera creates contemporary American cuisine with Oriental touches; fresh ingredients. Waikiki Joy Hotel, 320 Lewers; 926-8826; L

Chart House. Seafaring decor; reliable fresh fish and seafood dining overlooking Ala Wai Yacht Harbor. Dinner only. 1765 Ala Moana Blvd.; 941-6669; M

Eggs 'n Things. Hearty breakfast at midnight. Open overnight from 11 P.M. to 2 P.M. 1911B Kalakaua Ave.; 949-0820; B

Hau Tree Lanai. Al fresco dining beside beach in upper Waikiki. Built under enormous *hau* tree. Standard menu; good value. New Otani Kaimana Beach Hotel, 2863 Kalakaua Ave.; 921-7066; M

House Without a Key. Indoor dining and outdoor drinks at lawns beside Waikiki Beach. The best Hawaiian entertainment in town for old-style steel-guitar music at sunset. Halekulani Hotel, 2199 Kalia Rd.; 923-2311; M

Hy's Steak House. Wood paneling and hunting decor. Fine dining steak house; fish catch of the day. Excellent service. Entertainment in lounge. Waikiki Park Heights Hotel, 2440 Kuhio Ave.; 922-5555; L

Ilikai Yacht Club Restaurant. Pleasant surroundings overlook Ala Wai Yacht Harbor. Seafood and Pacific menu; indoor or outdoor dining. Escapes hotel atmosphere; good value. Dinner only. Live background music. Ilikai Hotel, 1777 Ala Moana Blvd.; 949-3811; M

Nick's Fishmarket. Traditional wood panel decor and seductive lighting. Fresh fish and seafood menu. Nick's Salad a long-time favorite with residents. Live music and rock dancing in bar. Waikiki Gateway Hotel, 2070 Kalakaua Ave.; 955-6333; L

Surf Room. Open, covered terrace right on the beach. Casual, dignified atmosphere for traditional food and service. Outdoor bar. Wonderful Sunday brunch. Royal Hawaiian Hotel, 2259 Kalakaua Ave.; 923-7311; L

Chinese

Golden Dragon. Ornate Chinese decor with dragons, teak, black lacquer, silk and gold paint. Beside lagoon. Cantonese menu with nouvelle touches; Beggar's Chicken a specialty (order in advance). Fine service. Pricey. Dinner only. Hilton Hawaiian Village, 2005 Kalia Rd.; 946-5336; L

Great Wok of China. Gold and red paint everywhere. Chinese style enclosed room. Popular with visitors; Cantonese menu. Upstairs at Royal Hawaiian Ctr., 2233 Kalakaua Ave.; 922-5373; B–M

Lotus Moon. Chinese decor. Cantonese menu. Good value. Princess Ka'iulani Hotel, 120 Ka'iulani Ave.; 922-5811; B

Continental and International

Bali by the Sea. Elegance in antiques and etched glass at oceanside. French and continental preparations of fish. Dinner only. Hilton Hawaiian Village, 2005 Kalia Rd.; 941-2254; L

Hanohano Room. Atop the tallest hotel on the beach. Pleasant room with window views of Waikiki Beach for continental dining. Fresh fish. Background music in evening. Sheraton-Waikiki Hotel, 2255 Kalakaua Ave.; 922-4422; L

Hofbrau. Oktoberfest all year long. Fun and noisy German beer-drinking crowd. Good dance floor with disc jockey. German menu; sausages. International Market Place, 2330 Kalakaua Ave.; 923-8982; B–M

Malia's Cantina. Hideway Mexican restaurant in heart of Waikiki. Traditional fare. 311 Lewers St.; 922-7808; B

Orchids. Open and airy beside the lawns at beachside. Fresh local ingredients with the continental touch. Game in season. Halekulani Hotel, 2199 Kalia Rd.; 923-2311; M

Roy's Park Bistro. Simple European decor for food by chef Roy Yamaguchi. Oriental touches to continental menu; fresh ingredients. Park Plaza Hotel, 1956 Ala Moana Blvd.; 941-7275; M

Tahitian Lanai. A Polynesian hideaway in open-sided room. Longtime local favorite for fresh fish with Tahitian influences. Active bar. 1811 Ala Moana Blvd.; 946-6541; B–M

Trellisses Garden Restaurant. Garden-like atmosphere and standard menu. Outrigger Prince Kuhio Hotel, 2500 Kuhio Ave.; 922-0811; B

W. C. Peacock. Open and airy overlooking Waikiki Beach. Named for a Waikiki resident long before tourism. Continental menu specializes in fresh seafood. Dinner only. Moana-Surfrider Hotel; 922-3111; L

French

Bon Appetit. Authentic bistro in Waikiki. Fresh fish, duck, and game in season prepared by owner-chef Guy Banal. Also, prix fixe gourmet dinner. Dinner only. Extensive French wine list. In Discovery Bay, 1778 Ala Moana Blvd.; 942-3837; M

Chez Michel. Classic, amiable bistro and authentic French menu. Good wine list.

Eaton Square, 444 Hobron Lane; 955-7866; L

La Mer. Elegant, seductive Hawaiian decor. Some ratings give it the top spot in the islands. Beautiful view of Diamond Head. Menu is strictly French; game in season. Flawless service. Jacket/tie required. Dinner only. Halekulani Hotel, 2199 Kalia Rd.; 923-2311; L

Michel's at the Colony Surf. Open and right above the sands of upper Waikiki Beach. Class-act establishment with fine French menu; evening piano music. Residents' favorite. Jacket required. 2895 Kalakaua Ave.; 923-6552; L

Italian

Baci. Italian decor and atmosphere, Beverly Hills style. Homemade pasta; rich sauces. Large portions. Waikiki Trade Ctr., 2255 Kuhio Ave.; 924-2533; M

Matteo's. Dark Italian surroundings with nice booths. Classic fare and game in season. Famed for its wine cellar. Dinner only. Marine Surf Hotel, 364 Seaside Ave.; 922-5551; L

Spaghetti! Spaghetti! Homey Italian atmosphere and standard menu at reasonable prices. Royal Hawaiian Ctr., 2233 Kalakaua Ave.; 922-7724; B

Trattoria. Exactly that, a trattoria with standard menu. Good value; slightly noisy. Dinner only. Edgewater Hotel, 2168 Kalia Rd.; 923-8415; M

Japanese

Benihana of Tokyo. Touristy; Japanese decor and menu. Teppanyaki—stir-fry at your table—colorful though hot. Hilton Hawaiian Village, 2005 Kalia Rd.; 955-5955; M

Daruma. Simple Japanese decor. You can order by photos of the standard menu. Royal Hawaiian Shopping Ctr., 2233 Kalakaua Ave.; 926-8878; B

Glory. Quiet, Japanese businessman's hideaway with standard menu and sushi. Dinner only. Waikiki Royal Suites, 225 Beach Walk; 926-5641; M

Kyo-Ya. Traditional Japanese pagoda; waitresses in kimono. Authentic fare; pre-arranged dinner in tatami-floored rooms with cushions upstairs. 2057 Kalakaua Ave.; 947-3911; M

CENTRAL O'AHU

Kemoo Farm. Old-time favorite overlooking Lake Wilson. Traditional American menu; some Japanese dishes. Quiet. Across the road from Schofield Barracks. 1718 Wilikina Dr., Wahiawa; 621-8481; B–M

Pearl City Tavern. Famed local place with a monkey bar where real monkeys cavort. Local style food; Japanese platter. Cactus nursery on roof. 905 Kamehameha Hwy., Pearl City; 455-1045 B–M

Shanghai Restaurant. Northern Chinese decor and menu; the accompaniment staple is wheat rather than rice. At Pearlridge Phase III, 98-151 Pali Momi St., Aiea; 488-9419; B

Stuart Anderson's Cattle Co. Traditional American steak-house. Good beef. In Pearl City at Times Square, 98-1262 Ka'ahumanu St.; 482-0054; M

LEEWARD O'AHU

Fogcutter. Pub-like steakhouse in rural Makaha. American menu. 84-111 Orange St., Makaha; 695-9404; M

Ilang Ilang. Named for a potently sweet tiny flower. Filipino menu. Tropicana Sq., 94-866 Moloalao St., Waipahu; 671-3707; B

Ka'ala Room. Pleasant continental surroundings and menu; fresh fish. At the only hotel on this coast. Nice for breakfast. Makaha Resort, 84-626 Makaha Valley Rd., Wai'anae; 695-9511; M–L

NORTH SHORE O'AHU

Ku Aina Sandwich. Super hamburgers and mahimahi burgers give it a rating of the best sandwich house on the island. Tiny and crowded; carry food to outside tables. 66-214 Kamehameha Hwy., Hale'iwa; 637-6067; B

Jameson's By the Sea. Elegant dining on the rural north shore; upstairs with beautiful view of Hale'iwa Harbor and sunsets. American menu; fresh fish and seafood. Downstairs terrace and bar serves chowder and burger lunch. 62-540 Kamehameha Hwy., Hale'iwa; 637-4336; M

Steamers. Indoor and outdoor service in casual surroundings. Popular bar; young crowd. Good fish and seafood at reasonable prices. Hale'iwa Shopping Plaza, Hale'iwa; 637-5071; B–M

The Cove. Hotel restaurant. American menu; fresh fish and seafood. Dinner only. Turtle Bay Hilton, Kahuku; 293-881; M

WINDWARD O'AHU

Bueno Nalo. Mexican restaurant in Hawaiian rural community. Traditional decor and menu; hefty portions. Bring your own liquor. Dinner only. 41-865

Kalaniana'ole Hwy., Waimanalo; 259-7186; B

Buzz's Original Steak House. Polynesian candlelit decor; American steak and seafood menu. Famed for its salad bar. Dinner only. Across from the beach in Lanikai on the fringe of Kailua town. 413 Kawailoa Rd.; 261-4661; M

Florence's. Long a tradition for family atmosphere and Italian food in Kailua town. Dinner only. 20 Kainehe St.; 261-1987; M

Jaron's. Pleasant California decor and menu; fresh fish with local ingredients. 201A Hamakua Dr., Kailua; 262-6768; M

L'Auberge. Swiss decor, cosy and pleasant. Swiss and continental menu by owner-chef Alfred Mueller. Dinner only. 117 Hekili St., Kailua; 263-4663; M

Marie Callender's. Pleasant coffee shop; standard American menu. Windward Mall, 46-056 Kamehameha Hwy., Kane'ohe; 235-6655; B

Orson's Bourbon House. Pub-like atmosphere; piano bar. Cajun menu; fresh seafood; steak. 5 Hoolai St., Kailua; 262-2306; M

Rabbit Island Bar & Grill. Open, airy marine surroundings; standard American menu; fresh fish. Lunch only. At Sea Life Park, Makapu'u Pt.; 259-9911; B

Saeng's Thai Cuisine. Simple Thai decor and good food with fresh local ingredients. 315 Hahani St.; Kailua; 263-9727; B

■ FESTIVALS

Up-to-the minute information is available from the telephone numbers listed; all are **area code 808.**

FEBRUARY

Narcissus Festival. Celebrates Chinese New Year; Chinatown Open House with lion dances, firecrackers, food booths, arts & crafts. Honolulu, O'ahu; Chinese Chamber of Commerce: 533-3181

Captain Cook Festival. Celebrates Cook's arrival; food booths, games, rides, parade, entertainment, 5k and 10k races. Waimea, Kaua'i; 338-1475

MARCH

Cherry Blossom Festival. Celebrates Japanese culture with crafts, drummers and dancers, games, tea ceremony, and *mochi* (sweets) pounding. Queen Kapi'olani Park, Waikiki, O'ahu; Japanese Junior Chamber of Commerce: 949-2255

Hawaiian Song Festival and Song Composing Contest Finals, Queen Kapi'olani Park Bandstand, Waikiki, O'ahu; Dept. of Parks & Recreation: 266-7654

St. Patrick's Day Parade. Post-parade party at the Hawaiian Waikiki Beach Hotel, from Ft. DeRussy to Queen Kapi'olani Park. Waikiki, O'ahu; 521-8693

Prince Kuhio Festival. Songs and dances from the Prince Kuhio Era; canoe races, *holoku* (gowns) pageant, and a royal ball. Prince Kuhio Park, Po'ipu, Kaua'i; 245-3971

A P R I L

Merrie Monarch Festival. A week of festivities honoring King Kalakaua, culminating with hula competitions. Hilo, Hawai'i; 935-9168

M A Y

Annual Lei Day Celebration. Features exhibits, lei-making competitions, entertainment, and crowning of lei queens. Queen Kapi'olani Park, O'ahu, Waikiki; Dept. of Parks & Recreation: 266-7654. Inter-Continental Wailea Hotel, Wailea, Maui; 879-1922; Kaua'i Museum, Lihu'e; 245-6931

Moloka'i Ka Hula Piko. Celebrates birth of the traditional hula; story-telling, performances; Hawaiian food, games, and crafts. Moloka'i; 553-3876; or O'ahu; 941-0444

J U N E

Annual King Kamehameha Floral Parade. Women horseback riders in *Pa'u* costume, bands, cultural arts & crafts demonstrations. From King & Richards streets in downtown Honolulu to Waikiki, O'ahu. State Council on Hawaiian Heritage: 536-6540

Kamehameha Day Celebration. Entertainment, crafts, food, Royal Court procession. Coconut Island, Hilo, Hawai'i; 935-9338

King Kamehameha Statue Draping. Statues draped in long leis. Honolulu, O'ahu and Kapa'au, North Kohala, Hawai'i. King Kamehameha Celebration Commission: 548-4512

Waiki'i Music Festival. Celebrates Hawaiian music and culture; concert. Waimea, Hawai'i; 546-4000

Annual Fancy Fair. Features food, entertainment, and crafts. Mission Houses Museum, Honolulu, O'ahu; 531-0481

JULY

Maui Jaycees Carnival. Features games, rides, entertainment, and food. Maui War Memorial Sports Complex, Wailuku, Maui; 879-0786

Annual Fourth of July Celebration and Parade. Floral floats; mainland, local and military bands; fireworks display. Finishes at Kailua Beach Park; Kailua, O'ahu; 261-2727

Na Hula O Ka'ohikukapulani. Annual hula exhibition by children. Kaua'i War Memorial Convention Hall, Lihu'e, Kaua'i; 335-5765 or 335-6466

Bon Odori Festivals. Buddhist evening ceremonies honoring souls of the dead; Lantern Boat Ceremonies/Bon Dances. Maui: Jodo Mission, Lahaina: 661-4304; O'ahu: Jodo Mission, Hale'iwa: 637-4382

Annual International Festival of the Pacific. Parade, athletic tournaments, music, and dances of the multi-ethnic people of the Pacific. Hilo, Hawai'i; 959-4248

Koloa Plantation Days. One-week celebration in honor of the birth of sugar plantations in Hawai'i. Historical parade, entertainment, crafts, games, and ethnic foods. Koloa, Kaua'i; 742-7444

Annual 'Ukulele Festival. Hundreds of 'ukulele players perform. Queen Kapi'olani Park Bandstand, Waikiki, O'ahu; 487-6010

AUGUST

Annual Ka Himeni 'Ana. Concert and contest of old-style Hawaiian singing without amplification. Songs are in Hawaiian and pre-World War II. Orvis Auditorium, University of Hawai'i, Honolulu, O'ahu; 842-0421

Kane'ohe Bay Fest. Entertainment, carnival rides, midway, water-sports competitions. Marine Corps Air Station, Kane'ohe, O'ahu; 254-2466

Annual Gabby Pahinui/Atta Isaacs Slack Key Guitar Festival. The best slack-key guitar artists perform. Waimanalo Beach Park, O'ahu; 522-7030

SEPTEMBER

Aloha Festivals (Aloha Week). Hawaiian entertainment, ethnic food, and crafts celebrated on all islands. County departments of Parks & Recreation; O'ahu: 523-4182; Hawai'i: 961-8311; Maui: 243-7389; Kaua'i: 245-8821

Annual Okinawan Festival. Cultural dances, arts & crafts, food. Queen Kapi'olani Park, Waikiki, O'ahu. The Okinawa Center: 676-5400

Hawai'i County Fair. Old-time country fair with food, music, and rides. Hilo, Hawai'i; 987-8016

Portuguese Heritage Festival. Food, entertainment, dances, cultural displays. McCoy Pavilion, Ala Moana Park, O'ahu; 845-1616

OCTOBER

Talking Island Festival. Four stages run concurrently with stories for children, followed by 3-week tour on other islands with performances in hotels; oral histories, Pacific tales. McCoy Pavilion, Ala Moana Park, Honolulu, O'ahu; Makia Malo, 949-4999 or Storytelling Assoc. of Hawai'i, P.O. Box 61036, Honolulu, HI 96839

NOVEMBER

Annual Kona Coffee Cultural Festival. A Kona coffee cupping and picking contest, parade, recipe contest, arts & crafts, ethnic foods, tours of coffee mills. Kona, Hawai'i; 322-4430

Hawai'i International Film Festival. Cross-cultural films by award-winning filmmakers from Asia, the Pacific, and U.S. (Free. Tickets required.) Honolulu, O'ahu; 944-7203 or 944-7007

Mission Houses Museum Annual Christmas Fair. Handmade crafts, food, entertainment. Mission Houses Museum, Honolulu, O'ahu; 531-0481

Annual Festival of Trees. Display of one-of-a-kind decorated trees, wreaths, decorations, and gifts. Amfac Plaza, Honolulu, O'ahu; 547-4780

■ CALENDAR OF SPORTS EVENTS

Up-to-the minute information is available from the telephone contacts listed. Numbers are O'ahu unless another island is indicated; all are **area code 808.**

JANUARY

Hula Bowl. Football; Aloha Stadium, Honolulu, O'ahu; University of Hawai'i Foundation; 956-4852

World Bodyboarding Championships. Banzai Pipeline, O'ahu; 396-8342

31-Mile Volcano to Hilo Marathon & Relay. Volcano, Hawai'i; 521-7686 (Hawai'i) or 935-7356 (O'ahu)

Senior Skins Pro-Am & Pro Golf Tournaments. Mauna Lani Course, South Kohala, Hawai'i; Aloha Section, PGA; 528-3700

Windsurfing Regatta. Amateur Windsurfing Assoc. sponsors these events once each month of the year; Kailua Bay, Oʻahu; Hawaiʻi; 247-5646

FEBRUARY

NFL **Pro Bowl.** Football; Aloha Stadium, Honolulu, Oʻahu; 486-9555, 486-9300
Annual Hawaiian Open PGA **Tournament.** Admission. Waiʻalae Country Club, Oʻahu; Hawaiian Open Office: 526-1232
Great Aloha Run. 8.2 miles (13 km), Aloha Tower to Aloha Stadium, Oʻahu; 735-6092
LPGA **Women's Kemper Open Golf Tournament.** Blue Course, Wailea, Maui; 879-2966 or 879-4465

MARCH

Pele's Cross Country Ski Cup. World's highest cross country race; Mauna Kea, Hawaiʻi; 737-4394 (Oʻahu)
Annual Maui Marathon. Maui Mall, Kahului to Whalers Village, Kaʻanapali; Maui Valley Isle Road Runners Assoc: 871-6441
Annual Oʻahu Kite Challenge. Kapiʻolani Park, Oʻahu; 922-5483
Annual 100K Saddle Road Relay & Ultramarathon. Hilo, Hawaiʻi; 521-7686 (Oʻahu)
Annual State Field Archery Championships. Archery Range, Kahului Harbor, Maui; 877-5555
Rainbow Wahine Invitational Golf Tournament. Klipper Course, Marine Corps Air Station, Kaneʻohe, Oʻahu. Aloha Section, PGA; 528-3700
Polo Season begins: **Honolulu Polo Club Games,** March–November, Saturdays at Waimanalo Polo Field, Oahu; 531-8020. **Hawaiʻi Polo Club Games,** March–August, Sundays at Mokuleʻia Polo Field, Oahu; 637-7656. Admission.

APRIL

Maui Invitational Windsurfing Championships. Hoʻokipa Beach, Maui; 572-4883 or 575-2169
Tin Man Biathlon. 1.7-mile (2.72-km) run, 800-meter swim; Ala Moana Beach Park, Oʻahu; 941-3344
Merrie Monarch Hula Competitions. Honors King Kalakaua with 3 nights of competitions; Hilo, Hawaiʻi; 935-9168

Honolulu Symphony Run. 4 miles. Fort Ruger Park, O'ahu; 942-2200
Annual 'Iao Valley 10K Run. Wailuku, Maui; Valley Isle Road Runners; 871-6441

M A Y

Carole Kai International Bed Race & Parade. Kapi'olani Park, O'ahu; Bed Race
Office: 735-6092
Annual Na Holo Wahine 5K, 10K All Women's Run. Wailuku, Maui; Valley Isle
Road Runners: 871-6441
Kapalua Tennis Jr. Veterans, Seniors Championships. Kapalua, Maui; 669-0244
Annual Bankoh Kayak Challenge. Moloka'i to O'ahu 38-mile (61-km) kayak
race; finishes at Hawai'i Kai, O'ahu; 254-5055
Annual World Cup of Windsurfing. Ho'okipa Beach Park, Maui; 579-9765
Golden Goddess Women's Fishing Tournament. Kailua-Kona, Hawai'i;
322-3832
Kona Gold Jackpot Fishing Tournament. Kailua-Kona, Hawai'i; 322-3832
Annual Keauhou Kona Triathlon. Endurance event equal to one-half the
Ironman: 1.2-mile (1.92-km) swim, 56-mile (89.6-km) bike race, 13.1-mile
(21-km) run; Keauhou Bay, Kona, Hawai'i; 329-2692

J U N E

Mauna Kea Polo Club. Season begins (Arena polo tournaments in July),
Kamuela, Hawai'i; 885-4445
Hawai'i State Clay Court Tennis Championships. Coco Palms, Kaua'i;
822-4921
Maui Kamehameha Day Archery Invitational. Archery Range, Kahului Harbor,
Maui; 877-5555
Kamehameha Day Canoeing Regatta. Kailua Beach Park, O'ahu; 261-6615
King Kamehameha Holua Ski Tournament. Dependent on availability of snow;
Mauna Kea, Hawai'i; 737-4394
Annual King Kamehameha Hula Competition. International competitions in
Kahiko (ancient) and *Auana* (modern) hula; chanting competitions; Blaisdell
Arena, Honolulu, O'ahu; 536-6540
Professional Championship Rodeo. Rodeo, country music, dancers; New Town
& Country Stables, Waimanalo, O'ahu; 235-3691
Hawaiian Islands State Bodybuilding Championships. Blaisdell Concert Hall,
Honolulu, O'ahu; 988-7887

Annual Pro-Am Golf Tournament. 54-hole event with 30 teams of one pro and 3 amateurs each. Mauna Kea Beach Hotel course, South Kohala, Hawai'i; Aloha Section PGA; 528-3700

Biennial Transpacific Yacht Race. Odd-numbered years San Francisco, California to Waikiki, O'ahu; Waikiki Yacht Club: 949-7141

JULY

Hanale'i Rodeo Stampede. Hanale'i, Kaua'i; 826-6777

Parker Ranch 4th of July Rodeo & Horse Races. Paniolo Park, Kamuela, Hawai'i; 885-7311 or 885-7655

Annual Makawao 4th of July Rodeo. Makawao, Maui; 572-9928

Walter J. MacFarlane Canoeing Regatta. Waikiki Beach, O'ahu; 689-6798

Hapuna Rough Water Swim. One-mile competition; Hapuna Beach, Hawai'i; 775-7718

Keauhou Wide-Open Fishing Tournament. Keauhou, Hawai'i; 322-3000

Kona Ahi/Marlin Fishing Tournament. Kailua-Kona, Hawai'i; 322-3832

Hawaiian International Billfish Tournament-Pro Am. Kailua-Kona, Hawai'i (also in August); 836-0974

Kilauea Volcano Marathon and Rim Run. Volcano, Hawai'i; 967-8222

Maui County Course Race Championships and Maui Slalom Series. Windsurfing, Kanaha Beach Park, Maui; 877-2111

Prince Lot Hula Competitions. Ancient and modern hula; Moanalua Gardens, Honolulu, O'ahu; 839-5334

AUGUST

Kenwood Cup International Yacht Races. Biennial (in even-numbered years); sailing series between the islands of O'ahu, Moloka'i, Maui, and Kaula Islet (off Kaua'i); 946-9061

Trout Season begins, Koke'e State Park; Kaua'i; Div. of Aquatic Resources: 241-3400

Annual Na Holo Kai Canoe Race. 90-mile (144-km) outrigger race from Poka'i Bay, O'ahu to Kalapaki, Kaua'i; 245-5822

Hawai'i State Windsurfing Course Racing Championships. Kailua Bay, O'ahu; 247-5646

Annual State Outrigger Canoe Racing Championships. Ke'ehi Lagoon, or Kane'ohe Bay, O'ahu; 689-6798 or 261-6615

Kaua'i Open Golf Tournament. Played on 3 Kaua'i courses; Aloha Section PGA; 528-3700

Duke Kahanamoku World Championship Paddleboard Race. Magic Island, south shore, to Kailua, windward shore, O'ahu; 732-1845

S E P T E M B E R

Annual Queen Lili'uokalani Long Distance Canoe Racing Championships. Hawai'i's biggest long-distance, outrigger canoe racing event. International competition in men's and women's single-hull and double-hull races on Labor Day Weekend; between Kailua-Kona and Honaunau, Hawai'i; 325-1417

Waikiki Rough Water Swim. 2.4 miles (3.8 km); Sans Souci Beach to Duke Kahanamoku Beach, Waikiki, O'ahu; 988-7788

USWA National Windsurfing Championships. Kanaha Beach, Maui or Kailua Bay, O'ahu; 247-5646

Annual Hana Relay. 54-mile (86-km) run; 6-person teams; Kahului to Hana, Maui; Valley Isle Road Runners: 871-6441

Annual Haleakala Run to the Sun/Ultramarathon. 36.2 miles (57.92 km) from sea level to 10,023 feet (3,047 m); Maui; Valley Isle Road Runners: 871-6441

Annual Na Wahine O Ke Kai Women's Outrigger Canoe Race. 40.8 mile (65 km) 6-person teams; West Moloka'i to Duke Kahanamoku Beach, Waikiki, O'ahu; 262-7567

Aloha Polo Match. Waiki'i Ranch, Waimea, Hawai'i; 885-0538

Aloha Seniors' Golf Championship. Klipper Golf Course, Marine Corps Air Station, Kane'ohe, O'ahu; Aloha Section, PGA; 528-3700

Annual Outrigger's Hawaiian Oceanfest. 6-day event; O'ahu

Hawaiian International Ocean Challenge. 6-person teams of world's best lifeguards in kayak, surf rescue, swim, paddleboard, and outrigger canoe races at Makapu'u Beach and Waikiki Beach.

Waikiki Kings Race. 4-part run, kayak race, and 1-mile (1.6-km) paddleboard race, Waikiki; Diamond Head Wahine

Windsurfing Classic. Professional women windsurfers in slalom and wave jumping competition; admission charge; Diamond Head Beach; 524-0722

Kapalua Open Tennis Tournament. Kapalua Tennis Garden, Maui; 669-0244

Century Bike Run. 25, 50, 75, and 100 miles (40, 80, 120, and 160 km). East and windward coasts of O'ahu, Hawai'i; Bicycling League: 735-5756

OCTOBER

Top Gun Hydrofest. Hydroplane races; Pearl Harbor, Oʻahu; 471-0818

Annual Ironman World Triathlon. 2.4-mile (3.84-km) swim, 112-mile (179-km) bike ride, and 26.2-mile (42-km) marathon; Kailua-Kona, Hawaiʻi; Ironman Office: 329-0063

Annual Molokaʻi Hoe Canoe Race. Men's 40.8-mile (65.28-km) outrigger race; West Molokaʻi to Fort DeRussy Beach, Waikiki, Oʻahu; 261-6614

Annual $1 Million Hula Bowl Hole-In-One. Ala Wai Driving Range, Honolulu, Oʻahu, and Muncipal Golf Course, Hilo, Hawaiʻi; 956-4852

USTA **Tennis Tournament.** Blue Course, Wailea, Maui; 879-1958

Makapuʻu Bodysurfing Class. Makapuʻu Beach Park, Oʻahu; 396-8342

NOVEMBER

Ultraman Endurance Challenge. 3-day international event covering 320 miles (515 km): 6.2-mile (9.92-km) swim, 261.4-mile (418-km) bike ride, and 52.4-mile (83.84-km) run; Hawaiʻi; 326-7946

State Marked-Animal Archery Championship. Archery Range, Kahului Harbor, Maui; 877-5555

Kapalua International Golf Tournament. Kapalua Plantation Course, Maui; 669-0244

Mauna Kea Invitational Golf Tournament. 54-hole men's and 36-hole women's tournament; South Kohala, Hawaiʻi; Aloha Section PGA; 528-3700 or 882-7222

Annual King Kalakaua Regatta. Canoe paddling and sailing, kayak and surfboard paddling races; Ala Wai Canal, Waikiki Beach, and Honolulu Harbor, Oʻahu; 956-4852

DECEMBER

LPGA **World Match Play Golf Championship.** Princeville Course, Kauaʻi; 826-5011

Annual Ted Makalena State Golf Open. West Loch Course, Pearl Harbor, Oʻahu; Aloha Section PGA; 528-3700

Annual Honolulu Marathon. Honolulu, Oʻahu; also **Honolulu Wheelchair Marathon.** Marathon Office: 734-7200

Makaha Pro-Am & Open Golf Tournament. Sheraton Makaha, Makaha, Oʻahu; Aloha Section PGA; 528-3700

Aloha Bowl. Football; Played on Christmas Day; Aloha Stadium, Honolulu, Oʻahu; 947-4141 or Stadium, 486-9555

Every month on the two nights of the full moon, **one-hour moonwalks**, family admission charge; take place at Waimea Falls Park, North Shore, O'ahu; 638-8511

■ GOLF COURSES

There are nearly 70 municipal, hotel, military, and country club golf courses in the islands, a total of more than 1,100 holes; most are 18-hole courses. International tournaments are frequent and televised; the most famous is the **Hawaiian Open,** held each winter at the **Wai'alae Country Club** course in Honolulu; 6,975 yards; par 72. Green fees vary widely; from under $10 at a municipal course, to $100 for non-hotel guests at the Mauna Kea course on the Big Island. A sampling of golf courses open to the public are listed; telephone numbers are **area code 808.**

■ HAWAI'I (BIG ISLAND)
HILO
Hilo Municipal Golf Course. 18 holes; driving range, pro shop, instruction & rentals, restaurant. Haihai St., Hilo; 959-7711

KONA
Kona Country Club. Championship courses, 36 holes, driving range, pro shop, instruction & rentals, restaurant & lounge. 78-7000 Ali'i Dr., Kailua-Kona; 322-2595

Mauna Lani Resort. Championship courses, 36 holes, driving range, pro shop, instruction & rentals, restaurant & bar. Francis I'i Brown Course, South Kohala; 885-6655

Waikoloa Beach Resort. Championship courses, 36 holes, driving range, instruction & rentals. Beach golf course and Kings' golf course, Waikoloa, South Kohala; 885-6060 (Beach course), and 885-4647 (King's course)

■ KAUA'I
PO'IPU
Kiahuna Golf Club. 18 holes, driving range, pro shop, instruction & rentals, restaurant & bar. Po'ipu; 742-9595

PRINCEVILLE

Princeville Resort. Site of LPGA Match Play Championship. 36 holes, driving range, clubhouse, golf shop, instruction & rentals, restaurant & bar, spa & weight room. Prince course and Makai course, Princeville; 826-5000 (Prince course), and 826-3580 (Makai course)

■ MAUI
KA'ANAPALI

Royal Ka'anapali Golf Courses. Championship courses, 36 holes, driving range, golf shop, rentals, clubhouse & restaurant. Two courses, Ka'anapali Beach Resort; 661-3691

MAKENA

Makena Resort. 18 holes, driving range (irons only), pro shop, instruction & rentals, restaurants & bars. 5415 Makena Alanui, Makena; 879-3344

PUKALANI

Pukalani Country Club. In Upcountry Maui; 18 holes, lighted driving range & putting green, pro shop, rentals, restaurant. 360 Pukalani Rd.; 572-1314

■ MOLOKA'I
WEST END

Kaluakoi Golf Course. Championship 6,618 yard, par 72 course; 18 holes. Driving range, pro shop, rentals. Kaluakoi Resorts, Moloka'i; 521-1625

■ O'AHU
CENTRAL

Mililani Golf Club. Championship 18-hole course. Night driving range, pro shop, instruction & rentals, restaurant & lounge. 95-176 Kuahelani Ave., Mililani; 623-2222

LEEWARD

There are two courses located here: **Makaha Valley Country Club**, 18 hole Country Club course; 84-627 Makaha Vly. Rd., 695-9578; and **Makaha Resort West Golf Course**, Championship 18-hole course, 84-626 Makaha Vly. Rd.; 695-9544. Both offer driving ranges, pro shops, instructions & rentals, restaurants & bars.

SOUTH SHORE

Ala Wai Golf Course. This is the busiest golf course in the state. Tee time begins at 6:30 A.M.; the last time slot is 5:06 P.M. 9 holes, driving range, pro shop, rentals, restaurant. 404 Kapahulu Ave., Waikiki, Honolulu; 296-4653

Hawai'i Kai Golf Courses. Championship 18-hole course (par 72); Executive 18 hole course (par 55). Driving range, pro shop, instruction & rentals, restaurant & bar. 8902 Kalaniana'ole Hwy., Hawai'i Kai; 395-3258

WINDWARD

Kahuku Golf Course. Rural golfing in Kahuku; 2,700 yards, par 35; 9 holes. No facilities; bring your own balls and cooler or water. Clubs may be rented up to 1:30 P.M.; 293-5842

Turtle Bay Hilton & Country Club. 18 holes, driving range, pro shop, instruction & rentals, showers (non-hotel guests, men only), snack bar. Kahuku; 293-8574

■ HAWAI'I'S STATE HOLIDAYS

January 1	New Year's Day	July 4	Independence Day
January 20	Martin Luther King, Jr. Day	August 21	Admission Day
mid-February	President's Day	early-September	Labor Day
March 26	Prince Kuhio Day	early-November	General Election Day
March/April	Good Friday	November 11	Veteran's Day
end of May	Memorial Day	late-November	Thanksgiving
June 11	Kamehameha Day	December 25	Christmas Day

■ MUSEUMS

All telephone listings are **area code 808.**

■ HAWAI'I (BIG ISLAND)

HILO

Lyman Museum. Open M–Sat.; admission. Gift shop. First-class museum. Exhibits of ancient tools, feather-lei making. *Kukui* nut candles, *kapa* cloth, and *awa* liquor-making. Largest mineral collection in the Pacific. Ethnic displays. 276 Haili St., Hilo, HI 96720; 935-5021

KONA

Hulihe'e Palace Museum. Open daily; admission. Gift shop. Collection of furniture of former Hawaiian royalty, and ancient artifacts including the war spears of Kamehameha I. 75-5718 Ali'i Dr., Kailua-Kona, HI 96740; 829-1877

Mauna Loa Royal Kona Coffee Mill & Museum. Open daily; no admission. Gift shop. Free cup of coffee, inspect the roaster. Photo gallery and old-time equipment. Learn how coffee is made. Middle Road, South Kona, between Captain Cook town and Kealakekua Bay; 328-2511

Ellison S. Onizuka Space Center. Open daily; admission. Gift shop. Features a scale model space shuttle, salute to the *Challenger* astronauts, Onizuka's space suit, a moon rock, hanging scale model of future space station, gyroscopes, and interactive exhibits. Keahole Airport, P.O. Box 833, Kailua-Kona, HI 96740; 829-3441

VOLCANO

Thomas A. Jaggar Museum. Open daily; no admission. Watch the seismic recorders, view instruments and learn about different kinds of lava. Displays of fire goddess legends. Hawai'i Volcano Observatory, Hawai'i Volcanoes National Park, Volcano, HI 96785; Park Hqs. Information: 967-7311

Hawai'i Volcanoes National Park Visitor Center. Open daily; no admission. Book shop. Exhibits, film, park rangers on duty to answer questions. Recorded information on current volcanic activity and directions to viewing sites. Volcano, HI 96785; 967-7311. Hotline; 24 hours: 967-7977

WAIMEA

Parker Ranch Visitor Center & Museum. Open daily; admission. Multi-media presentation of ranch history, and memorabilia room of Duke Kahanamoku. Hwy. 19 at the shopping center, Kamuela, HI 96743; 885-7655

■ KAUA'I

HANALE'I

Hanale'i Museum. Open M–F; no admission. Arts shop. Good photo gallery of rural life. Exhibits of taro and rice cultivation. Ancient implements and old bottles. Kuhio Hwy., Hanale'i, HI 96714; 826-6783

LIHU'E

Grove Farm Homestead Plantation Museum. Open M, W, Th; admission. Tours (reservations required). Finest example of plantation period. Furnished as though people still lived here. Hawaiian quilts. Complex of buildings. P.O. Box 1631, Nawiliwili Rd., Lihu'e, HI 96766; 245-3202

Kaua'i Museum. 4428 Rice St., Open M–F; admission with re-entry pass. Gift shop. Excellent exhibits including replicas of plantation shack, missionary bedroom, and Waimea at the time of Capt. Cook's arrival. Hawaiian quilts, canoes, instruments, tools you can pick up, and a continuous video with aerial views. Lihu'e, HI 96766; 245-6931

■ MAUI

HALEAKALA NATIONAL PARK

Park Headquarters. Open daily; no admission. Book shop. Exhibits address daily problems facing the park. Silverswords grow at the entrance and *nene* geese waddle in the car park. One mile inside park entrance; 572-9306

Haleakala National Park Visitor Center. Open daily; no admission. Book shop. Call before you go for recorded weather forecast. Exhibits of geology, archeology and ecology, and wilderness protection programs. Park rangers on duty. Eleven miles inside park at the summit; hotline, 24 hours: 572-7749

HANA ROAD AND HANA

Hana Cultural Center. Open daily (call before you go). Admission. One-room rural museum. Artifacts, photographs, carvings. Best exhibits describe pounding/soaking of mulberry bark to make *kapa* cloth, and fashioning Hawaiian brooms from coconut fronds. 'Uakea Rd., Hana town; 248-8622

Kahanu Gardens, Pacific Tropical Botanical Garden. Open Tu–F. Admission. 120 acres of herbal and medicinal plants; varieties of breadfruit and coconut. Garden is site of 14th century Pi'ilanihale He'iau largest *he'iau* (temple) on Maui, Kalahu Point. Ula'ino Rd.; turn off Hana Hwy. at the 31-mile marker; 248-8912

KAHULUI

Alexander & Baldwin Sugar Museum. Open M–Sat; admission. Finest photo gallery of sugar history in Hawai'i. Describes competition for water between Samuel Alexander/Henry Baldwin and Claus Spreckels. Explanations of sugar cultivation, model of cane crushing plant, and original immigrant labor contracts. Intersection of Hwy. 311 and Hansen Rd., Kahului, HI 96732; 871-8058

LAHAINA

Baldwin House Museum. Open daily; admission. Brochures. Oldest building in Lahaina. Missionary home with Connecticut furnishings. Front St., Lahaina, HI 96761; 661-3262

Whaling Museum. Open daily; no admission. Antique harpoons, scrimshaw, ship logs, and photos of whaleship wrecks. Hanging figurehead from the *Carthaginian* was carved for filming of James Michener's *Hawaii*. In Crazy Shirts store, 865 Front St., Lahaina

WAILUKU

Bailey House, Maui Historical Society Museum. Open daily; no admission. Gift shop. Largest artifact collection on Maui. Kapa cloth, missionary memorabilia, quilts, and paintings by mid-19th-century resident, Edward Bailey. 2375-A Main St., Wailuku, HI 96793; 244-3326

■ O'AHU
CITY AND COUNTY OF HONOLULU
Bishop Museum. Open M–Sat & first Sun of month; admission. Gift Shop; cafe; library; planetarium, shows day and evening (admission). Fine collection of Pacific artifacts. Exhibits describe cultural history of Hawai'i, Pacific peoples, flora & fauna. Well-known for research in Pacific ethnology and archeology. 1525 Bernice St., Honolulu, HI 96819; 847-3511

Contemporary Museum. Open daily except Tuesday; admission; free on Th. Gift shop, tea room. Housed in a former estate. Galleries of contemporary art by international and Hawaiian artists. Pavilion with permanent installation of David Hockney environmental work. 2411 Makiki Heights Dr., Honolulu, HI 96822; 526-1322

Foster Botanic Garden. Open daily; admission. Self-guided tour brochure; guided tours M-Tu-W. Gift shop. 20 acres of Asian and African spice trees, herb and orchid gardens, native O'ahu *loulu* palm; and bizarre cannonball, sausage and *Coco de Mer* trees. 180 N. Vineyard Blvd., downtown; 522-7065

Hawai'i Maritime Center. Open daily; admission. Gift Shop, waterfront restaurant. Ship models, hanging skeleton of whale, photos of old Waikiki. Good descriptions of early Polynesian voyaging techniques, and impact of shipping on Hawai'i. Rental tapes for self-guided tours. At dockside, *Falls of Clyde*, freighter/passenger sailing ship from turn-of-century; and *Hokulea*, replica of double-hulled voyaging canoe that made 2 extended modern voyages into the South Pacific. Pier 7, downtown; 536-6373

Honolulu Academy of Arts. Open Tue–Sun; no admission. Gift shop; cafe. Free guided tours. Foreign & art films in the theatre (admission). Pick up events calendar at front desk. Fine permanent collections of Asian, European, Pacific and American art. 900 S. Beretania St., Honolulu HI 96814; 638-1006

'Iolani Palace. Open W–Sat; admission. Excellent guided tours (reservations advisable). Only royal palace in the U.S.; official residence of last two monarchs. Extensively restored with original furnishings. Throne room. S. King & Richards Sts., downtown; 522-0832

Mission Houses Museum. Open M–Sat; admission. Periodic guided tours on weekdays; hourly on Sat. Living history programs Saturdays. Gift Shop. Original 3 buildings of the Sandwich Islands Mission. Frame house is oldest wooden building in Hawai'i. Missionary furnishings. 553 S. King St. across from Palace, downtown; 531-0481

Pacific Aerospace Museum. Open daily; admission. Traces history of Pacific exploration from celestial navigation of ancient Polynesian voyagers to modern-day space flight. "Great Skyquest Theater" includes footage of Pacific pioneers, Pan Am Clipper flights, Amelia Earhart, and attack on Pearl Harbor. Located in main concourse of Honolulu International Airport; 836-6413.

Queen Emma Summer Palace. Open daily; admission. Book shop. Airy home with European furniture; set of china, a gift of Queen Victoria; feather cloaks. 2913 Pali Hwy., Honolulu, HI 96817; 595-3167

USS *Arizona* Memorial. Open daily; no admission. Snack bar, gift shop, museum, theatre and memorial. Programs in several languages by National Park Service. Rangers on duty. Documentary film of Japan's attack on Pearl Harbor, December 7, 1941 and U.S. entry into World War II. U.S. Navy escorts visitors by launch to the memorial erected above sunken hull of USS *Arizona*. Best time to go is in early morning; there are always crowds here and guided tours are kept to medium-sized groups. Pearl Harbor, Honolulu, HI 96818. Visitor Center: 422-2771; hotline: 422-0561. Adjacent to the *Arizona* Memorial visitor center is **Bowfin Park.** Open daily; admission. Self-guided tour with radio receiver. WW II U.S. submarine. 423-1341

U.S. Army Museum. Open daily; no admission. Housed in a former gun battery emplacement. Excellent WW II dioramas. Exhibits describe Hawaiians and Hawai'i in war time. Fort DeRussy, Honolulu, HI 96815; 438-2821

■ ART GALLERIES

All telephone listings are **area code 808.**

■ HAWAI'I (BIG ISLAND)
HAMAKUA COAST

Kama'aina Woods. Open M–F. Fine quality thin-edged bowls of rare koa and milo woods, and mango wood. Lehua St., Honoka'a, HI 96727; 775-7722

KOHALA

Ackerman Gallery. Open daily. Works by artists on Hawai'i. Ceramics, carvings, and bowls in rare native woods, blown glass, paintings and jewelry. 961 Kapa'au St., Kapa'au, HI 96755; 889-5971

Mauna Kea Hotel. Guided art tours available. The hotel is a gallery of Asian and Pacific art (not for sale), mainly collected by the hotel's founder, Laurance Rockefeller. Its most important piece is a large 7th century. Indian Buddha. Hawaiian quilts on display. South Kohala, HI 96743; 882-7222

KONA

Blue Ginger Gallery. Open M–Sat. Represents 40 local artists. Painted silk scarves, jewelry, ceramics, and koa wood furniture; etched and stained glass. Hwy. 11, Kainaliu, HI 96704; 322-3898

Kimura Lauhala Shop. Open M–Sat. Finely-woven *lauhala* baskets, hats, and placemats. Intersection of Hualalai Rd. and Hwy. 180, Holualoa, HI 96725; 324-0053

Studio 7 Gallery. Open Tu–Sat. Oil and watercolor paintings by well-known owner Hiroki Morinoue. Wood block prints and metal sculpture, ceramics, blown glass and basketry by local artists who rate this gallery with high marks. Japanese environment. Mamalahoa Hwy., Holualoa, HI 96725; 324-1335

VOLCANO

Volcano Art Center. Open daily. Represents more than 100 local artists. Koa wood work, paintings, photographs, blown glass, ceramics and note cards; posters and T-shirts. Hawai'i Volcanoes National Park (next door to park hqs.), Volcano, HI 96785; 967-7511

■ KAUA'I
Hanalei Artisans Guild. Open daily. The gallery is downstairs in the museum. Works in every kind of medium from painters and artisans of the Hanalei art colony. Hanalei Museum, Hwy. 560, Hanalei, HI 96714

■ MAUI
In the side streets off Front Street, Lahaina town is filled with art galleries displaying the works of local artists. Open daily. Emphasis on whale paintings; pieces in other media. Artists available in the galleries on Friday evenings.
Maui Crafts Guild. Open daily. Two floors of works by Maui artists. Basketry, pine wood carved pieces, silk-screen fabrics, painted silk scarves. 43 Hana Hwy., Pa'ia, HI 96779; 579-9697

■ O'AHU
DOWNTOWN HONOLULU
A cluster of art galleries flanks Nu'uanu Avenue on the fringe of Chinatown. Contemporary works by local artists, and Pacific arts and crafts are featured. Some are:
Pegge Hopper Gallery. Open M–Sat. Paintings of Hawaiian women by Pegge Hopper; pastels. 1164 Nu'uanu Ave., Honolulu, HI 96813; 524-1160
Moratin Gallery. Open M–Sat. Landscape paintings by owner Moratin. Basketry and other small pieces. 3 N. Pauahi St., Honolulu, HI 96813; 521-9669
Ramsay Galleries & Cafe. Open M–F. Monthly displays by local artists. Cafe serves salads, canapes. Pen & ink fine-line drawings/prints by owner Ramsay, of historic buildings, skyline. 1128 Smith St., Honolulu, HI 96813; 537-2787
Waterall Gallery. Open M–Sat. Photographs by William Waterall; Oriental sculpture/crafts. 1160-A. Nu'uanu Ave., Honolulu, HI 96813; 521-6863

■ SPECIAL TOURS

Many tour activities in Hawai'i are advertised in free publications available at all major airports and tourist destination areas. Some unadvertised tours are highly recommended:

HONOLULU

The walking tours sponsored by **Kapiʻolani Community College** in Honolulu are rewarding, informative, and enjoyable experiences. These tours were pioneered by Glen Grant, who will take you on a downtown walk of **Mark Twain's Honolulu;** you'll feel you are actually in the year 1866. You can go on a ghost walk and hear Grant describe the Hawaiian fireballs that shoot around at night—if you know how to recognize them; or walk in graveyards to hear stories of gigolos, renegades, and Japanese *samurai.* You will need a reservation to take this tour, and there are additional tours offered by other leaders. Kapiʻolani Community College, Walking Tour Program, 4303 Diamond Head Rd., Honolulu, HI 96816; 734-9245.

Grant's "Journey To Old Waikiki" will give you a whiff of the Waikiki that once was a haunt of Kamehameha, kings, revolutionaries, and Robert Louis Stevenson. The tour is by reservation: Passport Hawaiʻi, P.O. Box 90884, Honolulu 96835; 924-1911.

MOLOKAʻI

To tour Kalaupapa, if you arrive by plane or walk or ride down the mule trail, the most informative pilgrimage around the peninsula is operated by Richard Marks. A third generation Kalaupapa resident, Marks is a walking library of Kalaupapa history, and an accomplished storyteller with a light touch. Damien Tours, Box 1, Kalaupapa, HI 96742; 567-6171. (If you'd like to spend the night at the Lighthouse, Marks also handles the arrangements and reservations.)

To arrange a wagon tour to IliʻIliʻopae Heʻiau on Molokaʻi, check with the Molokaʻi Destination Association; 553-3876.

■ Parks and Camping

■ COUNTY PARKS

No entrance, parking, or picnicking fees. Alcoholic beverages prohibited.

Hawaiʻi County: Tent and vehicle camping at 13 county beach parks. Camping permits and fees required. Maximum stay: 1 week in summer; 2 weeks at other times. Information and permits: Department of Parks & Recreation, County of Hawaiʻi, 25 Aupuni St., Hilo, HI 96720; 961-8311.

Kauaʻi County: Tent or vehicle camping at 7 county beach and inland parks. Camping permits and fees required. Maximum stay 7 days. Information and permits: Department of Parks & Recreation, County of Kauaʻi, 4396 Rice St.,

Lihu'e, HI 96766; 245-8821. After hours you can pick up a permit at the police station in Lihu'e (3060 Umi St.). Camping is also available at 4 forest reserve trailside camps in Waimea Canyon. Free camping permits and trail maps. Maximum stay 4 nights. Contact: Division of Forestry & Wildlife, P.O. Box 1671, Lihu'e, HI 96766; 245-4433.

Maui County: Tent camping on Maui leaves much to be desired. The island offers 2 county parks inland at northerly Pa'ia. Permits and fees required. Maximum stay 3 nights. Contact: Department of Parks & Recreation, County of Maui, 200 S. High St., Wailuku., HI 96793; 243-7389.

There is no camping on Lana'i; Moloka'i offers camping at 7 sites. Permits and fees required. Maximum stay 3 days. Contact: Department of Public Works, P.O. Box 526, Kaunakakai, HI 96748; 553-3221.

O'ahu, City and County of Honolulu: Tent and vehicle camping at 13 City & County beach parks. Camping permits required; no fee. Department of Parks & Recreation, Municipal Office Bldg. 650, S. King St., Honolulu, HI 96813; 523-4525.

■ **STATE PARKS**

The State Park system covers nearly 25,000 acres in 66 parks throughout most of the state. Environments vary from highly landscaped to wildland areas provided only with trails and primitive facilities. Most parks offer some landscaping for public safety and comfort. Alcoholic beverages are prohibited.

FEES AND PERMITS

State parks are open year-round. There are no entrance, parking, picnicking or tent camping fees. Camping permits are required; maximum stay 5 nights. Fees are charged for lodging accommodations in 6-person single and duplex housekeeping cabins; maximum stay 5 nights. Information, applications and permits may be obtained at district offices of the Division of State Parks; telephone numbers are **area code 808: Hawai'i:** P.O. Box 936, Hilo, HI 96721-0936, 933-4200

        Kaua'i: P.O. Box 1671, Lihu'e, HI 96766, 241-3444

        Maui: 54 South High St., Wailuku, HI 96793, 243-5354

        O'ahu: P.O. Box 621, Honolulu, HI 96809, 548-7455

GROUP ACCOMMODATIONS

Mauna Kea State Recreation Area, Hawai'i: maximum 64 persons. **Kalopa State Recreation Area, Hawai'i:** maximum 32 persons.

Reservations for lodging accommodations at **Hapuna Beach State Recreation Area,** Hawai'i; and **Koke'e State Park,** Kaua'i, are made through the concessionaires: Hawai'i Untouched Parks & Recreation, Inc., 4-person A-frame shelters, P.O. Box 5397, Kailua-Kona, HI 96745; 882-1095. Koke'e Lodge, P.O. Box 819, Waimea, HI 96796; 335-6061

■ NATIONAL PARKS

Hawai'i Volcanoes National Park. 3 drive-in campgrounds at varying elevations; maximum stay is 7 nights. No permit required. Information at the Kilauea Visitor Center, Park Headquarters, Volcano, Hawai'i. At the Namakani Paio Campground there are also cabins on rental from the Volcano House (hotel); reservations required. P.O. Box 53, Hawai'i Volcanoes National Park, HI 96718; 967-7321. Bring your own supplies.

Haleakala National Park. 2 drive-in tent camping grounds outside Haleakala Crater; maximum stay 2 nights. Permits are required and issued only on day you go. Also, 3 primitive cabins within the crater; reservations required. Information, permits, and reservations from Park Headquarters, one mile inside park entrance; Maui; 572-9306. Bring your own supplies.

■ HIKING

■ HOLOKA'I
For guided Nature Conservancy hikes into Kamakou Preserve, call the O'ahu office; 537-4508.

■ HAWAI'I (BIG ISLAND)
Hawai'i Volcanoes National Park. Back-country hiking requires pre-registration at the Kilauea Visitor Center at park headquarters, Volcano, Hawai'i. Trails are marked with *ahu,* (stone cairns). Trail maps are free.

There are many trails in the Coastal District where eruptions are possible at any time. Hikers should stay up-slope from active lava flows. In the event of a strong earthquake which may cause a *tsunami* (seismic sea wave), run for high ground. The 18-mile (29-km) Mauna Loa Summit Trail is a minimum 3-day, steep and difficult trek; snow and driving rain are possible any time of the year. There are two patrol cabins which may be used without charge; pre-register at park headquarters and report your return. Bring your own supplies and cooking fuel. The 6-mile (10-km) Observatory Trail to the Mauna Loa summit is even steeper and access to the trailhead is by reservation with the Mauna Loa Observatory; (808) 935-8482.

■ MAUI

Haleakala National Park. 36 miles (58 km) of trails. In back-country hiking be prepared for rain, heavy fog, and wind at all times. Average elevation of the crater floor is 6,700 ft. (2,042 m) and the summit is 10,023 ft. (3,055 m). Be alert to hypothermia; nighttime temperatures often drop to freezing. Use protection against sunburn. Carry water.

There are 3 main crater trails; Sliding Sands and Halemau'u trails descend 4 miles (6 km) to the crater floor; be mindful of the loose cinder surfaces and steep switchbacks. The 9-mile (14-km) Kaupo Gap trail exits the park and continues on private ranchland; rocky and steep.

■ HUNTING AND FISHING

Licenses are required for hunting and freshwater fishing; not for recreational ocean fishing. Licenses may be purchased from: State Department of Land and Natural Resources Division of Conservation and Resources Enforcement, 1151 Punchbowl Street, Honolulu, HI 96813; 587-0077; Hunter Education Office: 587-0200.

■ TOURIST INFORMATION

■ HAWAI'I (BIG ISLAND)

Chamber of Commerce. 180 Kino'ole St., #118, Hilo, HI 96720; 935-7178
Hawai'i Visitors Bureau. Open M–F. 250 Keawe St., Hilo, HI 96720, 961-5797; or 75-5719 W. Ali'i Dr., Kona Plaza, Kailua-Kona, HI 96740, 329-7787
Keauhou Visitors Assoc. Open M–F. 78-6831 Ali'i Dr., Suite 234, Keauhou, HI 96739; 322-3866

■ KAUA'I

Chamber of Commerce. P.O. Box 1969, Lihu'e, HI 96766; 245-7363
Hawai'i Visitors Bureau. Open M–F. 3016 Umi St., Lihu'e, HI 96766; 245-3971

■ **MAUI**

Chamber of Commerce. 26 N. Pu'unene, Kahului, Maui, HI 96732; 871-7711

Hawai'i Visitors Bureau Open M–F. 380 Dairy Rd., P.O. Box 1728, Kahului, HI 96732; 871-8691

Ka'anapali Beach Operators Assoc. 2530 Keka'a Dr., Lahaina, HI 96761; 661-3271

Wailea Destination Assoc. 161 Wailea Ike Pl., Kihei, HI 96753; 879-4258

■ **MOLOKA'I**

Destination Moloka'i Assoc. P.O. Box 233, Kualapu'u, HI 96757; 567-6255. Other numbers: O'ahu, 941-0444; Mainland U.S., (800) 367-4753; Canada, (800) 423-8973; Australia, 0014-800-125-569, #247. Brochures mailed; no office.

■ **O'AHU**

Chamber of Commerce. 735 Bishop St., Suite 220, Honolulu, HI 96813; 522-8800

Hawai'i Visitors Bureau. Open M–F. The main office is located at 2270 Kalakaua Ave., Suite 801, (Waikiki Business Plaza) Honolulu, HI 96815; 923-1811. A desk also located at Ala Moana Shopping Center, street level beside the escalator.

■ DISABLED VISITOR INFORMATION

The Hawai'i State Commission on Persons with Disabilities publishes a guide to facilities on the major islands available for the physically handicapped.

The guide lists hotels with wheelchair access and rooms with special facilities; shopping complexes, beaches, and parks with suitable access and conveniences. Medical equipment, nursing, and transportation services also are listed. In the section on O'ahu, major city and county curbs are graded for wheelchair access.

The guide is free if you pick it up; $3 by mail. The Commission office is at 5 Waterfront Plaza, Suite 210, Honolulu, HI 96813. Open M–F; (808) 586-8121.

■ RADIO STATIONS

Since many who visit Hawai'i spend quite a bit of time in a rental car, the following selection of radio stations should keep sightseers entertained:

■ HAWAI'I (BIG ISLAND)

KAHU, 1060–AM; Hawaiian music and oldies.

KEAU, 88.1–FM; Hawaiian Public Radio station featuring classical, jazz, and news.

KHLO, 850–AM; country music.

KIPA, 100.3–FM; rock station.

KKON, 790–AM; Hawaiian and contemporary music.

■ MAUI

HI PUBLIC RADIO, 90.7–FM; classical, jazz, and news.

KDLX, 94.3–FM; country music.

KMVI, 550–AM; Hawaiian music.

KNUI, 900–AM; contemporary and rock.

KPOA, 93.5–FM; Hawaiian music and jazz.

■ O'AHU

KCCN, 1420–AM; contemporary Hawaiian music

KCCN, 100–FM; traditional Hawaiian music.

KDEO, 102.7–FM; alternative rock.

KHPR, 88.1–FM; Public Radio station featuring classical music, news, and jazz in the evenings.

KPOI, 98.5–FM; rock music.

RECOMMENDED READING

THERE MAY BE MORE BOOKS AND PUBLICATIONS written about Hawai'i than any other island group in the Pacific. Bookshops on the four main islands offer extensive selections on a wide range of subjects. A recommended list:

■ HAWAIIAN MYTHS AND LEGENDS

Beckwith, Martha Warren. *The Kumulipo.* Chicago: University of Chicago Press, 1951/Honolulu: The University Press of Hawaii, 1972. The Beckwith translation of *The Hawaiian Creation Chant* is widely accepted. Extensive commentary brings insight into traditional hidden meanings in the Hawaiian language that are so evident in this cosmogonic and genealogical chant.

Cox, J. Halley with E. Stasack. *Hawaiian Petroglyphs.* Honolulu: Bishop Museum Press, 1970. Drawings. Discussion of imagery and symbolism at petroglyph sites island-wide.

Kane, Herb Kawainui. *Pele.* Captain Cook, Hawai'i: Kawainui Press, 1987. Color photos of paintings. Stories of Pele, fire goddess of volcanoes.

McBride, L. R. *The Kahuna.* Hilo, Hawai'i: Petroglyph Press, 1983. B & W drawings. During a long association with the National Park Service, McBride specialized in Hawaiiana, gathering stories and information on the ancient Hawaiian education system.

■ HISTORICAL NOVELS AND SHORT STORIES

Chock, Eric and Darrell H.Y. Lum, eds. *The Best of Bamboo Ridge, Hawaii Writers' Quarterly.* Honolulu: Bamboo Ridge Press, 1986. Diverse collection of local literature compiled by one of the best Hawaiian small presses.

Jones, James. *From Here to Eternity.* New York: Avon Books, 1951. Army personnel, conflicts, and love affairs, while stationed in Honolulu during WW II.

London, Jack. *Tales of Hawaii.* Kailua, Hawai'i: Press Pacifica, 1984. A trilogy on the plight of the leper in the islands, and the machinations of a Chinese patriarch to marry off his children.

Michener, James. *Hawaii.* New York: Random House, 1959. Michener's first sweeping saga. Begins with geologic origins; touches all historical eras up to statehood, and Hawai'i's modern population.

Tregaskis, Richard. *The Warrior King.* New York: Macmillan Publishing Co. 1973; Honolulu: Falmouth Press, 1984. B & W photos; genealogy charts. The definitive biography of Kamehameha the Great told by the master writer of men in war. Describes wars to unite islands, and the king's voluptuous love life.

■ CREATIVE NON-FICTION

Farber, Thomas. *On Water.* Berkeley: Okeanos Press, 1991. An intellectual voyage into the medium of water by a well-known novelist and short story writer.

■ HISTORY AND REFERENCE

Atlas of Hawaii. Honolulu: University of Hawai'i Press, Dept. of Geography, 1983. The most extensive all-around reference on Hawai'i.

Beaglehole, J.C. and R.A. Skelton, eds. *The Journals of Captain James Cook on His Voyages of Discovery, Vol. III.* London: Hakluyt Society, 1955-1969. Beaglehole's editorial masterpiece of Cook's logs from the third voyage.

Feher, Joseph. *Hawaii, A Pictorial History.* Honolulu: Bishop Museum Press, 1969. Fine collection of turn-of-the-century photos with commentary.

Forbes, David W. *Encounters With Paradise.* Honolulu: Honolulu Academy of Arts, 1992. Color plates. History and commentary of a once-in-a-lifetime exhibit; international collection of drawings and paintings covering period from Cook's 1778 voyage to 1941.

Fornander, Abraham. *An Account of the Polynesian Race.* New York: Trubner & Co., 1878. The definitive reference text on early Hawaiians and the Hawaiian ethos.

Ii, John Papa. *Fragments of Hawaiian History.* Honolulu: Bishop Museum Press, 1959. Ii lived in Kona during the time of Kamehameha I; eye-witness account of life under the *kapu* system.

Kaeppler, Adrienne L. *The Fabrics of Hawaii (Bark Cloth).* Leigh-on-Sea, England: F. Lewis Publishers, 1975. Scholarly work on the manufacture of *kapa.* Also by Kaeppler, *Feather Cloaks, Ship Captains, and Lords.* Honolulu: Occasional Papers, Bishop Museum, Vol. XXIV, No. 6, 1970. Stories of two cloaks taken to Scotland and returned to Hawai'i.

Kamakau, Samuel M. *Ruling Chiefs of Hawaii.* Honolulu: Kamehameha Schools Press, 1961. The accepted reference text on Hawaiian rulers; from Umi, eight generations before Kamehameha I, to the death of Kamehameha III.

Macdonald, Gordon A. and Douglass H. Hubbard. *Volcanoes of the National Parks in Hawaii.* Hawaii Volcanoes National Park, Hawai'i: Hawai'i Natural History Assoc., 1989. Color photos. Descriptions of Mauna Loa and Kilauea volcanoes, and the observatory on the Big Island; Haleakala on Maui. Volcanic activity from 1924-1989.

McGaw, Martha Mary, C.S.J. *Stevenson in Hawaii.* Honolulu: University of Hawai'i Press, 1950. Fine detailed account of Robert Louis Stevenson in Hawai'i.

Pukui, Mary Kawena and Samuel H. Elbert. *Hawaiian Dictionary.* Honolulu: University of Hawai'i Press, 1986. Hawaiian-English and English-Hawaiian. Authoritative collection; 30,000 entries.

Te Rangi Hiroa (Sir Peter Buck). *Arts and Crafts of Hawaii.* Honolulu: Bishop Museum Press, 1957/1988-1990. Series of 14 scholarly tracts on Hawaiian food, fishing, games, musical instruments, weapons, religion, ornaments, etc.

■ NATIONAL PARKS PUBLICATIONS

At park headquarters of Haleakala National Park on Maui and Hawaii Volcanoes National Park on the Big Island, many special interest and children's books are sold. Subjects include geology and volcanic eruptions, petroglyphs, flora and fauna, hiking guides, and the fire goddess Pele. Publications also available at Volcanoes National Park cover: Puʻuhonua O Honaunau National Historical Park, Hawaiʻi; Puʻukohola Heʻiau National Historic Site, Hawaiʻi; and Kalaupapa National Historical Park, Molokaʻi. Haleakala National Park Hqs., Maui, HI 96732. 572- 9306. Hawaii Volcanoes National Park Hqs., Volcano, HI 96785. 572-9306. 967-7311.

At the USS *Arizona* Memorial books are available concerning the attack on Pearl Harbor in 1941; the building of the Memorial; and the War-in-the-Pacific National Historical Park on Guam, 3,300 miles (5,311 km) west of Hawaiʻi. National Park Service, USS *Arizona* Memorial, Pearl Harbor, HI 96782. 422-2771.

■ NATURAL SCIENCES

Goodson, Gar. *The Many-Splendored Fishes of Hawaii.* Palo Alto, California: Stanford University Press, 1985. Color drawings. Small book with good identifications of reef and game fish.

Kimura, Bert Y. and Kenneth M. Nagata *Hawaii's Vanishing Flora.* Honolulu: Oriental Publishing Co., 1980. Color photos. Rare and endangered Hawaiian plants discussed for "semi-serious botanists."

Merlin, Mark David. *Hawaiian Forest Plants.* Honolulu: Oriental Publishing Co., 1980. Color photos. Description and usage of plants found in Hawaiian forests.

Miller, Carey D., *et al. Fruits of Hawaii.* Honolulu: University of Hawaii Press, 1945/1989. B & W photos. Description, nutritive value, and recipes.

TenBruggencate, Jan. *Wildlife of Hawaii.* (Booklet). Honolulu: *The Honolulu Advertiser,* 1986. Drawings. Descriptions of fish, bird, insect, turtle, toad, and plant life.

■ REMINISCENCES

Johnstone, Arthur. *Recollections of Robert Louis Stevenson in the Pacific.* London: Chatto and Windus, 1905. The editor of the *Pacific Commerical Advertiser,* friend of Robert Louis Stevenson, published the poem, *The High Winds of Nu'uanu* here for the first time.

The Kauai Papers. Lihu'e, Kaua'i: Kauai Historical Society, 1991. First-person stories and written oral histories from turn-of-the-century.

Lili'uokalani (Lydia Kamaka'eha). *Hawaii's Story.* Rutland, Vermont: Charles E. Tuttle Co., 1964/1990. Hawai'i's last monarch tells her story of historic events, from the time of her childhood to the overthrow of the monarchy: sorrow, prison, parole and a time to renew.

■ SURFING, DIVING, AND PADDLING

Jenkins, Bruce. *North Shore Chronicles.* Berkeley: North Atlantic Books, 1990. The *San Francisco Chronicle*'s ace sports columnist and avid surfer goes to the heart of big-wave surfing on the north shore of O'ahu.

McKissick, Mitch. *Surf Lingo.* Balboa, California: Coastline Press, 1987. "A complete guide to a totally rad vocab!"

Wardlaw, Lee. *Cowabunga!* New York: Avon Books, 1991. Surfing history, gear and etiquette. Where to catch waves; how boards are made.

Thorne, C. and L. Zitnik. *The Divers' Guide to Hawaii.* Kahului, Maui: Hawaii Divers Guide (Maui), 1984. Shore diving off the six major islands, with maps, hazards, and directions to sites.

Wallin, Doug. *Diving and Snorkeling Guide to the Hawaiian Islands.* Kahului, Maui: Pisces Books, 1984. Color photos. Diving and snorkeling off the four main islands.

Sutherland, Audrey. *Paddling Hawai'i.* Seattle: The Mountaineers, 1988. B & W photos and maps. When it comes to kayaking, Sutherland is the master. Explores secluded coves and wild coasts, many reachable only by water, at six islands; offers wealth of practical information for remote sites.

■ TRAVEL, EARLY DESCRIPTION

Bird, Isabella L. *Six Months in the Sandwich Islands.* London: John Murray, 1890/Rutland, Vermont: Charles E. Tuttle Co., 1974. This intrepid lady climbed on mules and trekked into remote villages and nearly impenetrable forests. Detailed prose in letters written home to Edinburgh in 1873.

Day, A. Grove, ed. *Robert Louis Stevenson, Travels in Hawaii.* Honolulu: University of Hawai'i Press, 1973. The frail Robert Louis Stevenson produced some of his finest stories in Hawai'i. Collection of his writings about, in, and from Hawai'i, mainly 1889 to 1893.

Day, A. Grove, ed. *Mark Twain's Letters from Hawaii.* Honolulu: University of Hawaii Press, 1975. The humor and heart of Twain became famous after these articles were written in Hawai'i for the *Sacramento Union* in 1866. The letters mark his lifelong love affair with the islands.

Maugham, W. Somerset. *Trembling of a Leaf.* New York: Doubleday & Co., 1921. "Honolulu" essay about a *haole* man in love with a Hawaiian girl.

Stevenson, Robert Louis. *The South Seas.* London: Chatto & Windus, 1912. Contains essays about Hawai'i often not included in subsequent editions.

Stoddard, Charles Warren. *South Sea Idyls.* New York: James R. Osgood & Co., 1873. Diary kept during second visit to Moloka'i, 1884. Contains the earliest and perhaps best description of Father Damien, the priest who cared for the lepers on Moloka'i.

■ TRAVEL, MODERN

Bisignani, J. D. *Hawaii Handbook.* Chico, California: Moon Publications, 1990. A thorough guide for the adventurous traveler.

Clark, John R. K. *The Beaches of the Big Island* (1985); *The Beaches of Kauai* (1990); *The Beaches of Maui County* (1989); *The Beaches of Oahu* (1977). Honolulu: University of Hawaii Press. If you plan to explore beaches, you'll want these detailed accounts of the history and geology of every beach. Includes water conditions.

Riegert, Ray. *Hidden Hawaii.* Berkeley: Ulysses Press, 1991. Describes little-known sites and remote regions island-wide. Great for hikers.

■ MISCELLANY

Blanding, Don. *Leaves From a Grass House.* Hilo, Hawaii: Petroglyph Press, 1972. Poetry written in Hawai'i in the early twenties.

Friends of 'Iolani Palace, ed. *'Iolani Palace.* Honolulu: 1988. Color photos. History, description and restoration of the Palace, residence of the last two reigning monarchs.

McDonald, Marie A. *Ka Lei.* Kailua, Hawaii: Press Pacifica, 1980. Color plates. Everything you always wanted to know about the lei.

Schleck, Robert J. *The Wilcox Quilts in Hawaii.* Kaua'i: Grove Farm Homestead Kaua'i: 1986. Color photos. Documents acquisition of quilts by the family; offers a glimpse into the lives of early quiltmakers.

PLAY OF DOLPHINS

*B*ack to the surface for air, up through the quicksilver interface, having overcome the quite palpable tug from below, and . . . there's life. Dorsal fins approaching: as if to confuse things further, the play of dolphins, the endless circling wheel of their surfacing and diving. And here they are, more or less: squadrons, armadas, flotillas, echelons, convoys, holding just below formation, in a display of skill, the Blue Angels of the deep blue. "Check this out," they seem to be saying, exhibitionists of this liquid Sahara. Forget the spinning, individual dolphins over and again surging up through the surface as if for a toke of gravity, try these group routines to make you *ooo* and *ahh* like the skating of the Rockettes at Rockefeller Center. So you look: there they are, perhaps 13 of them, one/four/two/four/two, front to back. But even as your eye sees this, the formation alters both depth and angle, though without visible movement, so that as the image is perceived it is already in jeopardy or is in fact lost. Another image taking its place at a different distance, or perhaps now the formation has also changed, is now one lead dolphin and a football-shaped cluster behind. Student body left. Even the MTV-trained eye now beginning to rebel against such transitions. At which point, click, a small pod is within touching distance, dolphins angling, right eyes staring, one's own eye now staring at the cookie cutter shark bites, which seem enormous even as one reminds oneself: *water magnifies.* Further confusing the eye/mind dialogue. The dolphins then not suddenly but suddenly, that is, without apparent use of any force, both simultaneously alongside and heading away, spiraling down in one of those primary patterns, the formula governing growth of the chambered nautilus/proportions of the human body/patterns of leaf growth/efficiency of projectiles in air.

—Thomas Farber, *On Water,* 1991

G L O S S A R Y

'A'a	Jagged, rough, broken lava
Ahupua'a	Land division, often a pie-slice shape extending from the mountains to the sea
'Aina	Land, earth
Akua	God, goddess, spirit, or ghost
'Aumakua	Personal or family gods; deified ancestors who may take other forms; they warn and scold in dreams
'Awa	Narcotic drink made from root of the *kava* shrub
Bento	Japanese box lunch
Haole	Any foreigner, usually Caucasian
Hau	Type of hibiscus; the wood once used for canoe outriggers; the bast for rope; the sap and flowers for tonics
Hau'oli	Happy, as in *Hau'oli Makahiki Hou* (Happy New Year)
He'iau	High place of worship; pre-Western contact
Hilo	First night of the new moon
Hukilau	Group fishing with a *seine,* or net
Hula halau	Hula school or troupe
'Iako	Outrigger boom
Imu	Underground oven
Kahuna	Skilled and wise in any profession; usually a priest, or healer
Kalo	Taro *(Colocasia esculenta)*
Kama'aina	Native born; literally, land child
Kane	Man, male
Kapa	(Tapa) cloth made from the bark of the paper mulberry tree
Keiki	Child; *keiki o ka 'aina:* child born on the land
Ki	Commonly known as *ti;* leaves used extensively by ancient Hawaiians for food wrapping, hula skirts, sandals
Kiawe	Algaroba tree (has sharp thorns); introduced in 1828
Kipuka	Calm place in a high sea; has come to mean a bit of land left isolated by flowing lava
Koa	Largest of native forest trees *(Acacia koa)*
Kohola	Coral reef flats; pronounced kohoLA: humpbacked whale
Kokua	Help, assistance

Konane	Ancient game similar to checkers played with pebbles in even lines on board; also, bright moonlight
Komo	To enter; *komo mai:* come in
Kumu	Teacher, tutor, model
Kupuna	Grandparent, relative or close friend; ancestor
Lanai	Veranda, porch
Lana'i	Lana'i island; literally, day of conquest
Laulau	Wrapped package; food wrapped in leaves and baked in ground oven *(imu)*
Lomi	To press or crush; raw lomi salmon, worked with fingers, mixed with onions and seasoned
Lu'au	Hawaiian feast; also *kalo* (taro) tops baked with coconut cream and chicken
Mahalo	Thank you
Maka'ainana	Commoner, populace
Makahiki	Ancient festival beginning about mid-October and lasting about 4 months; with sports and religious festivities and *kapu* on war
Makai	Towards the sea
Mauka	Towards the mountains or inland
Menehune	Legendary race of elves in the islands preceding the first Hawaiians
Moana	Open, deep ocean; *'aumoana:* to travel on the open sea
Mo'o	Legendary water spirit, dragon, or lizard
Mu'umu'u	Loose gown
'Ohana	Family, extended family; clan
Pahoehoe	Unbroken lava that flows rapidly in smooth folds
Pali	Cliffs
Pilikia	Trouble
Poi	Hawaiian staff of life made from *kalo* (taro)
Pupu	Appetizer; also shells
Pu'u	Protuberance; cinder cone hill
Saimin	Japanese noodle soup
'Ukulele	Instrument brought by Portugese in 1879; literally, leaping flea
Wahine	Woman, female
Wiki	To hurry; *hele wiki:* walk quickly

I N D E X

Each place name is followed by an abbreviation for the island on which it is found:
(H)=Hawai'i; (K)=Kaua'i; (L)=Lana'i; (Ma)=Maui; (Mo)=Moloka'i; (O)=O'ahu.

■ ABOUT THE AUTHOR

A resident of Honolulu, Moana Tregaskis writes regularly on Hawai'i for the *New York Times* Sunday travel section. Before concentrating on the curiosities of travel, she spent years as a correspondent traveling the Pacific and high mountain areas of Asia. Trained in war coverage by one of America's famous war correspondents, Richard Tregaskis, she covered wars on the Indian subcontinent and Southeast Asia for news services and is a member of the Overseas Press Club of America. Moana is a Fellow of the Royal Asiatic Society and the Royal Society for Asian Affairs. She and her husband live in Honolulu with a view overlooking Waikiki.

■ ABOUT THE PHOTOGRAPHERS

Wayne Levin lives on the Big Island's Kona Coast where he is famous for swimming far out to sea to photograph dolphins and whales; and for swimming closer in, among the big waves, to photograph surfers. He has had shows in Paris, Tokyo, and New York, and his photographs are in the collections of the Museum of Modern Art in New York as well as in Hawai'i at the Honolulu Academy of Art, the Contemporary Arts Center, and the State Foundation on Culture and the Arts. A recipient of the Photographers Fellowship of the National Endowment for the Arts, Levin has seen his photographs published in numerous magazines and journals including *Manoa, A Pacific Journal of International Writing;* and in *Kalaupapa: A Portrait,* a book illustrating the history and life of Moloka'i's leper colony.

Paul Chesley has been a freelance photographer with the National Geographic Society since 1975, traveling regularly throughout Europe and Asia. He was recently honored by the inclusion of his work in the Society's first major exhibition, "The Art of Photography at National Geographic: A 100 Year Retrospective" at the Corcoran Gallery of Art in Washington, D.C. Solo exhibitions of his work have appeared in museums in London, Tokyo, and New York; and his photographic essays are regularly featured in such magazines as *LIFE, Fortune, Bunte, Paris Match,* and *Connoisseur.* Over the past six years he has participated in ten *Day in the Life* book projects.